D0874085

WORKING
THE
RANGE

Essays on the History of Western Land Management and the Environment

Edited by
John R. Wunder

Contributions in Economics and Economic History, Number 61

GREENWOOD PRESS
WESTPORT, CONNECTICUT
LONDON, ENGLAND

Library of Congress Cataloging in Publication Data

Main entry under title:

Working the range.

(Contributions in economics and economic history,
ISSN 0084-9235; no. 61)
  Bibliography: p.
  Includes index.
  1. Land use—West (U.S.)—History—Addresses, essays,
lectures. 2. Land use—Environmental aspects—West (U.S.)—
History—Addresses, essays, lectures. I. Wunder,
John R. II. Series
HD209.W67 1985   333.76′17′0978   84-15693
ISBN 0-313-24591-6 (lib. bdg.)

Library of Congress Catalog Card Number: 84-15693
ISBN: 0-313-24591-6
ISSN: 0084-9235

First published in 1985

Greenwood Press
A division of Congressional Information Service, Inc.
88 Post Road West
Westport, Connecticut 06881

Printed in the United States of America

10 9 8 7 6 5 4 3 2 1

Copyright Acknowledgments

Grateful acknowledgment is given for permission to reprint in part the
following:
  "The Pueblos of New Mexico and the Protection of Their Land and Water
Rights" by Willard Rollings has appeared in a revised form as "Indian Land
and Water: The Pueblos of New Mexico (1848–1924)," *American Indian Cul-
ture and Research Journal* 6 (Winter, 1982): 1–21.
  "Agriculture, Mountain Ecology, and the Land Ethic: Phases of the Environ-
mental History of Utah" by Dan L. Flores has appeared in a revised form as
"Zion in Eden: Phases of the Environmental History of Utah," *Environmental
History* 7 (Winter, 1983): 325–344.

This anthology is dedicated to a celebration of the life of Charles L. Wood, agricultural historian at Texas Tech University. At the age of 44, Chuck Wood died in Lubbock, Texas, after a brief but heroic battle with acute leukemia. The loss to his family, friends, students, and colleagues is incalculable. But unlike many who perish, historians or not, Chuck left a legacy of wisdom in his writings—a legacy that this book will examine and complement with new contributions in his chosen field of agricultural history.

"Grass is the forgiveness of nature—her constant benediction.

Fields trampled with battle, saturated with blood, torn with ruts of cannon, grow green again with grass, and carnage is forgotten. . . .

Forests decay, harvests perish, flowers vanish, but *grass is immortal.*"

John J. Ingalls, long-time Kansas senator during the late nineteenth century

Contents

Tables

Acknowledgments

This book was realized only because the authors herein have contributed amply of their research, time, and attention. Willard H. Rollings, David Lanehart, Delmar Hayter, and Donald Abbe were students of Charles L. Wood; Paul H. Carlson, Dan L. Flores, Stephen P. Sayles, Benjamin H. Newcomb, David J. Murrah, and John R. Wunder were colleagues: Homer E. Socolofsky and Rita Napier were friend and teacher.

The "stylists," helpers of form and substance, are as important as the writers. Vicki Pachall, Linda Lester, and Vicky Vaughan endured typing countless drafts and redrafts; and Joan Weldon handled numerous administrative problems. Particular note should be made of David J. Murrah, Michael Hooks, Rebecca J. Herring, Janet Neugebauer, and Tommie Davis—all from the Southwest Collection of Texas Tech University—for their strong support of this project.

Several other persons aided greatly in this quest to recognize an historian of high merit. The aid came in an intangible form that sustained the effort throughout. Nina Potokova, historian from the Soviet Union and guest at Texas Tech University; Pamela Brink, Kansan par excellence, and Mary Hatfield; and Allan Kuethe and Briggs Twyman, interested and concerned colleagues, were most supportive. Susan Wunder, and Amanda and Nell Wunder—my family—and especially Alma Wood, and Mark, Greg, John, Marice, and Lisa Wood—Chuck's family—made this book a deep and most meaningful experience.

Introduction

The economic reality of living off the land has been fraught with complexity throughout American history. Physical control of the range has required force, vigilance, and political acumen. But the exercise of sovereignty was only a beginning. Individual and governmental efforts to influence land distribution rivaled environmental abuse as forces that those working the land had to face. Many failed to meet these challenges.

Walter Prescott Webb postulated that the environment altered human beings forever. He wrote that entering the Great Plains could be a life-changing experience. At the ninety-eighth meridian, "one sees what may be called an institutional *fault* (comparable to a geological fault) running from middle Texas to Illinois or Dakota. . . . At this fault," Webb postulated, "the ways of life and of living changed. Practically every institution that was carried across it was either broken and remade or else greatly altered."[1] Webb did not foresee the converse, however. The impact of human beings on the land was equally shattering ecologically.

James Malin was particularly concerned about the role the environment played in the working of the land, and he also discussed the influence of land policy and speculation. Malin recounted a story by "K," probably James Kirkwood, an engineer on the Missouri Pacific Railroad. "K" believed that successful settlement required land investment by railroad companies, because without railroads individual speculators would gain control and inhibit economic growth. Malin saw both forms of speculation as evil, as destructive to the agriculturalist. Tongue in cheek, Malin philosophized, "Desire endows a coveted object with charms unknown to the disinterested."[2]

Successful management of the land required a blend of entrepreneur and naturalist. These traits are not abundant in human beings and frequently repel each other, but one such person who thrived on western lands and who combined these personalities was Clarence B. Perry. Perry was an innovative southwestern Kansas rancher and farmer. According to Charles L. Wood, "Perry was motivated by a desire for profit and engaged in many enterprises, some of which were unsuccessful, to advance his interest. But he also wanted to make some lasting contribution to the development of the West by discovering some of the immutable laws of adaptation."[3] Perry, the pathfinder, discovered how to live and work on the land. He then took steps to preserve and share these discoveries with other farmers and ranchers.

The following collection of twelve original essays offers a variety of perspectives concerning working the range. These essays are presented to honor the work of Charles L. Wood, an agricultural historian who chronicled the relationship of settlers to their environment and who was especially interested in the environmental impact of the rise of twentieth-century agricultural industries on western lands.[4] They include articles describing group and individual responses to land settlement and factors causing such settlement to be a difficult process. The chapters are divided into four sections: native Americans and their lands, land speculation, land policy and entrepreneurship, and environment and land management. Each section discusses the temporal and spatial relationship of Americans to working western lands.

NOTES

1. Walter Prescott Webb, *The Great Plains* (New York: Grosset and Dunlap, 1931), pp. 8-9.

2. James C. Malin, *The Nebraska Question, 1852-1854* (Lawrence, Kans.: James C. Malin, 1953), pp. 60-61.

3. Charles L. Wood, "C.D. Perry: Clark County Farmer and Rancher, 1884-1903," *Kansas Historical Quarterly*, 39 (Winter 1973):476-477.

4. See Charles L. Wood, *The Kansas Beef Industry* (Lawrence: Regents Press of Kansas, 1980): idem, "Upbreeding Western Range Cattle: Notes on Kansas, 1880-1920," *Journal of the West* 16 (January 1977): 16-28; idem, "Cattlemen, Railroads, and the Origin of the Kansas Livestock Association—the 1890s," *Kansas Historical Quarterly* 43 (Summer 1977): 121-129; and idem., "Science and Politics in the War on Cattle Diseases: The Kansas Experience, 1900-1940," *Agricultural History* 54 (January 1980): 80-92.

I

NATIVE AMERICANS AND THEIR LANDS

"Outside my country we cannot raise a crop, but in it we can raise a crop almost anywhere; our families and stock there increase, here they decrease; we know this land does not like us, neither does the water."

Barboncito, Bosque Redondo,
May, 1868

The first Americans to claim real estate that would become a part of the United States approached the land in a multitude of ways. They either traversed it, taking carefully from it what it had to offer, or settled permanently, farming and irrigating the responsive soils. Discovery of what the lands could support and the competition for these lands punctuated the early native American experience.

For the non-Indians who flooded the domain of the native Americans, control of the land was paramount. They especially desired the areas that could sustain and increase agricultural activities. Consequently, sedentary and semi-sedentary tribes caught the brunt of the outpouring, each nation responding to the crisis as best it could.

The Pueblo and Navajo endured tremendous suffering and substantial land losses. Willard H. Rollings traces the fight of the Pueblo of New Mexico to maintain their agriculturally based city-states against pressures from the Spanish, Mexican, New Mexican, and United States governments. David Lanehart relates how the Navajo, after having their homeland—Dinetah—destroyed by a scorched-earth policy of the United States Army, made the long walk to a desolate reservation in eastern New Mexico only to find the region agriculturally inhospitable. After great expenditures of American finances and Navajo lives, the Peace Commission of 1867 miraculously allowed the Navajos to return to their homelands in the Four Corners region and to reside on a reduced land base. Still, these marginal successes of the Pueblo and Navajo were the exception to the general rule. Native Americans lost thousands of acres.

Four years after the Indian Peace Commission had gone to Fort Sumner, the United States government decided to end the treaty process whereby Indian nations were guaranteed lands and encouraged to become agriculturalists. It was a step fraught with many dangers to the homelands of Native American peoples. John R. Wunder describes the factors leading to passage of the Resolution of 1871 and how it was subsequently interpreted to be retroactive, placing all Indian treaty lands in peril. Not until the commencement of the post-World War II Indian Claims Commission hearings does a reversal of the momentum from Indian land confiscation to Indian land restoration begin. Still, the struggle for control of Native American lands continues today.

1 WILLARD H. ROLLINGS

The Pueblos of New Mexico and the Protection of Their Land and Water Rights

When the Spanish arrived in New Mexico in the sixteenth century, they found two groups of Native Americans already in residence. One group consisted of several nomadic nations—the Apache, Navajo, Ute—and the other consisted of sedentary agricultural tribes living in communal villages, or pueblos. Ancestors of the Pueblo Indians had lived in the area for thousands of years. While early Pueblo population centers were located north and west of the upper Rio Grande valley, Pueblo peoples had lived in villages along the river since 600 A.D. Beginning about 1300 A.D., there was a dramatic shift in population.[1] The Pueblo people began abandoning their villages along the San Juan drainage system (the Four Corners region of Arizona, Utah, Colorado, and New Mexico) and moved to the south and east. Some settled in the deserts of Arizona and New Mexico (Zuni and Acoma), but most joined those already living near or along the northern Rio Grande. These people lived communally in independent pueblos governed by secular and religious leaders.

The pueblos were small, compact villages, none larger than 2,000 inhabitants, where people lived together in adobe or stone-terraced houses usually constructed around ceremonial plazas. The people farmed by using stream irrigation and grew corn, squash, beans, and cotton. Although similar in many respects, these pueblos differed widely according to language and custom.[2]

At the time of initial Spanish contact, the pueblos numbered between 70 and 100.[3] However, destruction either by Spanish or the Apache or abandonment soon reduced these to about 20. Three of these, the Zuni, Acoma, and Laguna, were located east of the Rio Grande along the Pecos River. The remaining 16—Isleta, Sandia, Jemez, Santa Ana, Zia, San Felipe, Santo Domingo, Santa Clara, Cochiti, Tesuque, Pojoaque, Nambe, San Ildefonso, San Juan, Picuris, and Taos—were concentrated along the upper reaches of the Rio Grande in central and northern New Mexico.

The Spanish had conquered these Indians by the seventeenth century. But in 1680 the Pueblo united, attacked the Spanish, and drove them from the area. For twelve years these Indians were free from Spanish control, but the Pueblo coalition disintegrated and they were reconquered in a series of campaigns in the 1690s. Despite their conquest, these Indians retained their lands and their internal tribal government. The Spanish made a clear distinction between the conquered village (pueblo) Indians called *indios de los pueblos* and the unconquered, nomadic Indians who were called *indios barbaros* and enacted legislation to guarantee Pueblo Indian lands and local autonomy.[4]

Spanish policy toward the Pueblo Indians was established by a series of laws beginning as early as 1551. Various decrees in 1573, 1618, 1687, 1695, 1781, and 1811 established a protectorate policy,[5] by which Pueblo Indians were considered wards of the king. The Spanish government guaranteed Indian title to all land used or occupied. Although there is some controversy about the nature of these grants, it is generally agreed that the lands were granted to the pueblo, not to the individual, and were held in common by the pueblo. Only the viceroy, governor, and captain general could grant any further lands to the pueblo and approve any land sales made by the village.[6] The Pueblo Indians were given rights to all water that crossed or bordered their land, and all non-Indians were forbidden to live on Pueblo lands. Furthermore, the Spanish government provided legal protection and advice for the Indians.[7]

In 1821, the territory of New Mexico became a part of independent Mexico, yet Mexican policy in regard to the Pueblo Indians remained consistent with former Spanish practices. However, an important change came about as a result of Mexican independence; the Mexican government granted citizenship to the Pueblo Indians. The Mexican revolutionary proclamation, the Plan of Iguala (1821), called for Indian citizenship which later was incorporated into Mexican law in 1824.[8] Despite this grant of citizenship, the Mexican government continued to follow the paternalistic policies established by the Spanish government. All Spanish laws regarding the Pueblo in force prior to 1821 remained in effect, but the Mexican government was either unable or unwilling to prevent many non-Indians from encroaching upon Pueblo lands.[9] By 1846 many non-Indians had settled on and were cultivating Pueblo Indian land, and these illegal seizures caused friction between Indians and Mexicans. This situation was explosive by the time the United States captured New Mexico in the Mexican-American War.

New Mexico was seized and occupied in August 1846 by the Army of the West, commanded by General Stephen W. Kearny. Kearny established a system of government for the captured territory which included courts, judges, and a legislative body. The fact that the territory had only recently belonged to Mexico, and that the war had not yet ended, did not deter Kearny and his officers from establishing an American form of government. New Mexico officially became a part of the United States in 1848 by the terms of the Treaty of Guadalupe Hidalgo. Provisions of this treaty (section eight) granted Mexican citizens residing in New Mexico the option of retaining their Mexican citizenship or assuming United States citizenship. Residents were given a year to apply to keep their Mexican citizenship; if they did not apply within the year they would automatically become citizens of the United States. Since none of the Pueblo Indians requested to retain their Mexican citizenship, they became, in the eyes of many, United States citizens.[10] As citizens of the United States, therefore, they would have all of the traditional rights and privileges. But because they were citizens, the Pueblo were not wards of the federal government, and they did not have special federal protection. They had the right to sell or give away their land as they saw fit, and the adult males had the right to vote. This legal status stood in striking contrast to the rights and privileges granted to other tribes living within the United States: the other tribes were not citizens, but wards of the government who could not vote or dispose of their land without explicit federal permission.

Legally, then, the Pueblo Indians of New Mexico were free from federal control and protection. However, the situation quickly became confusing and ambiguous because the territorial government and the federal government were not consistent in their dealings with the Pueblo. In some instances they were treated as Indians in the traditional fashion, and at other times they were treated as United States citizens. Even before the approval of the Treaty of Guadalupe Hidalgo, Kearny's territorial legislature passed a law in 1847 that recognized the communal nature of the Pueblo's government and land titles, and in 1854 the legislature passed the following act:

That the Pueblo Indians of this territory for the present, and until they shall be declared by the Congress of the United States to have the right, are excluded from the privilege of voting at the popular elections of this territory.[11]

This act was an attempt to ignore the laws of citizenship and to deny the Pueblo their special status. The federal government said nothing about this law so it remained in force. However, other laws were passed by the territory that demonstrated New Mexico's recognition that the Pueblo Indians were indeed distinct from other tribes within the state. A law passed in 1853 prohibiting the sale of liquor to Indians included the provision that "the pueblo Indians that live among us are not included in the word Indian."[12]

The federal government contributed to this confusion. In 1851 the provisions of the Indian Intercourse Act of 1834 were extended to protect and control New Mexico Indians. The Act of 1834 had been enacted to guard "uncivilized" natives on reservations, yet the Pueblo Indians were not "uncivilized" and had not been placed on reservations. Their land title was based on Spanish and Mexican title, and the United States government, having never made a treaty with the Pueblo Indians, had never gained title to their lands. Indian agents in New Mexico were not allowed to enforce the 1834 act which did offer some protection, because Pueblo Indians were not classed as Indians.[13] At the same time, several Indian appropriation acts provided federal money for these same "Indians." The real status of the Pueblo would remain clouded for several years.

In 1869 the federal government attempted to enforce parts of the 1834 act and evicted a Mexican-American, José Juan Lucero, from Cochiti Pueblo lands. The Indian Intercourse Act made the unauthorized settlement of tribal lands a federal offense. The New Mexico Supreme Court dismissed the case (*U.S. v. Lucero*) because the 1834 and 1851 laws did not apply to the Pueblo Indians; " . . . by the express terms of the eighth article of the treaty (Guadalupe-Hidalgo), they (Pueblo Indians) became citizens of the United States, as they were previously citizens of the Mexican republic."[14] Furthermore, the court maintained that no treaties had been made with the individual pueblos, and the government had not provided an Indian agent for them, clearly demonstrating that even the federal government recognized that these peoples were distinct from other tribes.

This court, under this section of the treaty of Guadalupe Hidalgo, does not consider it proper to assent to the withdrawal of eight thousand citizens of New Mexico from the operation of the laws, made to secure and maintain them in their liberty and property, and consign their liberty and property to a system of laws and trade made for wandering savages and administered by the agents of the Indian department.[15]

Three years later the United States provided an agent for

the Pueblo and removed one of the grounds for the *Lucero* decision. Accordingly, in 1876 the government again tried to enforce the 1834 law. The government evicted a Mexican-American from the Taos Pueblo. The New Mexico Territorial Supreme Court again ruled that the 1834 law was not applicable to the Pueblo Indians. The government appealed this decision to the United States Supreme Court. Here the Supreme Court affirmed the territorial decision in *U.S. v. Joseph.* The Court ruled:

... if the Pueblo Indians differ from the other inhabitants of New Mexico in holding land in common, and in certain patriarchal form of domestic life, they only resemble in this regard the Shakers and other communistic societies in this country, and cannot for that reason be classed with the Indian tribes of whom we have been speaking.[16]

The Court also declared that the Pueblo Indians were citizens of the United States and Mexico, but because rights of citizenship were not further involved, it refused to rule on any other restrictions of these rights. The Court decided that the appointment of an agent for these Indians was not sufficient cause to change their status. Concerning land ownership, the Supreme Court found that, generally, title to Indian lands was held by the United States and that Indians had no right to transfer it without government consent. Yet,

The Pueblo Indians, on the contrary, hold their lands by a right superior to that of the United States. Their title dates back to grants made by the government of Spain before the Mexican Revolution, a title which was fully recognized by the Mexican government, and protected by it in the treaty of Guadalupe Hidalgo. ... If the defendant is on the lands of the pueblo, without the consent of the inhabitants, he may be ejected, or punished civilly by a suit for trespass. ... If he is there with their consent or license, we know of no injury which the United States suffers by his presence, nor any statute which he violates in that regard.[17]

The *Joseph* decision established the law governing New Mexico pueblos for almost forty years. Other rulings continued to affirm this Supreme Court decision. In 1891 the attorney general ruled that federal laws regulating Indian traders did not apply to the Pueblo.[18] In 1894 the Department of the Interior ruled that laws relating to the approval of leases of Indian tribal lands did not apply to Pueblo land.[19] The Pueblo's special status was reconfirmed several times. Only once was their status disturbed. In 1905 the territorial Supreme Court of New Mexico ruled that because of the *Lucero* and *Joseph* decisions the New Mexico pueblos would have to pay property taxes.[20] Congress intervened and passed an act that gave the pueblos a special tax exemption.[21] As a result of these decisions, many non-Indians purchased Pueblo lands in good faith, while others, assured that the federal government could not prevent it, settled on Pueblo lands illegally.

As long as New Mexico remained a territory the federal government left much of governmental control of all New Mexico Indians to territorial officials. However, when New Mexico became a state in 1912, control and supervision shifted from the territory to the federal government. As power shifted from Santa Fe to Washington, D.C., the Pueblo Indians began to be treated more like other Indian tribes. The first signs of this shift became apparent in 1910 prior to New Mexico's final admission to statehood.

Many people, Indian and non-Indian alike, were convinced that the Pueblo Indians needed federal protection, because without it they had lost much of their land while being denied the benefits of citizenship. Congress therefore added to the New Mexico Enabling Act of 1910 a provision that read "the terms 'Indians' and Indian country' shall include the Pueblo Indians of New Mexico and the lands now owned and occupied by them."[22] With the approval of this act in 1910, federal control was finally extended to the Pueblo Indians.

The constitutionality of this act was challenged in 1913. A Spanish-American, Felipe Sandoval, was arrested for introducing liquor onto the San Juan and Santa Clara Pueblos. In court, Sandoval's attorney argued the Pueblo were citizens and that the provisions of the New Mexico Enabling Act applying to the Pueblo were unconstitutional because it placed special conditions on New Mexico resulting in its admission on a different basis from other states. The federal district court concurred with Sandoval and dismissed the government's case. The government appealed the decision to the U.S. Supreme Court. In 1913 the Supreme Court reversed the *Joseph* decision in *U.S. v. Sandoval* and declared that the Pueblo Indians were indeed Indians by race, customs, and therefore government; that federal funds had been spent to improve Pueblo conditions; that Indian agents had been appointed for them; and that Congress had granted them tax exemptions. Hereafter, Pueblo Indians had the same status as other Indians and legally were wards of the federal government.[23] The pueblo could no longer sell their land and all sales since 1848 were invalid, reverting all land and water back to the Indians.

This decision was a victory for the Pueblo Indians because they could now regain lost farm lands and water; but the *Sandoval* decision also created an uproar in New Mexico. Approximately 12,000 people on 3,000 claims were threatened with possible eviction. It did not matter to the government that some had held title to the lands. According to the decision, all alienations were void. The 3,000 claims, titled and untitled, represented only about 10 percent of the total Pueblo lands, but almost all of the available water, vital for agricultural survival, was included in those claims.

The Tesuque pueblo's grant contained 17,471 acres of land. Of that, only 457 acres were claimed by non-Indians (2.62 percent). However, of those 17,471 acres, only 2,500 acres were irrigable. Of course the 457 acres claimed by non-Indians were out of this irrigable portion (18.2 percent). The Pueblo of San Juan had lost 3,000 of its 4,000 irrigable acres. Another pueblo just north of Santa Fe, San Ildefonso, possessed 12,000 acres, and of this only 1,250 were irrigable, yet by 1913 this pueblo contained less than 250 acres of irrigated land; at Nambe the Indians controlled only 360 acres of a possible 3,000.[24]

Land title in New Mexico was a complicated affair. Neither Spain nor Mexico had a system of land survey in New Mexico, and New Mexico Territory did not have one until 1856. Another complication involved the fact that many of the claims were based upon Spanish land grants; and often these grants contained vague or no longer existing boundaries. A typical deed written in 1727 described a tract of land as "Bounded on the north by the road which comes down from Tesuque, and on the south bounded by the ditch, and bounded on the east by the lands of Tomas Martinez, an individual, and bounded on the west by the lands of Jacobo Montoya, another individual."[25] Another read, "On the side of the town which looks toward the pueblo, 11 varas. From the road to a little cedar tree which divides the boundary of said Romero and Manuel Baca."[26] The road and ditch referred to in 1727 did not exist in 1913, so an exact boundary could not be determined. Also, the deeds between individuals could not always be verified as to whether the individuals were Indians or not, since many Pueblo had taken Spanish names.

In some instances non-Indians had purchased land in good faith from the Pueblo, both legal before and substantiated after the *Joseph* decision. In other instances Indian land had been loaned or rented to the non-Indians and by 1913 many non-Indians conveniently forgot that they had only rented the land. Other problems arose from the peculiar nature of Spanish and Indian land practices, which had no equivalent practice in United States land law. One such problem involved the Sandia Pueblo, just north of Albuquerque. Before New Mexico became a part of the United States a man named Garcia had helped the Sandia Pueblo. In return they granted him a life estate occupancy to a piece of Pueblo land. When he died his wife was allowed to remain on the Indian land until her death. Despite the fact that neither of the Garcias had children, several heirs continued to occupy the land until 1913.[27]

At Laguna in 1768, Baltasar Baca and his sons were granted a permit to graze their stock. They were specifically restricted from planting crops, building residences on the land or interfering with the Indians' use of the land, yet by 1913 the Baca family was living on the "grant" and claimed ownership.[28] While these encroachments were illegal, other examples were outright thefts. In 1917 a non-Indian began extending his fence to include more Pueblo land. An Indian agent investigated the situation and confronted the man. He produced a deed he claimed was forty years old. The agent pointed out to him that the Indian officials who had signed the deed were the present officials, not ones involved in 1877. The agent returned to the pueblo and took down the fence. The fence was soon restored by the non-Indian. When the agent again confronted the man, he produced a new deed "signed" by Indian officials who had served fifty years before.[29]

Prior to the *Sandoval* decision, the Indian Bureau had planned to file individual suits for the Pueblo to reclaim lost land and water. Before these suits could proceed, however, a survey was required to show the location of the non-Indian claims against the Indian land. In 1913 the Department of the Interior authorized the Joy Survey, which recorded only claims being made against the Pueblo; it did not substantiate them.

From 1913 until 1924, non-Indians sought every possible means to evade the consequences of the *Sandoval* decision, and tensions increased in New Mexico. In February of 1922 a group of Tesuque Indians tore down a fence erected by a non-Indian, E.B. Healy. Healy gathered ammunition and guns in preparation to attack the Indians. Violence was avoided only because Francis Wilson, an attorney for the Indians, intervened. In Taos, Indians tore down fences and burned crops. Clearly, an immediate solution to this complex situation was needed.[30]

The secretary of the interior, Albert Fall, a former senator from New Mexico and appointed to Harding's cabinet in 1921, asked Colonel Ralph E. Twitchell, a New Mexico scholar of Spanish history, to prepare a historical and legal report on Pueblo land titles. Fall, however, could not wait for Twitchell's report; he asked New Mexico senator Holm O. Bursum to introduce a bill to settle the controversy quickly. Bursum composed a bill that would simply confirm all non-Indian claims of title held since 1902, and he submitted the bill to Congress on May 31, 1921. Representatives of the Indian Rights Association visited Secretary Fall and protested that the bill was unfair to the Indians and asked him to reconsider. Fall agreed and allowed Bursum's first bill to die in the committee.[31]

Fall received Twitchell's report in the spring of 1922, which recommended that Congress enact special legislation to provide an exemption from the *Sandoval* decision. This would allow all non-Indians to remain on the disputed lands. But Twitchell was not completely indifferent to the indians' plight; he also suggested that something be done to protect Pueblo water rights and to end any further encroachments on Indian land.

Work on new legislation was postponed, however, because the indian commissioner Charles H. Burke had left Washington for New Mexico where he met with several Indians at the Santa Clara pueblo. He also met with Twitchell and Santa Fe attorney A.B. Renehan who had represented Sandoval in the *Sandoval* case. Renehan had also represented 155 non-Indians in a suit to settle title within the Santa Clara and San Ildefonso Pueblo grants. These men returned to Washington and met with Secretary Fall and Senator Bursum to draw up a compromise bill.[32] Entitled "A Bill to ascertain and settle land claims of persons not Indians within Pueblo Indian land, land grants, and reservations in the State of New Mexico" (Senate Bill 2855), it was known nationally as the Bursum bill.

The Bursum bill was sent to committee and was returned to the floor for action on September 11, 1922. Senator Bursum spoke in behalf of the bill and described why the bill was necessary, and how it was written.

An investigation was made by an agent of the Interior Department and of the Department of Justice. They investigated the whole question from the standpoint of the Government, from the standpoint of the Indians, and from the standpoint of the settlers. Finally the attorney for the settlers and the attorney for the Government met and conferred, and hearings were held before the Commissioner of Indian Affairs and also before the Secretary of the Interior. A bill was agreed upon vesting jurisdiction in the federal court of the state of New Mexico, providing a remedy whereby title might be quieted by settlers occupying lands on various grants.[33]

Bursum went on to explain that the bill simply provided the rules by which suits could be filed. On the surface the bill was just as Bursum implied. The Senate approved it and sent it to the House for action. Bursum admitted that no Indians had had direct involvement in the writing of the bill. Indeed, few Indians were even aware that the bill existed until after it had already been approved by the Senate. Once the Indians were made aware of the bill they were extremely upset, because it virtually confirmed all non-Indian claims and seriously interfered with internal Pueblo government.

Perhaps the most damaging feature to the Indians was Section Fifteen. This section revived the Joy Survey and declared that it would be used as *prima facie* evidence of boundaries. The survey had only been made to show claims, not to confirm title. Other sections were equally damaging to Indian claims. Despite the fact that Twitchell had urged protection of Indian water rights, the bill confirmed conditions as they existed in 1922 and stated that any further disputes would be decided according to New Mexico state law within state courts. The Pueblo Indians therefore had to recover any lost water in the unfriendly confines of New Mexico courts. According to Twitchell, "The local courts and juries have yet, in my judgment, to show where the Indian has ever received justice."[34] Furthermore, the state of New Mexico had a statute of limitations of four years on water claims, and most of the water taken from the Indians occurred prior to 1918, so according to the Bursum bill Indians could never regain their lost water rights.

Sections Seven and Eight specified conditions whereby non-Indians could receive title to the disputed lands. Any non-Indians who could prove possession by means of a title were to be granted all they claimed. Any non-Indian who had held land since June 20, 1910, "with or without color of title," and anyone who claimed land under a valid grant from either Spain or

Mexico "shall be entitled to a decree in their favor respectively for the whole of the lands claimed."[35] All non-Indians had to do was prove occupancy in order to acquire title. If non-Indians were still unable to prove their title, they could appeal to the secretary of the interior, and he was empowered to grant them title to their claims.

The Indians did have some, although minimal, protection. Lands lost to non-Indians merely on the basis of occupancy since 1900 were to be compensated. The government was to give to the Pueblo lands equal in size and quality and adjacent to the Pueblo. If equal land was not available the secretary of the interior would place an amount of money equal to the value of the land at an unimproved basis in the Pueblo's account. The Indians knew that irrigated land was at a premium in New Mexico, and that none was available in the public domain. Equally important, the bill did not provide for any appropriation to pay the compensation. Any losses of land to settlers who had proof of title would not be compensated.

The bill went beyond the land issue in Section Two which proposed to place all authority to deal with the Indian offenses within the federal court. Part E of Section Two allowed federal intervention into inner tribal affairs. Federal courts held jurisdiction over "all suits of a civil nature at common law or in equity, involving any question of internal affairs or the government of any of said Pueblos, including the right to hold offices in said pueblos in accordance with the customs and regulations of said Pueblos."[36] This gave the federal court the right to interpret Indian customs and traditions. People who might have no understanding at all of Indian culture would be empowered to interfere with tribal decisions.

Despite the passage of the bill in the Senate, the Pueblo were not without defenders. John Collier, a former social worker and college teacher from the East, had lived in Taos and had been inspired by the Pueblo Indians' lifestyle and customs. He formed, with members of the Taos artist community, a local organization to preserve, protect, and revive Pueblo traditions and culture. He became aware of the bill in the summer of 1922 and began fighting its passage. Collier was soon joined by Stella Atwood, the chairman of the Indian Welfare Committee of the General Federation of Women's Clubs, a national women's association.[37]

Collier and Atwood led the fight against the Bursum bill. They used their influence with various magazine publishers to launch a national campaign opposing Secretary Fall and the Bursum bill. *Sunset Magazine* defended the Pueblo and began to publish a series of articles in October 1922. These articles were often written by Collier and were highly emotional accounts. Their titles—for example, "The Pueblo's Last Stand," "Plundering the Pueblos," "Persecuting the Pueblos," and "Read the Shameful Story and Blush for America"—were guaranteed to elicit support for the Indians.[38] The editors of the magazine distributed copies of these magazines to every member of Congress and other influential government officials.[39] In New Mexico the Santa Fe *New Mexican* owned by Bronson Cutting, a Progressive-Republican and political foe of Bursum and Fall, led the New Mexico attack: "The Indian is the most historic of all underdogs. . . . Wading through the maze of legal phraseology in this bill, we do not gather that it is giving the Pueblo Indian any the best of it."[40]

Collier worked with the Pueblo and organized their resistance. He traveled through the pueblos with Antonio Luhan, a Taos Indian, and urged the Pueblo to unite to oppose the bill. At Cochiti one of the Indian leaders reminded them all of the Revolt of 1680 and said that the Pueblo must unite "as we did long ago when we drove the Spaniards out."[41] On November 5, 1922, representatives of all the Pueblo met at Santo Domingo and drafted an appeal to the American people to defeat the Bursum bill. The appeal described several attempts made by the Indians to get an explanation of the bill from government agents. Pueblo officials "have always been put off and even insulted," they declared.[42] The Indians closed their appeal with an emotional plea:

The Pueblos, as is well known, existed in a civilized condition before the white man came to America. We have kept our old customs and lived in harmony with each other and with our fellow Americans.

This bill will destroy our common life and rob us of everything we hold dear—our lands, our customs, our traditions.

Are the American people willing to let this happen?[43]

The Indians united to fight the bill and decided to raise money to send a delegation to Washington to campaign in person against it.

Atwood hired a Santa Fe attorney, Francis Wilson, who had represented the government in the *Sandoval* case, to help defeat the bill. Wilson wrote Senator William Borah, a powerful legislator from Idaho and member of the Senate Committee on Public Lands and Surveys, and described the problems involved in the bill. Borah was able to recall the bill from the House, and he called for hearings before the committee in January. Secretary Fall was outraged and he wrote an emotional letter to Borah protesting his actions. Fall defended the bill and explained that the settlers deserved special consideration because they paid taxes and the Indians did not.[44]

Fall threatened to evict all non-Indian settlers from the land. In the tense atmosphere of New Mexico, mass eviction would certainly cause violence, and many were convinced that Fall wanted to do this to create a panic in New Mexico. It would make the opponents of the bill appear to be "ruthless extremists driving thousands of innocent non-Indians off their lands."[45] Collier, Atwood, and Wilson asked Fall to wait and allow Congress to write a law guaranteeing justice for all participants.

Fall refused to stop and continued his threats, but by December pressures created by the opposition to the Bursum bill were exaggerated by the Teapot Dome scandal. Fall believed he had lost all influence in the Harding administration and feared a loss of influence at home in New Mexico. He began to consider resigning from the Cabinet and never followed through with the evictions. In January 1923 the White House announced that Fall would leave office in March because of personal business reasons. However, Fall continued to support the bill and testified before both the Senate and House committee hearings.

Before the Senate committee began its hearings, Francis Wilson drew up an alternative bill which was introduced by the senior senator from New Mexico, Andrieus A. Jones. The bill, known as the Jones-Leatherwood bill, proposed a three-person commission, appointed by the president with congressional approval, to examine claims and grant or reject titles. In addition the bill provided for extensive irrigation projects for the Pueblo. The Senate Committee of Public Lands and Surveys and the House Indian Affairs Committee began hearings in January and February and investigated the situation to decide the fate of the proposed bills.

Bursum bill opponents Collier, Atwood, Wilson, and Isleta Pueblo Indian Pablo Abeyta testified in favor of the Jones bill and against the Bursum bill. Before both committees Wilson pointed out the damaging sections and explained how they would destroy the Pueblo communities. When Fall testified before the committees, he explained that the bill was a just one and admitted that changes, such as use of the Joy Survey, were needed. He denounced the opponents of the bill and their public relations campaign: "If we are to have a government by propaganda, not by the three departments of government, the present conditions in Soviet Russia would constitute a political paradise . . . compared to what we have here."[46] Fall also criticized the Jones-Leatherwood bill as being much too expensive and ended his Senate appearance by refusing to be questioned by attorney Wilson. The House hearings which had begun after the Senate hearing were noticeably anti-Pueblo. They began with a sharp attack on Atwood, reducing her to tears. Wilson took the stand and while explaining the harmful effects of the bill remarked that the Indians were industrious and were worthy of help. To this, Republican Representative Homer Snyder from New York, chairman of the House Committee on Indian Affairs, answered: "If those Indians were really thrifty, hardworking Indians, they are the first tribe or bunch of Indians that I ever saw that were."[47] Despite the animosity present in the House committee, neither the Bursum nor the Jones bills were passed to the floor.

In February a compromise bill, the Lenroot bill, was created by the Senate Committee on Public Lands and Surveys. This bill established a presidential lands board made up of three people. The board was empowered to investigate and grant title to contested lands. Settlers who had possessed title for twenty years and settlers without title who had occupied the land for thirty years were to be granted guaranteed title to their land.[48] Francis Wilson gave his approval for the bill because it eliminated the objectional provision contained in the earlier Bursum bill and, he thought, did provide, justice for those non-Indians who had been on the land for a long time. However, Collier rejected the bill and denounced Wilson. Collier maintained that the bill still allowed Pueblo trespassers to obtain title and did not provide any compensation for lost lands for the Indians. While the controversy raged within the pro-Indian movement in Washington, Senator Bursum rewrote his bill and reintroduced it in the Senate. Collier also wrote an alternative bill and Senator Charles Curtis of Kansas submitted it for him. Collier returned to New Mexico to prevent the split between Wilson and himself from destroying the Indian movement.[49] He also returned to gather support for his bill and arranged for another Pueblo delegation to travel to Washington to testify in behalf of his bill.

Things had changed in Washington since the Indians had last been there. Secretary Fall had been replaced by Dr. Hubert Work in March. Due to the outcry over the Pueblo Indians, Work had created an advisory committee of 100 people—Indians, conservatives, scientists, reformers, missionaries, and such notables as Bernard Baruch, Oswald Villard, and William Jennings Bryan—selected to investigate Indian conditions in the United States and make recommendations.[50] Little was done concerning the Pueblo Indians, however, and Collier was thoroughly disappointed with the committee.

Collier had better luck with the Senate Committee on Public

Lands and Surveys. Attorneys for the settlers and the Indians met with the committee and drew up a compromise bill, entitled the Pueblo Lands Act. The Pueblo Lands Act created a lands board made up of the secretary of the interior, attorney general, and a third member appointed by the president. Because this board had offices in Santa Fe, the attorney general and secretary of the interior were empowered to appoint assistants to take their places. The board was given the power to investigate, determine, and report the boundaries of all the New Mexico pueblos. In order to extinguish Indian title the board would have to reach a unanimous decision, and its findings would be filed in the federal court in New Mexico to bring suit to quiet title. Non-Indian settlers with color of title had to demonstrate continuous adverse possession since January 6, 1902 (twenty years), supported by payment of taxes on the land. Non-Indian settlers without color of title had to demonstrate continuous adverse possession since March 16, 1889 (thirty-five years), supported by payment of taxes. If the same land had been granted to both an Indian and a non-Indian by the Spanish or Mexican government, the Indian was allowed the prior claim. Indians were to be compensated for any lost land or water, and this money had to be used to purchase land for the Pueblo, or construct irrigation projects. If the Indians did not agree with the board's findings they could appeal the decision to the federal district court within sixty days. Non-Indians could also appeal the decisions to the federal district court and could apply for compensation from the Department of the Interior. This bill was written to end the land problems in New Mexico and to prevent any further disputes over Pueblo land.

No right, title, or interest in or to the lands of the Pueblo Indians of New Mexico to which their title has not been extinguished as herein before determined shall hereafter be acquired or initiated by virtue of the laws of the State of New Mexico, or in any other manner except as may hereafter be provided by Congress, and no sale, grant, lease of any character, or any other conveyance of lands, or any title of claim thereto, made by any pueblo as a community, or any Pueblo Indian living in a community of Pueblo Indians, in the state of New Mexico, shall be of any validity in law or equity unless the same be first approved by the Secretary of the Interior.[51]

This compromise bill was passed by the Senate on May 13 and the House on June 5, and President Calvin Coolidge signed it into law on June 9, 1924. With the passage of the Pueblo Lands Act of 1924 the special status that had long been granted to the Pueblo Indians officially ended, and their lands were finally given the status of other tribal lands in the United States.

The Pueblo Land Board began settling claims and soon its decisions were challenged in court. These challenges were turned back and the constitutionality of the act was upheld.[52] The Pueblo Lands Act did not end the controversy surrounding the Pueblo Indian lands because the board continued working well into the 1930s, yet this act finally did provide some protection for the Pueblo Indians.

The Pueblo Indians had occupied a unique place among Native Americans in the United States. As citizens they had been forced to accept the responsibilities of citizenship while being denied the benefits. The federal governments of both Mexico and the United States showed little understanding and concern for these people and their special situation, and as a result they were victimized and cheated throughout most of the nineteenth century.

Finally in 1910, control and protection was extended to the Pueblo Indians. This change in policy caused tremendous problems in New Mexico, particularly in regard to land ownership. Initially, local politicians working under the guise of protecting the Indian attempted to deprive them of much of their land by means of national legislation. Fortunately for the Pueblo, by the 1920s many Americans were concerned with the plight of the American Indian. These people joined with the Pueblo, demanded, and eventually got fair treatment for the Pueblo Indians too long denied.

NOTES

1. John C. McGregor, *Southwestern Archaeology*, 2d ed. (Urbana: University of Illinois Press, 1965), p. 20.

2. Among these pueblos there were five different languages spoken: Piro, Tiwa, Towa, Tewa, and Keresan. The five languages were distinct and were not understood by the different pueblos. See Richard I. Ford, Albert H. Schroeder, and Stewert L. Peckham, "Three Perspectives on Puebloan Prehistory," in *New Perspectives on the Pueblos*, ed. Alfonso Ortiz (Albuquerque: University of New Mexico Press, 1972), pp. 19-39.

3. Albert H. Schroeder, "Rio Grande Ethnohistory," in *New Perspectives on the Pueblos*, ed. Ortiz, pp. 47-48.

4. Felix Cohen, *Handbook of Federal Indian Law* (Washington, D.C.: Government Printing Office, 1942; reprint, Albuquerque: University of New Mexico Press, 1971), p. 383.

5. Ibid., pp. 383-384.

6. Myra Ellen Jenkins, "The Baltasar Baca Grant: History of an Encroachment," reprint from *El Palacio* 68 (Spring, Summer 1961):50.

7. Herbert Brayer, *Pueblo Land Grants of the Rio Abajo* (Albuquerque: University of New Mexico Press, 1938), p. 16.

8. Cohen, *Federal Indian Law*, p. 384.

9. Jenkins, "Baltasar Baca Grant," pp. 60-61.

10. Cohen, *Federal Indian Law*, p. 384.

11. Ibid., p. 385.

12. Ibid.

13. Leo Crane, *Desert Drums: The Pueblo Indians of New Mexico, 1540-1928* (Boston: Little, Brown and Company, 1928; reprint, Glorieta, N.M.: Rio Grande Press, 1972), p. 277.

14. *United States v. Lucero*, 1 N.M. 440 (1869).

15. Ibid., p. 441.

16. *United States v. Joseph*, 94 U.S. 617, 618 (1876).

17. Ibid., pp. 618–619.

18. Cohen, *Federal Indian Law*, p. 388.

19. Ibid.

20. *Territory of New Mexico v. Delinquent Taxpayers*, 12 N.M. 139, 76 Pac. 316 (1904).

21. Act of March 3, 1905, 33 Stat. 1048.

22. Act of June 20, 1910, 36 Stat. 557.

23. *United States v. Sandoval*, 231 U.S. 28 (1913).

24. U.S. House of Representatives, Committee on Indian Affairs, *Hearings on H.R. 13452 and H.R. 13674, Pueblo Land Titles*, 67th Cong., 4th sess., 1923, pp. 170, 214-215, 258.

25. Crane, *Desert Drums*, p. 284.

26. Committee on Indian Affairs, *Hearings*, p. 229.

27. Crane, *Desert Drums*, p. 299.

28. Jenkins, "Baltasar Baca Grant," pp. 98-99.

29. Committee on Indian Affairs, *Hearings*, p. 152.

30. U.S. Senate, Subcommittee on Public Lands and Surveys, *Hearings on S. 3865 and S. 4223, Pueblo Indian Lands*, 67th Cong., 4th sess., 1923, pp. 307-308.

31. Donald R. Moorman, "A Political Biography of Holm O. Bursum: 1899-1924" (Ph.D. dissertation, University of New Mexico, 1962), p. 309.

32. Ibid.

33. Congressional Record, 67th Cong., 4th sess., December 21, 1922, vol. 64, pt. I, pp. 808-809.

34. Crane, *Desert Drums*, p. 304.

35. Congressional Record, pp. 12324-12325.

36. Ibid., p. 12324.

37. Kenneth R. Philp, *John Collier's Crusade for Indian Reform, 1920-1954* (Tucson: University of Arizona Press, 1977), pp. 26-27.

38. *Sunset Magazine*, November 1922-December 1923.

39. Philp, *Collier's Crusade*, p. 33.

40. Santa Fe *New Mexican*, November 6, 1922.

41. John Collier, *From Every Zenith: A Memoir and Some Essays on Life and Thought* (Denver: Sage Books, 1963), p. 132.

42. Santa Fe *New Mexican*, November 6, 1922.

43. Ibid.

44. *Congressional Record*, p. 809.

45. Subcommittee on Public Lands and Surveys, *Hearings,* pp. 173-174, 254.

46. Committee on Indian Affairs, *Hearings*, p. 253.

47. Ibid., p. 160.

48. Philp, *Collier's Crusade*, p. 45.

49. Ibid., pp. 46-49.

50. Ibid., p. 50.

51. Cohen, *Federal Indian Law*, p. 390.

52. Ibid., pp. 390-391.

Regaining Dinetah: The Navajo and the Indian Peace Commission at Fort Sumner

June 1, 1868, is recognized as a major turning point in Navajo history. The once-powerful Navajo, or Diné, had been militarily overcome and removed from their homeland, Dinetah. For almost five years these Indians were held as prisoners of war. While incarcerated they regressed into a pitiful state of poverty and despair. Then a special commission, sent under the authority of the United States Congress, allowed the Navajo people to return to their homeland. The Peace Commission of 1867 gave the Navajo a new beginning.

Prior to their removal to the Bosque Redondo, the Navajo inhabited a large region in the American Southwest. This land was located between four mountains, which the Navajo believed were created for them by their sacred ancestors. Bounded on the north by Mount Hesperus in Colorado, on the west by the San Francisco Mountains in Arizona, on the south by Mount Taylor in New Mexico, and on the east by Mount Blanca in Colorado, this area contained a Navajo population, estimated in 1848, of more than 13,000.[1] They were traditionally a farming nation, but by the time the United States seized the area in 1846 the Navajo had adopted the horse and had become a seminomadic sheep raising people. They also had learned the art of raiding and become proficient at stealing livestock.[2]

Although the United States had made seven different treaties with the Navajo between 1846 and 1861, these Indians had never been restrained, subdued, or confined. Consequently, in 1862 when Brigadier General James H. Carleton became commander of the Military District of New Mexico, he instituted military action against nomadic Indians of the territory and intended either to exterminate them or confine them to reservations. His policy was successful, and the Navajo nation became one of his victims.[3]

Carleton ordered Colonel Christopher (Kit) Carson, with four companies of New Mexico volunteers, to conquer the Navajo. From 1863 until 1865, Carson carried out a war of agricultural attrition against them. He never engaged in a major battle. Instead he captured and dispersed Navajo herds and flocks and destroyed their fields and orchards. Starving Navajo soon began to surrender in large numbers.[4]

Carleton had selected a site known as the Bosque Redondo, or Round Grove, as the reservation for the Navajo. The military post, Fort Sumner, and the Bosque Redondo were located about 140 miles southeast of Santa Fe, on the Pecos River. Since November 1862, it had been inhabited by about 500 Mescalero Apache. The Navajo who were sent to this 40-square-mile tract eventually numbered over 7,000.

The Bosque Redondo was a poor choice for the location of a reservation and military post. An examination of the site in May 1859 for a proposed military installation had produced a report declaring it unfit for a post. The water in the Pecos and the surrounding earth were impregnated with alkali, and for miles around there was nothing but a desolate sandy prairie. Aside from the few cottonwood groves near the river, the vegetation consisted mainly of grama grass, with cane cacti, yucca plants, and random mesquite bushes. The location was far from existing supply routes, and literally everything had to be transported. Territorial Governor Henry Connelly was apparently misinformed when, in his annual report to the territorial legislature in 1864, he stated, "this reservation has been chosen with great care as to soil, climate, and location."[5]

On November 30, 1862, Fort Sumner was officially established.[6]

The Navajo's stay at Bosque Redondo was not a pleasant one. The Navajo concentration camp was the buffer zone between the Plains warriors on the east and the Mexicans on the south and west and vulnerable to both. Depredations against them were constantly being made by other Indians, principally the Comanche, and by the Mexican citizens of the Territory of New Mexico. Captured Navajo women and children were in demand by both the Plains Indians and the Mexicans. Livestock was stolen and murders were committed frequently.

General Carleton, intent on civilizing the Navajo, thought he could teach them to farm. He believed that within a couple of years the Navajo would become self-sufficient. He did not realize that the Navajo were traditionally agriculturalists who were quite successful in raising crops in their homeland. At the Bosque Redondo, however, there was never a successful harvest. Insects, hail, floods, and drought devastated Navajo fields each year, until in 1868 they simply refused to plant. Even if there had been high yields each year, the Navajo could not have been self-sufficient. It would have been impossible to feed 7,000 people off the products of only 3,500 acres of nonirrigated, alkali-soaked soils.[7]

Since the Navajo were unable to provide for themselves, the government was forced to provide for them. The cost was unbearably high. A.B. Norton, superintendent of Indian affairs for New Mexico, was convinced that the government had spent at least $10 million on the Bosque Redondo fiasco from its inception until mid-1867. He estimated that it took $1.5 million annually to maintain the establishment. Navajo agent Theodore H. Dodd reported the cost for Navajo subsistence only at approximately $750,000. Congress, which was forced to pay the bill, soon took a closer look at the plight of the Navajo.[8]

From its inception, the Bosque Redondo, as a reservation for the Navajo, was a controversial issue. Dr. Michael Steck, Norton's predecessor as superintendent of Indian affairs in New

Mexico from July 1863 until May 1865, actively opposed Carleton's Navajo policy. Due to Steck's urging, Commissioner of Indian Affairs William P. Dole advised J. P. Usher, secretary of the interior, not to assume responsibility for the Navajo while at the Bosque Redondo. The reservation remained a War Department liability until after the controversy had become a national issue. It existed as an actual prisoner of war camp until late 1867, when the Bosque Redondo was turned over to civilian control.[9]

Public opinion, stirred by local newspapers, turned against Carleton and his Navajo experiment as early as 1864. Washington officials were aware of this discontent, and in March 1865 Congress appointed a joint committee to inquire into the condition of all American Indians.[10] The Doolittle Committee, as it was known, visited the Navajo that summer and was shocked at their situation. Even so, little was done to improve the state of the Navajo directly by the Doolittle group. But once back in Washington, the committee requested that the Department of the Interior make its own investigation. Julius K. Graves, special agent of the Office of Indian Affairs, was then sent to New Mexico in late 1865. After consulting with civilian and military officials, and after a council with Navajo headmen, Graves filed his report. He generally agreed with Carleton's policy, but found that civil and military leaders in the territory were literally at each others' throats over the temporary reservation. Graves advised the government to decide whether or not the Bosque Redondo was to be a permanent reservation for the Navajo. He also believed that the military should provide for the Indians adequately or shift that authority to civilian control.[11]

Meanwhile, Superintendent Steck became weary of the running feud with Carleton and resigned in disgust. When A. B. Norton replaced Steck in early 1866, he began where Steck left off. Along with the new Navajo agent, Theodore H. Dodd, Norton foresaw the imminent failure of the Bosque Redondo experiment. Norton's advice was ignored by Commissioner of Indian Affairs D. N. Cooley in 1866, but Cooley was soon replaced by Charles E. Mix, who actively espoused the recommendations of Norton. By mid-1867, the Office of Indian Affairs was endorsing removal of the Navajo from the Bosque Redondo.[12]

At about the same time, the Territorial Legislature of New Mexico had been successful in its efforts to get rid of Carleton. It applied enough pressure on the War Department, by sending a memorial to President Andrew Johnson stating Carleton's incompetence, to force Secretary of War U.S. Grant to relieve Carleton from his New Mexico post. Soon after, steps were put into motion to transfer the Navajo to civil control. The Bosque Redondo became a reservation, under the authority of the Office of Indian Affairs, on November 1, 1867. It was about this same time that officials began talking seriously about sending representatives of the new Indian Peace Commission to the Bosque Redondo.[13]

The Indian Peace Commission was created by Congress in the summer of 1867 to assuage and make peace with the Plains Indians who had declared war against the United States. Closer contact between the Indian and non-Indian had come as a result of the end of the Civil War. Due to increased east-west travel, the continued construction of the railroads, the search for precious metals and the rapid push in the westward line of settlement, the Indians of the Plains became uneasy and alarmed. The sparks that had set the Plains on fire were the Sand Creek Massacre and the Fetterman Massacre, and the army seemed incapable of defending the frontier, having been drastically reduced in size after Appomattox. Congress, with considerable debate, concluded that it would be far less costly to make peace with the Indians, even if they had to be fed and "civilized", than to fight them. Therefore, Congress established the commission on July 20, 1867.[14]

The act provided that the president appoint a commission consisting of three army officers who, along with N.G. Taylor, the commissioner of Indian affairs, John B. Henderson, chairman of the Senate Committee on Indian Affairs, Samuel F. Tappan, and John B. Sanborn, would have the authority to call together and meet with the leaders of all Indian nations in the western territories and remove, if possible, the causes of the hostilities and make treaties of peace. It also provided for the commission to find a suitable location to remove these Indians beyond the reach of white settlement, out of the routes of travel, and out of the routes of the proposed railroad lines. President Johnson appointed Generals William T. Sherman, William S. Harney, and Alfred H. Terry. General Christopher C. Augur was later added to the commission.[15]

The peace commission functioned in an official capacity from August 1867 until late 1868. It met with all of the major Indian groups on the Great Plains and made treaties and agreements with them to fulfill its obligations. Within that time, the commission signed nine treaties and made peace with all Indian nations at war between the Mississippi River and the Rocky Mountains.[16]

At its first meeting on August 6, 1867, in St. Louis, the members decided to meet first with those tribes generally viewed as most troublesome on the frontier. Post commanders, superintendents, and agents were instructed to inform the Indians that councils would be held to discuss grievances and make peace. The Indians of western Dakota were to meet the commission at Fort Laramie in September, the Indians south of the Arkansas River were to meet the commission near Fort Larned in October.[17]

From St. Louis the commission toured the northern Plains by boat on the Missouri River and met with various peaceful bands of Sioux in Nebraska and Dakota before returning to Omaha. From there they took the Union Pacific Railroad to North Platte, Nebraska, and held councils with some groups of Sioux and Northern Cheyenne. However, the Northern Sioux were waging war in the Powder River country and were unable to attend those talks. An invitation was sent to them requesting their presence at Fort Laramie when the commission returned in September.[18]

The commission then moved to meet with the southern nations on Medicine Lodge Creek near Fort Larned, Kansas. It was at this great council that treaties were made with the Kiowa, Comanche, Arapaho, Kiowa-Apache, and Cheyenne in late October. The commission then went back to Fort Laramie, hoping that a successful treaty could also be made with the Sioux. The commission was met at Fort Laramie, however, by only the Crow, who informed them that the Sioux, under Red Cloud, would not come. Word was sent to the Sioux that the commission would return the next summer to make peace. Then the commission went back to Washington, D.C., and prepared its report to the president.[19]

The next year the commission returned as promised and held talks with the Indians of the northern Plains. In late April and early May it was successful in negotiating treaties with the Sioux, Arapaho, Crow, Northern Cheyenne, and Northern Arapaho. Two other treaties were made that summer, one with the Navajo at Fort Sumner, New Mexico Territory, in June and the other with the Eastern Band of Shoshone and Bannock at Fort Bridger, Utah Territory, in early July.[20]

The Commission had discussed the removal of the Navajo as early as September 1867,[21] however, nothing was decided about the matter until Congress in early 1868 directed the commission to go to the Bosque Redondo.[22] Finally, on May 9, 1868, it was decided that only Sherman and Tappan would go to the Navajo reservation.[23]

Before the commissioners traveled to the Bosque Redondo there had been no question that the Navajo would be moved. The commission had decided upon it, Congress ordered it, and the Navajo knew it. The only question was where they would be moved. Two alternatives had been considered: the Indian Territory (Oklahoma) or the Navajo homeland west of the Rio Grande. Sherman had been an early advocate of Navajo removal to the Indian Territory, and still held that opinion upon his arrival in New Mexico. Tappan's position was never voiced, but from all indications he sided with western removal.[24]

On May 27, Sherman and Tappan arrived at the reservation. The talks began the next day at eleven o'clock. Because the day was hot, a large canvas was erected to shade the participants.

The commissioners sat between General George W. Getty, commander of the Military District of New Mexico, and post commander Brevet Brigadier General Benjamin S. Roberts. Across from them sat the principal chief, Barboncito, with six other headmen behind him.[25]

At first the participants were unable to find anyone who could translate Navajo into English, but finally two interpreters were selected. A Mexican named Jesus Arviso, a one-time Navajo captive, was serving as post translator. Since he knew only Spanish and Navajo, another interpreter was necessary. James Sutherland, who was fluent in both Spanish and English, served as the second translator. The procedure of double translation was tedious and time consuming, and the talks moved slowly. It is possible that this awkward system produced misunderstandings. Nevertheless, the council ran smoothly.[26]

The dialogue of the council was almost totally between Sherman and Barboncito. Tappan's voice was heard only once during the three days of negotiation when he asked a simple question concerning the number of Navajo still held captive by the Mexicans. The only other vocal participant was Ganado Mucho, who was added to the Navajo delegation on the last day of the talks. He simply expressed his happiness at the prospect of returning to his homeland. Apparently both sides knew exactly what they wanted to say, and stood united behind their respective spokesmen.[27]

Sherman opened the council by stating the reasons for the presence of the commissioners at Fort Sumner. He said he had been informed that the Navajo had worked hard, but were as poor as they had been when they were brought to Bosque Redondo. He stated that he and Tappan had come to learn about the condition of the Navajo and asked them to tell the commission about their past and express their opinion of the reservation.[28]

Barboncito then painted a sad picture. His tone was not one of anger, contempt, or defiance, but of sadness and despair. He explained that the Navajo god had given them a good land to live in and had told them never to move east of the Rio Grande or west of the Little Colorado. The deaths, poverty, and misery at the reservation Barboncito attributed to Navajo noncompliance with this divine commandment. Barboncito feared "that when the last of [the other chiefs present at the council] is gone the world will come to an end."[29]

The Indian spokesman then related the story of the Navajo at Bosque Redondo. In the five winters they had lived there not one successful crop had been harvested, even though they worked the fields diligently. Almost all of their stock had died and those who had been rich were now poor. Even firewood was unavailable, no closer than twenty-five miles from Fort Sumner. This lack of fuel led to sickness and death from cold during the winter. Barboncito also emphasized the productiveness of his homeland in relation to the reservation. He stated: "Outside my country we cannot raise a crop, but in it we can raise a crop almost anywhere; our families and stock there increase, here they decrease; we know this land does not like us, neither does the water."[30]

Barboncito concluded his eloquent speech by stressing that the Navajo wished to leave the reservation and return to their homeland. "If we are taken back to our own country," he said, "we will call you our father and mother, if you should only tie a goat there we would all live off it, all of the same opinion. I am speaking for the whole tribe, for their animals from the horse to the dog, also the unborn." In the end the chief told Sherman that he was speaking to the general as if Sherman were a spirit and asked when the spirit was going to take the Navajo home.[31]

Sherman acknowledged that he believed what Barboncito had said was true. Then with very little rhetoric, the general proposed that the Navajo consider a reservation in the Oklahoma Territory as a new home. There was plenty of water there, and crops could be cultivated without irrigation. Over the years the Indians there had been productive. Sherman suggested that several Navajo leaders take a tour of the Indian Territory, at government expense, and see if they liked the area. Barboncito's reply was brief, but to the point. The chief said, "I hope to God you will not ask me to go to any other country except my own. It might turn out [to be] another Bosque Redondo. They told us this was a good place when we came, but it is not."[32]

The Navajo insistence to return to their ancestral home convinced Sherman to accede. He instructed the headmen to assemble the entire tribe the following morning and to select ten men to act as a council to settle the boundary of their new reservation. Sherman then adjourned the meeting, to convene again at ten o'clock the following morning.[33]

The Navajo did as they were told, and on the morning of the twenty-ninth selected the ten men to act as delegates for the signing of the treaty. These principal men were then directed to select a chief from their ranks, and Barboncito was unanimously chosen. The Navajo then promised always to obey Barboncito and agreed that the Navajo nation would be bound by the acts of their ten selected delegates.[34]

Barboncito then expressed his concern about several matters. He said he did not know one of the bands, the Cibollettas, and did not know if they wanted to return to their old country. The chief also said that he believed it was wrong to confine the Navajo behind a boundary line, because the Navajo wished to hunt and trade beyond the line. He also brought up the subject of the Navajo captives among the Mexicans.[35]

Commissioner Sherman replied that if they wanted, the Cibollettas could live among the Mexicans, but if they did, they would be unable to enjoy the advantages of the treaty. The general assured Barboncito that it was permissible to trade and hunt outside the boundary lines, but that the Navajo farms and homes had to be located inside. The Navajo had no claim to the land outside the stipulated boundaries. As to the Navajo captives, Sherman explained that peonage or slavery was illegal and that by approaching the civil courts and land commissioners, the Navajo would obtain justice. He stated that the peace commission had no authority over such matters. Having satisfied Barboncito, Sherman asked if the Navajo would like schools, blacksmith shops, and carpenter shops on their new reservation. Barboncito said yes. They then adjourned to meet at nine o'clock the next morning.[36]

Next day the commissioners met with the ten headmen to discuss any changes in the treaty which had been prepared. After the manuscript was read and interpreted, it was approved. Sherman explained that the reservation did not include all of the territory previously occupied by the Navajo, the total area was now only about 100 square miles. The chief said that the Navajo were happy with the treaty, which gave them the heartland of their old country. He said it was more than they had expected. After accepting two additional members to the Navajo council, Sherman asked for and received an endorsement of old Fort Defiance as the site for the new agency. They adjourned until nine o'clock on Monday, June 1, 1868, at which time the treaty was officially endorsed. Then the Navajo went home.[37]

In the Treaty of 1868, both the United States government and the Navajo received what they wanted. The government saw removal of the Navajo to their old home as an economic measure, the officials believing that these Indians could provide better for themselves in their own country. This was no guess. The Navajo had maintained themselves for hundreds of years in their mountain domain, but at the Bosque Redondo they could not even manage one successful harvest. The government had wasted millions of dollars each year on the Fort Sumner-Bosque Redondo establishment. Removal of the Navajo west of the Rio Grande seemed to be a logical response to a basically economic problem.

For the Navajo, the signing of the treaty was a matter of survival. The Navajo population had dwindled and had become poverty stricken due to the extreme conditions at Bosque Redondo. They could not succeed at the reservation, no matter how hard they tried. If it had not been for the Treaty of 1868, the Navajo nation might have perished as did other Indian tribes. How long they would have remained is a matter of speculation. Some authorities at that time predicted that the

Navajo would have soon attempted an escape en masse, as did other Indian groups. If so, the Treaty of 1868 saved the Navajo from the fate which met the Nez Percé, Comanche, and other Indian nations. Thus, the Navajo were able to begin a new, more prosperous life in their regained ancestral home.

NOTES

1. U.S., *Annual Report of the Commissioner of Indian Affairs for 1866*, p. 135.

2. Lynn R. Bailey, *The Long Walk: A History of the Navajo Wars, 1846-1968* (Los Angeles: Westernlore Press, 1964), pp. 2-3.

3. Gerald E. Thompson, ed., "'To the People of New Mexico': General Carleton Defends the Bosque Redondo," *Arizona and the West* 14 (Winter 1972):349.

4. Ibid.

5. "Governor's Message to the Territorial Legislature of New Mexico, December 6, 1864," in U.S. Department of State Territorial Papers, New Mexico, 1851-1972, Record Group 59, National Archives Microfilm Publications, Washington D.C., microcopy no. T17, roll 3.

6. Thompson, "'To the People of New Mexico,'" p. 349; Frank McNitt, "Fort Sumner: A Study in Origins," *New Mexico Historical Review* 45 (April 1970): 102, 107-111.

7. "Letter from the Secretary of War relative to the unsuitableness of the Bosque Redondo Reservation in New Mexico for the location of the Navajo Indians," House Exec. Doc. 248, 40th Cong., 2d sess.

8. U.S., *Annual Report of the Commissioner of Indian Affairs for 1866*, pp. 146, 150; U.S., *Annual Report of the Commissioner of Indian Affairs for 1867*, p. 190.

9. Lynn R. Bailey, *Bosque Redondo: An American Concentration Camp* (Pasadena: Socio-Technical Books, 1970), p. 117.

10. The report of the Doolittle Committee was read before Congress on January 26, 1867, *Congressional Globe*, 39th Cong., 2d sess., 1867, p. 763.

11. Bailey, *Bosque Redondo,* pp. 121, 130-133; U. S., *Annual Report of the Commissioner of Indian Affairs for 1866,* pp. 131-35.

12. Ibid., pp. 144-150; U.S., *Annual Report of the Commissioner of Indian Affairs for 1867,* pp. 11-12, 189-91, 198-203; Bailey, *Bosque Redondo,* pp. 133-34.

13. Bailey, *Bosque Redondo,* pp. 137-38.

14. Wilcomb E. Washburn, *The American Indian and the United States: A Documentary History,* vol. 3 (New York: Random House, 1973), pp. 1488-1617.

15. The Act of July 20, 1867, can be found in *Appendix to the Congressional Globe,* 40th Cong., 1st and sp. sess., 1867, pp. 44-45.

16. "Transcript of the Minutes and Proceedings of the Indian Peace Commission appointed by an Act of Congress approved July 20, 1868," Records of the Office of the Secretary of the Interior, Indian Division, Records of Treaty Commissions, Record Group 48, National Archives, Washington, D.C. Hereafter Peace Commission proceedings.

17. Ibid.

18. Ibid.

19. Ibid. A reprint of the report to the president can be found in Washburn, *The American Indian and the United States,* vol. 1, pp. 134-63.

20. Texts of all of these treaties may be found in Charles J. Kappler, *Indian Affairs, Laws and Treaties,* vol. 2 (Washington, D.C.: Government Printing Office, 1904), pp. 977-1024.

21. Peace Commission proceedings, meeting of September 13, 1867.

22. Discussion in Congress pertaining to Navajo removal can be found in *Congressional Globe,* 40th Cong., 2d sess., 1868, pp. 1184, 1789-1790, 2110-2121.

23. Peace Commission proceedings, meeting of May 9, 1868.

24. "Telegram from Lieutenant General Sherman, relative to the removal of the Navajo and Ute Indians," House Exec. Doc. 308, 40th Cong., 2d sess.; Peace Commission proceedings, meeting of April 1, 1868.

25. Valentine Wolfenstein Diary (excerpts), Frank McNitt

Papers, New Mexico State Records Center and Archives, Santa Fe, New Mexico.

26. David M. Brugge, "Story of the Interpreter for the Treaty of 1868," *1966 Navajo Tourist Guide*, p. 12B.

27. "Proceedings of the Council held with the Navajo by Commissioners Sherman and Tappan, May 28-30, 1868," Office of the Secretary of the Interior, Indian Division, Records of Treaty Commissions, Record Group 48, National Archives, Washington, D.C.

28. Ibid.

29. Ibid.

30. Ibid.

31. Ibid.

32. Ibid.

33. Ibid.

34. Ibid.

35. Ibid.

36. Ibid.

37. Ibid.

No More Treaties: The Resolution of 1871 and the Alteration of Indian Rights to Their Homelands

In the spring of 1981, the United States Congress and Air Force discovered that the $33.8-billion missile system proposed for construction in eastern Nevada would violate a 117-year-old Indian treaty, the Treaty of Ruby Valley made in 1863 between representatives of President Abraham Lincoln and Timoak, Moho-a, Buck, and nine other leaders of the Western Shoshone nation. That treaty recognized the formal boundaries of the Western Shoshone in portions of the present states of Utah, Idaho, and Nevada. This land was designated the home of the Western Shoshone where today over 4,000 descendants of the signers reside.[1]

The Treaty of Ruby Valley was one of over 350 treaties made between the United States and American Indian tribes. Treaties had been made until 1871, the year Congress abolished all future treaty-making powers with Native Americans. The treaty abolition rider was attached to the Indian Appropriations Act for the fiscal year of 1871 and it stated:

That hereafter no Indian nation or tribe within the territory of the United States shall be acknowledged or recognized as an independent nation, tribe, or power with whom the United States may contract by treaty: Provided further, That nothing herein contained shall be construed to invalidate or impair the obligation of any treaty heretofore lawfully made and ratified with any such Indian nation or tribe.[2]

Briefly, Congress with the approval of President Ulysses S. Grant had statutorily altered a basic practice of foreign policy based upon constitutional precedent. Inherent within the law was the bold new power of the House of Representatives to determine, along with the Senate, which nations could be recognized for treaty-making purposes.

The circumstances behind and the ramifications of this rather unusual step, that of abolishing future treaty-making powers, have not been the subject of specific scholarly scrutiny. How did this most significant legislation affecting Indian-United States relationships and general diplomatic actions evolve? What arguments were used to justify such a drastic change? And what would be the immediate legal outcome of the implementation of the Resolution of 1871? These fundamental questions need to be probed and answered in order to understand the nineteenth-century framework of demands upon the lands of the Native Americans.

The origins of Indian-United States treaty dealings begin in colonial America. Probably the very first such agreement among sovereign powers was consummated between England and the Powhatan Confederacy. When one Christopher Newport returned to Jamestown from Britain, he carried instructions to bestow presents upon Powhatan, leader of the most powerful coalition of the Chesapeake region; and Newport was told to crown Powhatan as a gesture of subservience to the English monarchy. Powhatan was invited to Jamestown for the crowning, but he refused. He noted that he was also a king and while he would be happy to receive the gifts from England, he would accept them only as a fellow sovereign. Eventually Newport journeyed to Powhatan, gave him the presents, and placed a crown upon Powhatan's head.[3]

The Powhatan agreement was a familiar treaty relationship that England and later the United States entered into with various Indian tribes. It represented a bargain struck by two autonomous powers who desired peace and friendship. There would be other treaties that would represent a change in the power nature of the relationship and require an agricultural economic activity. Some would acknowledge American power over the diplomatic affairs of tribes; others would require cessions of land or removal from lands in exchange for moneys, other lands, or future considerations; and some treaties would divide lands previously held in collective ownership into allotments. Many treaties combined several of the above provisions in one document.[4]

The process by which treaties were made between various Indian groups and Euro-Americans remained remarkably stable throughout the seventeenth, eighteenth, and early nineteenth centuries. This stability was directly related to the balance of power on the North American continent. Above all, these pre-mid-nineteenth century diplomatic negotiations were based upon the political and legal equality of the participants.[5]

Indian-United States relations of the nineteenth century, however, underwent significant change. After the War of 1812 and before the Civil War, Americans were relatively free to concentrate upon reshaping their diplomacy. Armed with new war technologies and massive population resources, the fragile international structure east of the Mississippi River was forever altered by the rushing, emergent new republic. Treaties that once were negotiated in the dual interests of each party now became more major-minor diplomatic agreements. Moreover, the 1820s and 1830s witnessed the federal government gripped by a national mood demanding Indian removal. Oftentimes removal required questionable treaty interpretations, unethical treaty signings, and blatant violations of human rights and international law.[6]

The uproar created by removal necessitated a redefinition of the legal relationships of Indians and the United States, and John Marshall and his court confronted the issues. In *Cherokee Nation v. Georgia*, Marshall indulged in some curious legal fiction in order to provide a means of recognizing the recently changed diplomatic forces. He explained that an Indian tribe was not a foreign nation. Instead, "They may, more correctly, perhaps, be denominated domestic dependent nations. They

occupy a territory to which we assert a title independent of
their will, which must take effect in point of possession when
their right to possession ceases. Meanwhile they are in a state
of pupilage. Their relation to the United States resembles that
of a ward to a guardian."[7]

The next year, Marshall again embraced these complexities
and further defined the state of Indian treaties. In *Worchester
v. Georgia*, Marshall stated: "The words 'treaty' and 'nation'
are words of our own language, selected in our diplomatic and
legislative proceedings, by ourselves, having each a definite
and well understood meaning. We have applied them to Indians, as we have applied them to the other nations of the
earth. They are applied to all in the same sense."[8]

Marshall had confused basic concepts of sovereignty. He con-
stitutionally recognized the treaty-making power of Indian
tribes, and yet he called them domestic dependent nations.
Historically, treaties were made among independent nations,
to be sure of varying military strengths.[9] Marshall meant to
distinguish between internal and external forms of sovereignty, and he concluded that Indian tribes, at least by the 1830s in
Georgia, no longer held much external sovereignty over their
collective lives.

Nevertheless, treaties between Indians and the United
States government continued to be contracted, some honorably
negotiated and some dishonorably imposed. With continental
expansion completed by the time of the Civil War and with the
mining rushes and accompanying settlers moving west, more
and more contact was made with the trans-Mississippi tribes.
Antebellum treaties again reflected pre-1812 documents. They
varied in specifics but they did embellish the interests of more
equal foreign powers. Indeed, the Sioux nation controlled the
north Plains throughout this era. But once the Civil War was
over, military attention centered upon establishing United
States physical hegemony, and treaties became more the product of war than peace, more the result of imposition than
negotiation. Still, as historian Wilcomb Washburn relates,
"Even after the military power of the Indians was broken, their

legal political existence as distinct political bodies, at least for particular purposes, continued."[10]

In the decade that preceded the Resolution of 1871, a number of significant events helped shape the ultimate outcome. Minnesotans experienced a major outbreak of violence in 1862 when the Santee Sioux, confined to reservations and denied treaty-guaranteed provisions, broke out and vented their anger on local settlements.[11] Reaction was swift. Termed a "national war," not a local outbreak, by Minnesota governor Alexander Ramsey, federal troops were ordered west.[12] General John Pope, disgraced for Union army war failures, instructed Colonel Henry H. Sibley that no treaties could be made with the Sioux. Pope described the Sioux as maniacs and wild beasts who deserved extermination. By October the Sioux were defeated and President Lincoln in response urged Congress to remodel Indian-United States relations.[13]

Congress proved anxious to comply, especially the House of Representatives. In 1862, during the Sioux Uprising, a bill had become law formally breaking any treaty with an Indian tribe that committed hostile acts against the United States. Abrogation occurred if such action came within federal interests. The merit of any grievances as justification for hostility need not be considered.[14]

Five years later the House originated a section in the 1867 Indian Appropriations Act forbidding the expenditure of money by the president, secretary of interior, or commissioner of Indian affairs for treaty negotiations without express congressional authorization. This provision was dropped several months later when Congress realized that it would hinder the efforts of the newly constituted Indian Peace Commission.[15]

Appointed by an act of Congress in July 1867, eight leaders in past negotiations were charged with investigating abuses within the treaty system and making recommendations for reform that would restore peace to the trans-Mississippi West. These men included Indian Commissioner N. G. Taylor as chairman; army or militia volunteer officers William S. Harney, William T. Sherman, John B. Sanborn, Alfred H. Terry,

Christopher C. Augur; and Samuel F. Tappan and Senator John B. Henderson from Missouri. All of the military men had participated in major Indian campaigns such as the Black Hawk War, the Seminole Wars, the Brule Sioux Action, and the Sand Creek Massacre.[16]

The commission traveled extensively in the Great Plains region and collected testimony. The words offered by Bishop Henry B. Whipple of Minnesota on October 7, 1868, were typical. He prefaced his advice to the group by relating personal feelings:

I know by the bitterness of our experience the horrors of savage warfare. I have too many friends in nameless graves to offer one plea for savage violence. But, even this does not and cannot release us from the claims of justice, of humanity and of our fear of God. We are writing history, and as true as God's words are true, if we continue the course we have followed, his curse will fall on us and our children. There is no question that our Indian system is a blunder more than a crime, because its glaring evils would have been redressed if it had ever been calmly considered.[17]

Then Whipple offered an explanation for the serious problems in United States-Indian relations. To him, changing United States governmental attitudes toward treaties would make the difference. Treaties, he argued, should be contracted fairly and scrupulously upheld.

We recognize them as nations, we pledge them our faith, we enter on solemn treaties and these treaties are ratified, as with all foreign powers, by the highest authority in the nation. You know every man who ever looked into our Indian Affairs knows it is a shameless lie. The treaties are often conceived in fraud, and made solely to put money in some white man's pocket. . . . The savage, left without law to protect, with no incentive to labor, with harpies to plunder, vice and crime holding a carnival of death, until maddened with frenzy, he wreaks his vengeance on the innocent people of the border.[18]

The next day, October 8, General Sanborn, influenced by Whipple's testimony, proposed that the commission recommend to Congress and the president that treaties remain in force only with those Indians abandoning their nomadic ways. All other treaties under the Sanborn proposal should be declared null and void.[19] General Terry rephrased Sanborn's motion:

Resolved: that it be recommended that henceforth, the Government shall cease to recognize the Indian tribes as domestic dependent nations, except so far as it may be absolutely required to so recognize them by existing treaties and that hereafter the Indians individually shall be considered and held to be personally subject to the laws of the United States, like other persons owing allegiance to the Government. That, hereafter no treaties shall be made with any Indian tribe but that their rights of person and property and the duties of the Government toward them shall be defined by statute law. That existing treaties shall be maintained and respected, until their violation by the Indians themselves shall justify the Government in abrogating them, severally, and that whenever any treaty shall be so violated, it *shall* be abrogated and declared null and void, and the Indians violating it shall be thence forward governed and controlled without reference to such treaty.[20]

No further action was taken that day, but in the evening Taylor and Tappan no doubt consulted because they had consistently been outvoted 5-2 on other issues. The next day Taylor tried to dilute the Terry proposal and failed. Then after much debate, Taylor and Tappan, persuaded by humanitarian arguments such as those presented earlier by Bishop Whipple, joined the military in unanimously urging Congress to curtail future treaty-making with Indian tribes.[21]

The substance of the Terry proposal was noteworthy on three accounts. First, the notion of considering Indians as domestic dependent nations was scuttled for the future and seriously curtailed for past treaties. Second, hints at a severalty program were articulated, a "reform" finally implemented by the federal government in the 1880s. And third, new preconditions were to be imposed upon past treaties in order to invalidate them. The underwritten goal was total treaty abolition, present, future, and *past*. Whatever the implications of the

Terry proposal, it was included in the final report of the commission and was seriously received by members of Congress.

Also during the decade of the 1860s, the United States accelerated its treaty-making initiatives with Indian nations. Countless councils were held and fifty-nine treaties were actually ratified and sanctified. The 1860s represents the most intense era of Indian and United States treaty making; three tribes—the Shoshone, Sioux, and Cheyenne—were the most extensively involved. They alone accounted for over one-third of all treaties made in the 1860s.[22]

As is evident from the vast number of treaties entered into during the 1860s the process was not a successful enterprise. The treaty system itself was riddled with administrative problems, but there were also other factors that contributed to its demise. The Shoshone, Dakota, and Cheyenne represented some of the strongest of the trans-Mississippi tribes, and they were accustomed to dealing with international relations from a position of superiority or equality. Their first treaties with the United States had been made with certain concessions on their part, but it was obvious to all sides that any failure to live up to the agreements most assuredly meant war. By being unable to meet federal treaty obligations, whether it was by Mormon settlers overrunning Shoshone lands, miners invading the sacred Black Hills of the Sioux, or Reverend John Chivington's Colorado militia's barbaric mutilations of Black Kettle's Cheyenne, the United States would simply have to embark upon the politics of confrontation. The diplomacy of all parties would no longer matter, and the Resolution of 1871 would simply ratify international reality.

The crisis of Indian-United States diplomacy of the 1860s, especially with Great Plains tribes, and Congress's careful ponderance of the recommendations of the Indian Peace Commission provided the backdrop for the debate surrounding the Resolution of 1871. The desire of the House of Representatives to infringe upon the traditional foreign affairs powers of the Senate and the coalescing of fiscal conservative sentiment, anti-Indian attitudes, and reformer conversion to the idea that the treaty system unfairly took advantage of Indian parties spelled an immediate doom to Indian-United States diplomatic parity.

Debate centered around the Indian Appropriations Act which originated in the House. Argument over these appropriations exhibited numerous forms. Those who disliked the present system by which the United States conducted Indian affairs were divided into anti-Indian and humanitarian groups. Some, like Representative Thomas Fitch of Nevada—possibly the one who uttered the infamous remark, "The only good Indian is a dead Indian"—charged that the treaty system wasted money and fostered corruption. In addition, the army performed incompetently, necessitating volunteers. To this group the best policy was no policy. Fitch felt natural extermination would be best for all concerned.[23]

Others critical of the treaty system could not stomach the Fitch bravado. Aaron Sargent of California saw treaty negotiations as comedies. He cited treaties with 38 Umpquas and 236 Rogue River Indians as absurd. They were not nations, he claimed, and he seemed to equate the usage of the treaty power to numbers of persons within a nation. "Eighty or a hundred years ago, perhaps," Sargent reflected, "when there were great confederated nations upon our borders, not entirely upon and owned by ourselves, we might treat with them in order to keep the peace; but now the whole thing is changed."[24]

This practical diplomatic philosophy also included calls for a moral accounting. Eugene M. Wilson of Minnesota reasoned that if anything was wrong with Indian treaties, it was that they did not stand up under strict contractual scrutiny. In a major speech, he called for

a future policy [to be] adopted in which no treaties should be made. I think it would be better. But this propriety for the future does not authorize us to repudiate the past. Much sympathy is expressed by eastern gentlemen for the suffering Indians, and we are told that their outrages are but retaliations for the bad acts of our frontiersmen. Let me tell them that the wrongs done the Indian have been the failure to carry out treaty stipulations.[25]

Those who favored the Indian treaty system recognized its faults, but they argued that it worked. If the goal was peace, survival of human beings, or economy, the treaty and concomitant appropriations were desired.[26] Besides, asked Massachusetts's Henry L. Dawes, was there not any reasonable alternative? Dawes viewed the Fitch approach as butchery: "As between butchery and humanity, I prefer humanity," he declared.[27] Others like James A. Garfield noted that this policy prevented Indian massacres.[28]

Many who supported the treaty system believed that the ultimate solution had to be assimilation through severalty.[29] Alloting lands would bring the Indian out of his domestic dependent national status. If those who favored severalty, such as Dawes, could be convinced that abolishing or abrogating treaties would lead to their desired reform, then that long honored diplomatic process would be abandoned.

The Indian Appropriations Act passed the House with a number of minute additions and deletions from its original form, with the most curious amendment occurring after a provision for additional moneys to be given to the Yankton Sioux. Congressman William Lawrence of Ohio amended the act to read as follows:

Provided, That nothing in this act contained shall be construed to ratify any of the so-called treaties entered into with any tribe, band, or party of Indians, since the 20th July, 1867.[30]

Lawrence argued that the House needed to assert its powers in foreign relations.[31] This amendment created considerable comment culminating in an exchange between Representatives Clarkson N. Potter, Horace Maynard, and Eugene Wilson. All three agreed that the fundamental question focused upon whether Indian tribes were foreign nations. Potter believed it to be a matter of judgment. Who decides? To Potter, it was the House *and* the Senate. Wilson disagreed; he strongly felt the Supreme Court made such decisions. The Potter position prevailed, although no language prevented future treaties.[32]

The Senate did not receive the House version very kindly. Many senators thought that the House was too extravagant.[33] Others objected to innuendos such as "so-called" before treaties.[34] Senator Samuel C. Pomeroy of Kansas noted that to ignore past treaties was to commit "a burlesque upon the history of the country, and upon the legislation of the country."[35] Senator Frederick A. Sawyer of South Carolina believed large appropriations encouraged fraud, and Senator Henry Wilson of Massachusetts saw the lawyers who would be attached to the treaty process as creating the bulk of the problems with their contingent fees.[36] As in the House, Indian haters and admirers alike expressed chagrin with the treaty system.

Defenders such as Iowa's James Harlan tried desperately to uphold treaty commitments. He argued that Indians were like the recently emancipated slaves, that keeping treaties was the international duty of a civilized nation, and that fulfilling treaties kept the peace and a stable economy.[37] But he was unable to stem the criticism. Senator Henry W. Corbett of Oregon correctly gauged the sentiment of the upper house when he suggested that, in an era of limited means, Congress had a choice of funding the army for Indian wars or appropriating enough to keep Indians on reservations. The latter was cheaper but harder to defend.[38]

After the Senate finished with the bill, clearly the Indian Appropriations Act needed a conference committee to compromise the differences. Speaker of the House James G. Blaine and Vice President Schuyler Colfax selected a conference committee which began to work on a compromise package on February 28, 1871.[39] By March 1, they had agreed upon the restructured bill that included a completely new clause outlawing future treaties. Aaron Sargent brought the revised proposition back to the House where he gloated over the power he had absconded from the Senate and the millions of dollars to be saved.[40] Sargent continued to extol the virtues of this "new" bill even though ratification clauses and "so-called" treaty clauses had been trimmed in conference. He did make clear, however, that all past treaties should be honored. The bill was quickly approved.[41]

The Senate did not acquiesce as easily. The change was discovered immediately, and Senator Garrett Davis of Kentucky urged strong opposition. He saw the new provision as counter to international law and justice. Harlan and Eugene Casserly tried to delay by asking that the report be printed. Senator Cornelius Cole successfully opposed this move, and Harlan gave in. He noted that the Osage had been "civilized" without benefit of treaties so others were likely to obtain the same results.[42]

Pomeroy held out. He considered the new clause to violate the treaty powers of the Constitution. The bill, at best, he countered, "is a sort of toadyism to the House of Representatives."[43] Davis now became most passionate. He argued that the checks and balances of the Constitution were being upset and that the law would conflict with the decisions previously made by the Supreme Court. Yes, treaties were not infrequent, and yes, the military relationships of the tribes to the United States had changed, but this alone could not justify diluting the treaty powers of the entire federal government.[44]

The only member of the conference committee to answer these objections was Senator John P. Stockton of New Jersey. He insisted that the central question to be answered once again was whether Indian tribes were foreign nations. He strangely reasoned that they were not nations because they could become territories and states in the Union. Thus, to Stockton, Congress classified who were and were not foreign nations.[45]

The Senate seemed exhausted and desirous to end their present session. Without even taking the yeas and nays, the report was approved. President Grant then signed the Indian Appropriations Act and the Resolution of 1871 became law.

By passing the Act of 1871, Congress abolished the treaty system of dealing with Indian nations in the future, but it in no way ended any past relationships between the United States and the tribes. The passage of the resolution simply allowed

Congress after 1871 to deal with the Indian nations through ordinary legislation instead of by treaty. Past recognitions of sovereignty in Indian tribes were maintained.

It would be inevitable for congressional legislation concerning Indians to be challenged in the United States court system, especially if the legislation affected *prior* treaties. Several important decisions were made at the Supreme Court level in the years subsequent to the Resolution of 1871, judgments that continue to carry precedent. The major controversies in these cases concerned the power of congressional legislation over and against previous Indian treaties.

Less than a year before, in the *Cherokee Tobacco Case*, the Supreme Court began the assault on Indian treaties. Elias Boudinot and Stand Watie, Cherokee leaders, refused to pay federal taxes on tobacco produced on the lands of the Cherokee nation. The court held that the Internal Revenue Act of 1868 prevailed over the Cherokee Treaty of 1866. It held that

A treaty may supersede a prior act of Congress, and an act of Congress may supersede a prior treaty. In the cases referred to these principles were applied to treaties with foreign nations. Treaties with Indian nations within the jurisdiction of the United States, whatever considerations of humanity and good faith may be involved and require their faithful observance, cannot be more obligatory. They have no higher sanctity; and no greater inviolability or immunity from legislative invasion can be claimed for them. The consequences in all such cases give rise to questions which must be met by the political department of the government. They are beyond the sphere of judicial cognizance. In the case under consideration the act of Congress must prevail as if the treaty were not an element to be considered. If a wrong has been done the power of redress is with Congress not with the judiciary, and that body upon being applied to, it is to be presumed, will promptly give the proper relief.[46]

The *Cherokee Tobacco Case* in conjunction with the Resolution of 1871 proved to be a lethal combination for not only future but past Indian treaties. The "political question" doctrine introduced in the *Cherokee Tobacco Case* and silently ratified by Congress became a strong influence in two early twentieth-century Supreme Court decisions that broadened further the impact of the Resolution of 1871.

In *Cherokee Nation v. Hitchcock* (1902), the Cherokee sought to enjoin the secretary of the interior from authorizing mineral and oil leases on Cherokee land, an action which Congress had authorized by legislation. The Cherokee argued that such action was an abrogation of certain treaty rights promised by the United States to that Indian nation. In finding for the federal government, the Court made it clear that they were not

concerned in this case with the question whether the act of June 28, 1898, and the proposed action thereunder, which is complained of, is or is not wise, and calculated to operate beneficially to the interests of the Cherokee. The power existing in Congress to administer upon and guard the tribal property, and the power being political and administrative in its nature, the manner of its exercise is a question within the province of the legislative branch to determine and is not one for the courts.[47]

The next year in *Lone Wolf v. Hitchcock*, another case involving Indian tribal property rights—this time Comanche, Kiowa, and Kiowa-Apache—the Court specifically stated that "The power exists to abrogate the provisions of an Indian treaty." The Court upheld the constitutionality of the Resolution of 1871, arguing that when "treaties were entered into between the United States and a tribe of Indians, it was never to be doubted that the *power* to abrogate existed in Congress."[48] The standard for abrogation was whether the congressional action was in the best interests of the United States and the Indians personally and individually. And once appeal was made to the highest court of the land, the Court would never question the motives of Congress.

The *Lone Wolf* case represented the culmination of legal and political destruction of Indian sovereignty and the treaty process. The Marshall decisions of earlier times had been seriously eroded if not overruled, and the Resolution of 1871 had been substantially modified if not misinterpreted. The Court had decided that treaties were the supreme law of the land, until Congress altered them. The same rule applied to mere executive agreements. In other words, no Indian treaty was safe from the changing whims of Congress.

The danger of this doctrine to diplomatic actions of the United States has been recognized by post-1945 Congresses and Supreme Courts. Modern decisions of the Court and the Indian Claims Commission have attempted to uphold the sanctity of treaties with the tribes. Not to do so would cause future allies to be very suspicious and jeopardize delicate international relationships. The Resolution of 1871 not only represented an end to pretense in Indian relations, but it also meant a serious modification and violation of international law and a threat to the diplomacy of the United States.

Even so, laws and treaties have a way of surviving long after their origins have been erased or obscured. The Native American-United States treaty binge of the 1860s left its residue. Although their failures culminated in future treaty prohibitions, they have remained vibrant and useful in the twentieth century. Indeed, in the years to come the little-known treaties will no doubt become the object of national focus and debate. Once again sovereign nations of varying strengths will have to reconcile long-standing disagreements—perhaps in a treaty council.

NOTES

1. See *Indian Claims Commission Findings on the Shoshoni Indians* (New York: Garland, 1974); and Maurine Carley and Virginia Trenholm, *The Shoshonis: Sentinels of the Rockies* (Norman: University of Oklahoma Press, 1964).

2. U.S., *Statutes at Large* 16 (1971): 566.

3. Wilcomb E. Washburn, *The Indian in America* (New York: Harper and Row, 1975), pp. 80-81.

4. Ibid., pp. 97-98.

5. Francis Jennings, *The Invasion of America: Indians, Colonialism, and the Cant of Conquest* (New York: W.W. Nor-

ton and Company, 1976), pp. 120-124; Wilcomb E. Washburn, *Red Man's Law and White Man's Law: A Study of the Past and the Present Status of the American Indian* (New York: Charles Scribner's Sons, 1971), p. 73.

6. See Arthur H. DeRosier, Jr., *The Removal of the Choctaw Indians* (New York: Harper and Row, 1970); Grant Forman, *Indian Removal*, Norman: University of Oklahoma Press, 1953); Joseph C. Burke, "The Cherokee Cases: A Study in Law, Politics, and Morality," *Stanford Law Review* 21 (February 1969):500-531; Mary Young, "Indian Removal and Land Allotment: The Civilized Tribes and Jacksonian Justice," *American Historical Review* 64 (October 1958):31-45; Ronald N. Satz, *American Indian Policy in the Jacksonian Era* (Lincoln: University of Nebraska Press, 1974).

7. *Cherokee Nation v. Georgia*, U.S. (5 Pet.) 1 (1831) at 7.

8. *Worchester v. Georgia*, U.S. (6 Pet.) 515 (1832) at 532-533.

9. See Frederick Ross Boundy, *Handbook to Indian Legal Problems* (Seattle: University of Washington, 1971), pp. 52-55.

10. Washburn, *Indian in America*, p. 81.

11. See Roy W. Meyer, *History of the Santee Sioux* (Lincoln: University of Nebraska Press, 1967); Kenneth Carley, ed., "As Red Men Viewed It: Three Indian Accounts of the Uprising," *Minnesota History* 38 (1962): 126-149.

12. Richard N. Ellis, *General Pope and U.S. Indian Policy* (Albuquerque: University of New Mexico Press, 1970), p. 12.

13. Ibid.; see also U.S., *Annual Report of the Commissioner of Indian Affairs for 1862*, p. 15.

14. U.S., *Statutes at Large* 12 (1862): 528.

15. U.S., *Statutes at Large* 15 (1867): 7, 18.

16. For Henderson, see *Biographical Directory of the American Congress, 1774-1971* (1971), p. 1103. For Sanborn and Augur, see *The National Cyclopaedia of American Biography* (New York: James T. White, 1907), vol. 5, p. 287, and vol. 4, p. 327. For Harney, Sherman, and Terry, see *Webster's American Military Biographies* (Springfield, Mass.: G & C Merriam Company, 1978), pp. 166, 382-384, 433.

17. Records of the Office of the Secretary of the Interior, RG-48, "Transcript of the Minutes and Proceedings of the Indian Peace Commission Appointed by an Act of Congress, July 20, 1867," p. 162.

18. Ibid.

19. Ibid., p. 176.

20. Ibid., p. 177.

21. Ibid., p. 185. The first annual report of the Board of Indian Commissioners of 1869 and the *Annual Report of the Commissioner of Indian Affairs for 1869* contained this recommendation.

22. See Charles J. Kappler, *Indian Affairs: Laws and Treaties*, 5 vols. (Washington, D.C.: Government Printing Office, 1903-1941).

23. *Congressional Globe*, 41st Cong., 3d. sess., 1871, pp. 730-736.

24. Ibid., p. 765.

25. Ibid., p. 766.

26. Ibid., pp. 731, 733-737, 765-769.

27. Ibid., p. 733.

28. Ibid., p. 737.

29. Ibid., pp. 730-737, 762-769.

30. Ibid., p. 763.

31. Ibid.

32. Ibid., pp. 767-769.

33. Ibid., pp. 1112-1114.

34. Ibid., p. 1112.

35. Ibid.

36. Ibid., pp. 1485.

37. Ibid., pp. 1483, 1491-1497, 1499-1504, 1507, 1564, 1568-1573, 1822.

38. Ibid., pp. 1503-1504.

39. Ibid., pp. 1756, 1771; *Biographical Directory of the American Congress, 1774-1971* (1971), pp. 570, 764-765, 747, 1070, 1656, 1760. Blaine appointed James B. Beck, Aaron Sargent, and Sidney Clarke, and Colfax selected Cornelius Cole, James Harlan, and John P. Stockton. The composition of the

committee did not reflect any strong commitment for treaty making aside from Senator Harlan, who had been visibly weakened by the Senate debate. Of the six members, all except Clarke were lawyers, Stockton had served as minister (ambassador) to Italy and none had any previous experience with Indian wars or treaty negotiations. Four were Republicans and two, Beck and Stockton, were Democrats. They generally represented areas no longer confronted with on-going Indian relations. Except for Kansas (Clarke), inactive Indian regions gaining recognition included Kentucky (Beck), California (Sargent and Cole), Iowa (Harlan), and New Jersey (Stockton).

40. *Congressional Globe*, 41st Cong., 3d sess., 1871, p. 1811. The credit, Sargent noted, went to a representative from Pennsylvania who was not a member of the committee, William H. Armstrong. Armstrong had prepared the clause preventing future Indian treaties. Although he only served one term in Congress and had had no previous experience in Indian Affairs, President Grant would offer him the office of Commissioner of Indian Affairs for his effort. Armstrong wisely turned this position down.

41. Ibid., pp. 1810-1812.

42. Ibid., p. 1822.

43. Ibid.

44. Ibid., pp. 1823-1824.

45. 1bid., p. 1823.

46. *Two Hundred and Seven Half Pound Papers of Smoking Tobacco, Elias C. Boudinot et al. (Claimants) v. United States*, 78 U.S. (11 Wall) 616 (1870) at 620-621.

47. *Cherokee Nation v. Hitchcock*, 187 U.S. 294 (1902) at 308.

48. *Lone Wolf v. Hitchcock*, 187 U.S. 553 (1903) at 566.

II
LAND SPECULATION

"Everyone was imbued with a reckless spirit of speculation. The mania, such as it undoubtedly was, did not confine itself to one particular class, but extended to all. Even the reverend clergy doffed their sacredotals, and eagerly entered into competition with mammon's votaries, for the acquisition of this world's goods."

Levi Beardsley, New Yorker-gone West,
Reminiscences, 1852

The largess of lands in North America provoked numerous responses from their inhabitants and their would-be occupants. Environmental considerations entered the minds of but a small minority, and rules and regulations created by absentee governments touched many, but it was to the speculator that the lands first fell. The introduction of agriculture, whether subsistence farming or modern ranching, inevitably had to endure the initial investor and the subsequent on-the-scene consolidator.

Land speculation in North America was strongly influenced by the first English settlers. Benjamin H. Newcomb suggests that large landholders in colonial New York and New Jersey were able to protect their thousands of acres from divestiture by political action in their respective legislatures. It appears that manor lord families in New York, such as the Livingstons or the Nicolls, and proprietors in New Jersey, such as the Morris family, played important political roles but were not overhanded in a class sense. Only on issues of taxation of un-inhabited lands were the lines firmly drawn between speculator and settler advocates.

Further away in time and space, Donald Abbe documents the development and decline of large ranch holdings in the Texas South Plains county of Lynn. Here during the last portion of the nineteenth century one of the later agricultural frontiers was opened to purchase. Outsiders first obtained the range of Lynn County, and then large ranches, such as the T-Bar, successfully accumulated thousands of acres, much of it in leaseholds. But unlike their colonial forebears, Texas pioneer ranching speculators were not able to prevent unfavorable legislation and court opinions that forced a dramatic change from a ranching to a farming economy.

Charles K. Warren, according to David J. Murrah, represented a many-sided speculator. His venture into Mexican ranching included the interests of an absentee colonialist but also because of the Mexican Revolution required a sensitivity to local needs, conditions, politics, and law. Eventually, the Warrens, like the Slaughters and Edwards families in Lynn County, and the Van Rensselaers and Beekmans of colonial New York and New Jersey, would be forced to consolidate their holdings and pay heed to the democratic yearnings for those poised on the agricultural lands.

Land speculation, then, usually predated development and settlement. Some have termed it a "necessary evil," while others have found it to be a parasitic outrage. Nevertheless, speculation has permeated the history of agriculture on the lands that would become the United States and beyond.

The Great Landholders and Political Power in Colonial New York and New Jersey

Several characteristics common to twentieth century America shaped the political life of New York and New Jersey in the forty years before the outbreak of the American Revolution: ethnic variety, religious diversity, mixed economies, and a combination of urban growth and agricultural prosperity. One characteristic, anachronistic rather than modern, that deserves exploration and analysis is the privileged political position enjoyed in the two colonies by great landowners. In New Jersey these were the proprietors; in New York manor lords or large patentees.

Proprietors and manor lords in these two colonies occupied positions different from the upper-class leaders of most other colonies. In New England there were none so great in land and privilege. In the southern colonies aristocrats in varying circumstances did equal those of New York and New Jersey, or surpass them, but the social and economic setting, that is, plantation slavery, was so greatly different as to reinforce and add singular solidity to aristocratic dominance. The neighboring colony of Pennsylvania was most like New York and New Jersey; but its landed aristocrats, the Penn proprietors, were absentee landlords.

The aristocrats of New York and New Jersey were involved in a freer system that was more permissive of political tension, a system in which other economic and social groups were more at liberty to oppose the dominant class. The lowest class in these two colonies, also had some power of political complaint, if not opposition, and could more readily join with a group that had political power for purposes of confrontation. In short, unlike other colonies, the aristocratic claims of proprietors and manor lords were under challenge from equals—that is, merchants and wealthy lawyers—and from unequals—small farmers and tenants.[1]

The course and process of the assertion of political privilege is the subject of this study. An assessment of the success of the landholder elite in retaining and using political power is important for the understanding of how politics developed in the colonies. Some historians have argued that in the early eighteenth century the aristocrats of the American colonies staged a "feudal revival," a strengthening of the economic status and to a lesser extent the political status of the great landlord class. The Revolution then cut short any fuller institution of the archaic system. The notion of feudal revival has not been widely taken up as a device for interpreting colonial American social development generally, but, because New York and New Jersey had privileged and powerful landlords, the validity of the application of the concept could be readily tested there.[2]

The economic circumstances of the proprietors and manor lords are not the principal concern here, but they should be generally noted as background to the political circumstances. Being a large landholder around 1750 was not merely a speculation because the holdings were paying off at greater rates, or at least as well as ever before. The New York manor lords, as a group, were wealthier than were the New Jersey proprietors. The Van Rensselaer family held two major grants: the Manor of Rensselaerwyck and Claverack, totaling 1 million acres—the bulk of Albany County. The neighbor of the Rensselaers to the south was the lord of the Manor of Livingston. Robert Livingston, Jr., manor lord for the twenty-five years before the Revolution, in 1765 was netting £100 per week from his iron works and grist mills; this was the greatest income of any American. South of this bonanza was the Livingston's lower manor called Clermont, owned by another Robert Livingston, uncle of the manor lord. This Livingston territory totalled 150,000 acres. Slightly larger in extent were the two major holdings of the Philipse family: the Highland patent in southern Dutchess County and the Manor of Phillipsborough, extending along the east side of the Hudson River. The Manor of Cortlandt, in northern Westchester County, was only 86,000 acres; after 1750 it became divided among many owners. Roughly the same size were the two patents of the Beekman family in Dutchess County, which were not denominated manors but, like them, were populated by tenants.[3]

Some manors were much smaller. For example, an 850-acre Manor of Bentley on Staten Island was owned by Christopher Billop, assemblyman from Richmond County, just as was Henry Beekman from Dutchess. More imposing were such smaller manors as Morrisana, at the southern tip of Westchester County and owned consecutively by Lewis Morris I, II, and III, all assemblymen; Islip on Long Island, 100 square miles belonging to three generations of the Nicoll family all of whom served in the legislature; and Fox Hall in Ulster County, owned by Colonel Abraham Gaasbeck-Chambers, assemblyman and stepson of the patentee.[4] Small or large, the manors seemed to prosper. The owners recorded no major economic difficulties, and they translated economic status into political prominence.

The New Jersey proprietors at the beginning of the eighteenth century had resigned the troublesome task of governing but they had not relinquished their land rights. There were no large manors with tenants; the business of the New Jersey proprietors was land sales and quit-rents. The West Jersey proprietors were numerous; no one group monopolized the land, although a few of the proprietors held substantial tracts. The governing body of the proprietors, the Board or Council, divided up the allocated land among the large number of proprietors at fairly frequent intervals, rather than hold it for speculation. This policy was of more advantage to the smaller landowners of West Jersey, whom the West Jersey Board best represented, than to those larger holders with speculative interests.[5]

Lewis Morris, East Jersey proprietor and later governor, epitomized the difference between his constituency and that of the West Jersey Board by referring to the West Jersey Board as the "mob interest." The group of proprietors from the eastern side was smaller in number, much wealthier, and concentrated in and around the city of Perth Amboy, a metropolis of some 1,500 by 1775. Samuel Neville, assemblyman from Perth Amboy and Middlesex County, 1743-1765, was the wealthiest, claiming 5 1/4 proprieties, or 21.9 percent of the undivided land of East Jersey. Other prominent proprietors were the Johnston family of Perth Amboy and their in-laws, who were rich merchants and lawyers; the Morris family of New York, particularly Lewis, Sr., and his son Robert H.; and prominent New York lawyer James Alexander, who Richard Peters of Pennsylvania said "has the most immoderate Thirst for Land of any man I Know."[6]

The East Jersey proprietors held onto their land as speculators, declaring few dividends or divisions of their holdings, and were content to wait for the value to increase. This policy brought them into conflict with timber poachers and land-hungry squatters. They evidently considered themselves a breed apart from the common herd, without any redeeming features of civic duty and solicitude for lesser economic classes that was more characteristic of the New York manor lords. Thus Lewis Morris Ashfield, proprietor, councilor, grandson of Lewis Morris, arrogantly cursed a constable—"God Damn You with your King's Laws"—and horsewhipped him. Ashfield, of course, was exonerated.[7]

No one questioned that the economic domination of the proprietors and manor lords should rightly be accompanied by political power. That this power was formally established for some New York manor lords merely put in writing the traditional rule by the landed elite that originated long before the establishment of British colonies. Merchants and lawyers were more pressed to justify their governing power; those of landed estate automatically qualified.

The institutional channels for expressing this political power varied among the two colonies, as political conditions changed. Either governor, council, or assembly was potentially susceptible to elite domination. At times governors in New York and New Jersey did join with members of the landed elite for mutual advantage. Only the DeLancey family of New York, not primarily landed but mercantile, gained control of the governorship, and this occurred because of an extraordinary combination of events and influence. Under normal circumstances the proprietors and manor lords could not depend on the governor to further their cause, any more than could other colonial interest groups.[8]

For the resident landed elite, the governor's council would appear a more likely place to exert political power. There was a certain obvious analogy with the British House of Lords— though a very feeble one—and indeed the East Jersey proprietors in particular were firmly entrenched in the council. Of the thirty-two councilors appointed from 1738 to 1775, fifteen were East Jersey proprietors. Only five were prominent West Jersey proprietors, though others may have had small proprietary shares. New York manor lords, in contrast to the East Jersey proprietors, did not show much interest in the council. At one time or another all the great houses were on the council, but no Philipse served after 1721, no Morris after 1729, no Van Rensselaer after 1746 (the manor lords were minors or young men), no Van Cortlandt after 1748, and no Livingston after 1750.[9]

The council was clearly not the place for the landed elite to make its political mark. The New York manor lords seem to have seen this more readily. The East Jersey proprietors as a group did not; but their chief spokesmen and most able leaders, Samuel Neville and Cortlandt Skinner, never served on the council. Proprietors and manor lords as a group gained little or nothing politically from council office. The economic advantages to being councilor were important; land grants were easy for New York councilors to obtain. Councils, however, were not strong and stern enough to escape the influence of the governor. Governors, with little extensive patronage to bestow, lacked important political influence except within the circle of councilors. As a result, councils were respondent and managed. Any particular economic interest on a council would have to accommodate itself to the governor. Moreover, a council would not be powerful enough, if the governor were of contrary mind or disposed toward compromise, to forestall policies pushed by whatever majority controlled the assembly.[10]

For the proprietors and manor lords of New York and New Jersey to be involved in the activities of the popular branch of government would appear to be almost lowering oneself. However, they realized that real political control and power came only with dominance of the legislature. They did not expect total hegemony, for legislatures did not work that way. There must be give-and-take, bargains, alliances, and *quid pro quo* arrangements, in which some things are gained and some given up. The landed elite hoped to surrender very little, however, and at the same time to enlarge the scope of their authority, or at least prevent encroachments on their economic interests and social position. Two specific circumstances helped to make them powerful in the legislative bodies: numerical strength and holding leadership positions.

In regard to numerical strength, the manor lords of New York were at great advantage. The Manors of Rensselaerwyck, Livingston, and Cortlandt had direct representation in the legislature. Rensselaerwyck attained the right in the 1680s probably chiefly because of its great size. Livingston manor was granted representation in 1715, and Cortlandt in 1717 to put them on a par with the larger manor and to reward Robert Livingston I for his political alliance with Governor Robert Hunter and Lewis Morris, lord of Morrisana. In these three seats either the lord of the manor or a close relative served as representative. In addition to these three, other assembly seats were frequently held by manor lords prominent in that county, sometimes for years in succession. Thus in the forty-five years before the outbreak of the Revolution, eighteen manor lords— 14.1 percent of all legislators—served eighty-nine terms in the New York house, or 27.1 percent of all terms.[11]

West Jersey proprietors were the most numerous of any of the proprietary groups in the legislatures. In the period 1738-1772, sixteen West Jersey proprietors served thirty-eight assembly terms, comprising 23.5 percent of all West Jersey assemblymen and 26.4 percent of all terms of office. During the same period thirteen East Jersey proprietors served. Of these, nine of them served twenty-one of the twenty-four assembly terms from Perth Amboy, and the other four served five of twenty-four terms from Middlesex County. In West Jersey, because proprietors were widely distributed geographically and not necessarily very large landholders, the large proportion of proprietors serving does not represent exclusive inner-group domination, though it does represent domination by the more affluent. In East Jersey the proprietors were top ranking in wealth and social position.[12]

The number of manor lords and proprietors in the assemblies was of course greatly out of proportion to their number in the general population; the almost direct representation they enjoyed in New York, and their considerable political influence in New Jersey, assured that they would be heard in the assembly to an extent that no other group could be. The voice of the elite agricultural landholder would be strong enough to work the will of this group. Indeed the proprietors and manor lords had great influence. Further analysis of the legislatures, and the course of events in regard to how key issues were resolved in the assemblies, show that the landholders were not dominant, but, like other interest groups, compelled to share political power to obtain only a portion of what would benefit them.

Within the assemblies the proprietors and manor lords did not play the most dominant leadership roles. An evaluation of leadership in the assemblies of the two colonies identifies top leaders: the relatively few who dominate a group; second ranking leaders, more numerous and of less prestige; ordinary members; and inactives. Tables 4.1 and 4.2 show that the proprietors and manor lords in New York and New Jersey were not as important in playing leadership roles as were merchants and lawyers.

Table 4.1
Assembly Political Leadership in Colonial New York, 1728–1775

	Top Rank ($N = 15$)	2nd Rank ($N = 21$)	Inactive ($N = 26$)
Lawyers ($N = 6$)	33.3% (5)	4.8% (1)	0
Merchants ($N = 36$)	46.6% (7)	42.9% (9)	0
Manor lords ($N = 18$)	20% (3)	42.9% (9)	7.7% (2)

Put another way, in New York all the lawyers were leaders, two thirds of the manor lords were, and 44.4 percent of the merchants were, but the merchants dominated the top rank of leaders, with lawyers also important.

Table 4.2
Assembly Political Leadership in Colonial New Jersey, 1738–1775

	Top Rank ($N = 15$)	2nd Rank ($N = 18$)	Inactive ($N = 34$)
Lawyers ($N = 8$)	33.3% (5)	11.1% (2)	0
Merchants ($N = 19$)	13.3% (2)	11.1% (2)	2.9% (1)
East Jersey proprieters ($N = 13$)	33.3% (5)	5.6% (1)	2.9% (1)
West Jersey proprietors ($N = 16$	0	22.2% (4)	9.5% (3)

Proprietors played a somewhat larger role in New Jersey than they did in New York, approximately equaling the leadership of the lawyers.[13]

No one group dominated the assemblies, and the proprietors and manor lords were compelled to share power with other members of the elite. The landed elite could not match the lawyers in the kind of ability needed to draft and put through legislation. Merchants might also have advantages of education, and, being near the capital or in it, often had the advantage of being more readily available for the work of the committee of correspondence or greater familiarity with accounts, that the assembly might need in its work. Indeed, several of the proprietor-manor lord leaders were also lawyers and merchants. Speakers Adolph Philipse, Samuel Neville, and Cortland Skinner were of this category; all were very able house leaders. But few were clearly over their heads. The most obvious example was the lord of the Manor of Fox Hall, Colonel Abraham Gaasbeck-Chambers.

There are few records of assemblymen condemned by contemporaries for incompetence; Gaasbeck-Chambers was the only one so generally described. He was an inactive, though serving in seven assemblies in New York from 1717 to 1747 from Ulster County. For Cadwalader Colden he was "the most senseless & silliest Creature in the House." He had "so little Credit or Reputation that no man would trust Any of his private affairs of the least consequence to his Arbitration." In 1738 one of his constituents brazenly confronted him saying he was "a Rogue and Liar, and that he would prove him such; and likewise, that he was a Fool, and no fit Person to be an Assembly Man, and that he was always drunk, and the other Assembly Men, or his Mates, could always make him do as they had a mind."[14] The rural great landowners, though some were educated and experienced men, were in political perspicacity not up to the abilities of the lawyers and merchants. They were not all as incompetent as Gaasbeck-Chambers, but they had less skill than their urban counterparts.

To determine the significance of the proprietor-manor lord

class as a political group entails looking at their political activity from two perspectives. First is to determine if they regularly cohered in voting behavior. In New York and New Jersey the proprietors and manor lords already possessed substantial affinities of class and wealth. To what extent would they join together and advocate the same issues in the legislatures?

Coherence in New York and New Jersey can be measured because roll call votes were taken on many issues for the forty or so years before 1775. Coherence of the proprietors and manor lords thus is measured first by identifying them in the legislature and then comparing their votes. Each proprietor-manor lord legislator of the two colonies was compared with every other proprietor-manor lord legislator of that colony to determine on what roll calls both participated and the number of times their votes agreed. Percentages of agreement were thus derived for each proprietor-manor lord legislator paired with every other proprietor-manor lord legislator.[15]

The results of comparing the votes of the individual manor lords of New York indicates that they were generally not likely to agree with their fellow manor lords. Of the eighteen manor lords who could be compared in regard to their voting behavior, only seven agreed with more than half the manor lords with whom they could be paired. Thus Frederick Philipse II, assemblyman, 1726-1750, could be compared with ten other manor lords since 1737 and agreed with eight of them, scoring a significant percentage of agreement on the roll calls in which he and his pairs participated. His uncle Adolph, assemblyman, 1722-1745, who also could be paired with ten other manor lords, agreed with only three.[16] Out of eighty-one total pairings of the eighteen manor lords who participated in a meaningful number of roll calls, thirty-five total pairings were at a percentage of agreement that was significant. Clearly New York manor lords did not register significant agreement with their fellow manor lords and did not cluster in a manor lord bloc in the legislature. The tendencies that they showed toward voting together were very weak.

The East Jersey proprietors were the most cohesive. Of the eleven East Jersey proprietors who could be compared with one another in regard to their voting behavior, all but one agreed at a significant percentage of roll call votes with all the other proprietors with whom he could be compared. These agreements were at a high percentage; all were over 90 percent in agreement on roll calls. The instance of Samuel Neville is instructive. He agreed with three other proprietors at a remarkably high percentage: John Johnston—97.8 percent, Philip Kearney—100 percent (23/23 votes), John Stevens—96.8 percent. He failed to agree significantly with Samuel Leonard on ten roll calls in 1743-1744, agreeing with him on eight of the ten, which is one fewer than required for a significant percentage of ten roll calls.[17]

The East Jersey proprietors cohered for reasons only indirectly related to their wealth and social position. First, they were active in the East Jersey Council of Proprietors, which encouraged them to concert their efforts in a common interest. Second, they were all from Perth Amboy and Middlesex County, giving them a strong regional interest. This in itself was not sufficient reason, though; there were plenty of legislators in New Jersey who did not vote similarly to their colleagues from the same district. Third, for much of the period they felt beset by the rival land claimants, whom they generally termed rioters. And fourth, they felt it important to back the governor and the power of the administration to preserve all aspects of authority. The whole social and economic milieu in which the East Jersey proprietors operated demanded their political coherence.

Those contemporaries who saw the West Jersey proprietors as a large, amorphous, and generally complacent group, insofar as regarded influencing the government to act in any particularly proprietary interest, were correct. Fourteen pairs of West Jersey proprietors agreed on a significant percentage of roll calls out of a possible thirty-nine pairs (35.9 percent). Only three West Jersey proprietors in the house, out of sixteen who could be compared with one another, voted at a significant level of agreement with a majority of those proprietors with whom they could be compared. Two of these instances were in the 1761-1768 session of the legislature. Ebenezer Miller, serving in the House from 1754 to 1771, is an example of the above. He agreed with six other West Jersey proprietors on a significant percentage of roll calls, out of a possible ten:

Samuel Clement	75.7 percent (56/74)
Richard Hartshorne	69.0 percent (49/71)
Abraham Hewlings	64.0 percent (48/75)
John Hinchman	70.2 percent (52/74)
Aaron Leaming	62.1 percent (105/169)
Thomas Rodman	92.3 percent (12/13)

Four West Jersey proprietors with whom Miller did not agree on a significant number of roll calls were as follows:

Samuel Clement, Jr.	57.9 percent (11/19)
John Ladd	53.1 percent (34/64)
George Reading	62.5 percent (30/48)
Isaac Sharp	62.1 percent (18/29)

The agreement percentages are rarely high, and two are close to the minimum required for significance in testing for cohesion. These West Jersey proprietors were substantial landholders, but their general differences originated in regional interests and perhaps religious background. They had none of the tight common feeling that the East Jersey proprietors had.[18]

A general agreement of this elite group, a general cohesion, a forming of a political bloc in the legislature, would occur only among the particular circumstances of the East Jersey proprietors, not among large landholders widely dispersed throughout a colony and having no other community of interest than their large landholdings.

A second aspect of the political behavior of the landholding elite concerns particular issues of importance to landholders. For the aristocratic manor lords and proprietors, there was no issue more important economically than that of land taxes.

There were two particular taxes that concerned them: one was generally to encourage as low a real estate tax as possible assessed on their extensive landholdings, and the second was to prevent the enactment of any tax on the unimproved lands held as speculation. The two colonies took somewhat different approaches to taxation, but a gradually increasing burden on the rural backcounty areas, which also included some proprietor-manor lord interests, seems to have occurred.

Taxes in New Jersey were always low, and in fact not levied at all for the support of the colonial government in the period 1732-1751. All groups, and certainly landholders, benefited from the lack of taxation. The public expenses were paid by the interest revenue from the loan office. Governor Morris charged that the borrowers were the "poor and necessitous," and that taxation would have been a more equitable way to raise money, but there were no complaints from the inhabitants.[19]

New York also relieved the backcounties of much of the tax burden by pushing it off on New York City. This practice developed during the early part of the eighteenth century, and was apparently foisted on the city by the agricultural interests of Long Island and the Hudson River Valley. In 1693 the quota of tax revenues that New York County had to raise was one-sixth of the total for the colony. By 1729 it had increased to one-half and remained virtually at that level through 1744. In 1729 the population of New York City and County was about 17 percent of the total for the colony, and in 1744 it was 18 percent of the total. The inequity caused criticism. In the early 1730s a political broadside inquired "How unreasonable is it, that Gentlemen should possess large Tracts of uncultivated lands, without paying Taxes, and yet these Tracts undeniably increase in Value by the Industry of the poorer Sort, and other Inhabitants who pay Taxes." It was probably good propaganda, though not accurate, to accuse the elite manor lords of profiting most; the ordinary farmers of Long Island and the Hudson Valley had as much to do with the unfair taxation system as the very rich did.[20]

The 1744 tax was passed by a considerable majority (17-9) on the key vote in the house. There were nine manor lords in the house; five voted for the heavy assessment of New York, and four voted against it. Manor lord William Nicoll drew up the tax bill. With the effort to pass a further tax bill for emitting £10,000 in February 1746, the city attempted to fight back, but to no avail. A remarkable division into two blocs held firm in the house for a total of seventeen roll calls, voting that to redeem £10,000 in bills of credit New York County was to raise in the next three years £4687 10 shillings. Of the seven manor lord landholders in the house, three voted for the heaby assessment imposed on New York, andfour voted against. The vote pattern of 1746 was different from 1744; Philp Verplanck of Cortlandt Manor shifted to a position opposed to lower taxes for the city, while Henry Beekman and J.B. Van Rensselaer now supported the city.[21]

The council threw out the tax bill in late February and the house had the job to do over in April 1746. This time the slight shift toward lightening the tax burden of the city, perceptible in the February votes, became a breakthrough. A Long Island motion that the old tax apportionments be continued was defeated 14-7, and by the same vote major modifications of the tax quotas for each county were adopted. Of the five manor lords in the house, four supported the city. Their shifts in voting had helped to form an alliance among representatives from New York, Westchester, and Albany Counties that made the tax system more equitable. Kings, Queens, Suffolk, and Ulster Counties, which had lived off the high New York County tax quota for so long, had their quotas substantially increased. Table 4.3 compares the shift in tax burden in key counties from 1744 to 1746.[22]

The manor lords, in changing their votes to support New York County's position, may have been recognizing that the Westchester and Albany interests were closer to those of New York County—with its commercial, social, political, and landholding interests weaving out of the city and up the river—than they were to those of the small farmers of Long Island. The new proportions of quotas for the counties did not

Table 4.3
County Taxation in Colonial New York, 1744–1746

County	Percent Population, 1745	Percent Tax, 1744	Percent Tax, 1746
New York	18.0	49.0	33.3
Albany	15.4	16.1	14.3
Westchester	13.6	5.1	5.5
Kings	3.3	3.9	5.8
Queens	12.0	5.5	11.2
Suffolk	12.9	5.2	10.0
Ulster	7.0	5.1	9.1

mean that heavy taxes would now be levied by those counties on the manor lords. More of the increased tax burden fell on the tenants of the manors who had to pay the taxes on their improved lands than on the manor lords who yet paid little or nothing on tracts held for speculation.[23]

New Jersey, in contrast, in the late 1740s and early 1750s did attempt to shift the tax burden more onto the great proprietors. Emissions of the loan office were expiring, the receipts of interest money had been more than halved in the period 1741-1749, and it was necessary by 1748 to levy taxes. Contrary to precedent, the assembly majority attempted to tax lands of the proprietors, including their unimproved lands. The council, where the East Jersey proprietors held sway, rejected seven tax bills sent up by the house in the years 1748-1751.[24]

Rejection of the tax bills meant no support for the government and no salary for the governor. Governor Jonathan Belcher in 1751 dissolved the old assembly to try to break the deadlock, and in the succeeding assembly the East Jersey proprietor representatives proved amenable to compromise. The house determined to institute valuation ranges for lands to be taxed. The proprietor assemblymen agreed to a low minimum valuation, which had scattered support from other representatives, but a high minimum valuation, roughly double or two and one-half times the low minimum valuation favored by the proprietors, was approved by the house in October 1751.[25] The council still balked, and a compromise more agreeable to the proprietors was worked out in the tax bill of February 1752. The proprietor assemblymen and a group of other assemblymen from West Jersey, who were not proprietors, apparently had reached a general agreement outside the house on the desirable minimum valuation for lands. This proposed minimum was higher than the one the proprietor assemblymen had supported in 1751; it was generally 60 to 80 percent of the high minimum valuations that the house had approved in October 1751. With this West Jersey support for a compromise, the proprietor side obtained a tax bill more to its liking, and the tax bill passed assembly and council.[26]

These two detailed examples of the development of legislation indicate that the political views of the manor lords and proprietors had to find their expression in compromise with other groups in the assemblies. The coherence of the East Jersey proprietors served to make it more necessary for other assemblymen to try to compromise with them and settle issues. Voting almost exactly alike was probably an effective and necessary tactic for them. New York manor lords, never closely cohering, individually shifted from one position to the other, reaching accommodation with the commercial interests of New York and Albany.

That the landed elite was obliged to compromise and shift its ground and that, except for the entrenched East Jersey proprietors, large landholders did not closely combine with one another to form a formidable bloc indicates that they were not participating consciously in any sort of revival or increase of the political power of their group; there was no feudal revival in these two colonies. Of course they sought to retain their prerogatives of membership in the legislature and did not relinquish the strong, but not dominant, leadership positions that they held in this period. But they could not stand alone and aloof from the other members of the legislature. They were compelled to play not the role of claiming ancient privileges but the part of modern political operators, seeking the fulfillment of their political interests in combination with other interests that approximated theirs and with whom they would negotiate as virtual equals.

NOTES

1. For general appraisals of the political situation of the middle colonies, see Douglas Greenberg, "The Middle Colonies in Recent American Historiography," *William and Mary Quarterly* 36, 3d ser. (1979): 396-427; and Patricia U. Bonomi, "The Middle Colonies: Embryo of the New Political Order," in *Perspectives on Early American History: Essays in Honor of Richard B. Morris*, ed. Alden T. Vaughan and George Athan Billias (New York: Harper and Row, 1973), pp. 63-92.

2. Rowland Berthoff and John M. Murrin, in "Feudalism, Communialism, and the Yeoman Freeholder: The American Revolution Considered as a Social Accident," in *Essays on the American Revolution*, ed. Stephen G. Kurtz and James H. Hutson (Chapel Hill: University of North Carolina Press, 1973), pp. 271-272, admit that the concept of feudalism that they employ is "grossly imperfect," and make more of the economic gains that the great landholders made in the eighteenth century than they do of the political privileges the landholders enjoyed, but they do specifically mention, without analysis, the proprietors of Pennsylvania and New Jersey. The concept is utilized by Edward Countryman in "'Out of the Bounds of the Law': Northern Land Rioters in the Eighteenth Century," in *The American Revolution: Explorations in the History of American Radicalism*, ed. Alfred F. Young (Dekalb: Northern Illinois University Press, 1976), p. 42, but no other historian has taken up this matter.

3. Patricia U. Bonomi, *A Factious People: Politics and Society in Colonial New York* (New York: Columbia University Press, 1971), p. 187, provides a map outlining the location and approximate extent of the great manors and patents. Acreage figures are from Irving Mark, *Agrarian Conflicts in Colonial*

New York, 1711-1755 (New York: Columbia University Press, 1940), p. 60. For the Livingston properties, see Robert Livingston, Jr., to James Duane, November 30, 1765, Duane Papers, New York Historical Society, New York City, New York; Peter R. Livingston, Heads of a Case [1792?], Peter R. Livingston Papers, Livingston-Redmond Collection, Hyde Park, New York; George Dangerfield, *Chancellor Robert R. Livingston of New York, 1746-1813* (New York: Harcourt, Brace, and Co., 1960), p. 29. Loyalist Frederick Philipse III valued his estate at £150,000 and posed as a soft-hearted landlord, as reported in Hugh Edward Egerton, ed., *The Royal Commission on the Losses and Services of American Loyalists, 1783 to 1785, Being the Notes of Mr. Daniel Parker Coke, M.P.* (1915; reprint, New York: Burt Franklin, 1971), pp. 241-243. For Beekman holdings, see Philip L. White, *The Beekmans of New York in Politics and Commerce, 1647-1677* (New York: The New York Historical Society, 1956), pp. 118-119, 162.

4. Ina K. Morris, *Memorial History of Staten Island, New York*, vol. 1 (New York: Memorial, 1898-1900), p. 142-143; Martha B. Flint, *Long Island before the Revolution: A Colonial Study* (1896; reprint, Port Washington, N.Y.: Iva J. Friedman, 1967), p. 259; City of New York, *Abstracts of Wills on File in the Surrogate's Office*, New York Historical Society Collection, vol. 26: pp. 296-298 and vol. 33, 89-91; Marius Schoonmaker, *The History of Kingston, New York* (New York: Burr, 1888), pp. 63-64, 492.

5. Edgar Jacob Fisher, *New Jersey as a Royal Province, 1738 to 1776* (New York: Columbia University Press, 1911), pp. 174-176; Donald L. Kemmerer, *Path to Freedom: The Struggle for Self-Government in Colonial New Jersey, 1703-1776* (Princeton: Princeton University Press, 1940), p. 192.

6. Lewis Morris to [?], July 18, 1728, Robert Morris Papers, Rutgers University Library, New Brunswick, New Jersey; Samuel Neville, *A Bill in the Chancery of New Jersey, at the Suit of John Earl of Stair and Others, Proprietors of the Eastern Division of New Jersey* (New York: James Parker, 1747), p. 3; Thomas L. Purvis, "The New Jersey Assembly, 1722-1775"

(Ph.D. dissertation, Johns Hopkins University, 1979), p. 54; Richard Peters to Thomas Penn, June 20, 1752, Penn Papers, Historical Society of Pennsylvania, Philadelphia, Pennsylvania.

7. Kemmerer, *Path to Freedom*, p. 191; Fisher, *New Jersey*, pp. 172-174; Lewis Morris Ashfield, *Journal of the Governor and Council*, October 3, 1751, and May 23, 1753, in *Archives of the State of New Jersey*, 1st ser., vol. 16 (Trenton: 1890-1893), pp. 324-326, 401-402.

8. James DeLancey gained power in New York because his sister's husband was a British national hero and the confidant of both the Duke of Bedford and the Earl of Sandwich. He became governor when a newly arrived appointee committed suicide. See Stanley N. Katz, *Newcastle's New York: Anglo-American Politics, 1732-1753* (Cambridge: Harvard University Press, 1968), pp. 210-212, 241. Pages 119-132 of this book analyze manor lord Lewis Morris's failure to exert any meaningful influence in London against Governor William Cosby in 1735.

9. Lists of councilors are in Kemmerer, *Path to Freedom*, pp. 357-360, and Bonomi, *Factious People*, pp. 312-314. Biographical data for New Jersey councilors are scattered through the *New Jersey Archives*.

10. On the general weakness of the colonial council, see Bernard Bailyn, *The Origins of American Politics* (New York: Alfred M. Knopf, 1967), pp. 73, 131-133. Bailyn's remarks on pp. 75-80 on the lack of patronage power of the governors omit mention of means available to them to reward councillors with plural offices.

11. On the representation of Livingston manor, see Bonomi, *Factious People*, pp. 86-87. Bonomi also provides the Livingston, Morris, and Philipse genealogies on pp. 289-291. For the Van Rensselaer family, see Sun Bok Kim, *Landlord and Tenant in Colonial New York: Manorial Society, 1664-1775* (Chapel Hill: University of North Carolina Press, 1978), pp. 416-417. See notes 3 and 4 on these pages for sources on other manor lords. Calculations of service are from the *Journal of the*

Votes and Proceedings of the General Assembly of the Colony of New York (New York City and Albany, 1764-1820), hereafter *N.Y. Votes.*

12. Proportions of the New Jersey proprietors in the house are calculated from *The Votes and Proceedings of the General Assembly of the Province of New Jersey* (New York City, Philadelphia, Burlington, Woodbridge, 1739-1775) hereafter, *N.J. Votes*; and biographical material in *Calendar of New Jersey Wills, Administration, Etc., New Jersey Archives*, vols. 24, 30, 32-42 (Paterson and others: various publishers, 1901-1949); and in *New Jersey Archives*, vols. 1-10 (Newark: various publishers, 1880-1886), in various footnotes.

13. The assessment of leadership is made on the basis of offices held by assemblymen, such as speaker, chairman of committees of the whole, service on important standing committees, and bringing in bills to the house. Those who served as speaker or chaired committees of the whole over a considerable part of their tenure were categorized as top rank; those who served on numerous committees were designated second rank leaders. Committee service for the first two years was weighted heavily to equalize among those who served for long and short periods. Inactives were those who had scant official function in the house, except that those who served short terms, thus not having a real chance to prove themselves, were not counted as inactives. Thomas L. Purvis, ("'High-Born, Long-Recorded Families': Social Origins of New Jersey Assemblymen, 1703 to 1776," *William and Mary Quarterly* 37, 3d. ser. [1980]: 605) designates many of the same persons as leaders but has too many top leaders (29) and fewer of second rank (18).

14. Cadwalader Colden, "History of Cosby's Administration," Colden Papers, vol. 68, *New York Historical Society Collection*, p. 355; *N.Y. Votes*, September 20, 1738. In *N.Y. Votes*, October 19, 1738, the house recorded giving Gaasbeck-Chambers a certificate that he was sober and discreet—probably a case of protesting too much.

15. Significant percentages indicating true cohesion and

party agreement rather than chance or casual agreement were adapted primarily from the work of political scientist Peter Willetts. See his "Cluster-Bloc Analysis and Statistical Inference," *American Political Science Review* 66 (1972): 569-582. With a table on p. 574, he details the significance levels of percentage cutoff points for cluster-bloc analysis. Common participation in five roll calls is the minimum for comparison. This method of cluster-bloc analysis is discussed also in Lee F. Anderson, Meredith W. Watts, Jr., and Allen R. Wilcox, *Legislative Roll Call Analysis* (Evanston, Ill.: Northwestern University Press, 1966), pp. 59-75.

16. Frederick Philipse agreed with the following at the significant percentage as noted:

Henry Beekman, 71.6 percent
Abraham Gaasbeck-Chambers, 69.6 percent
Robert Livingston, Jr., 73.0 percent
Lewis Morris, Jr., 77.4 percent
Adolph Philipse, 78.7 percent
Jeremiah Van Rensselaer, 72.1 percent
Philip Verplanck, 88.0 percent

He did not have a significant percentage of agreement when compared with Lewis Morris (25 percent) or with William Nicoll (25 percent). Roll calls for all vote comparisons are in *N.Y. Votes*, passim.

17. *N.J. Votes*, passim, for roll calls. Willetts, "Cluster-Bloc Analysis," p. 574, for significance. In all, eight pairs of legislators, out of a possible nine, agreed on a significance percentage of roll calls.

18. *N.J. Votes*, passim. According to the Willetts table, the percentage of agreement required for significance decreases as the number of roll calls on which both legislators compared votes increases.

19. On the low level of taxation, see Frederick R. Black, "Provincial Taxation in Colonial New Jersey, 1704-1735," *New Jersey History* 95 (1972):23; and Purvis, "New Jersey Assembly," p. 605. See Morris's view in *N.J. Votes*, April 5, 1745.

20. Edward Countryman, "The Revolutionary Transforma-

tion of New York," in *New Wine in Old Skins: A Comparative View of Socio-Political Structures and Values Affecting the American Revolution*, ed. Erich Angerman, Marie-Luise Frings, Herman Wellenreuther (Stuttgart, Germany: Ernst Klett Verlag, 1976), p. 78, for the general tax treatment of New York County. The 1729 and 1744 tax apportionments are from *The Colonial Laws of New York* . . . (Albany: J. B. Lyon, 1894-1896), vol. 2, p. 531; vol. 3, pp. 404-405; and *N.Y. Votes*, September 4, 1744. Population percentages interpolated from the censuses of 1731, 1737, and 1746 in E.B. O'Callaghan, ed., *Documents Related to the Colonial History of the State of New York* (Albany: Weed, Parsons, 1853-1887), vol. 5; pp. 702, 929, and vol. 6, p. 133. See also the broadside "John Sydney" (New York, 1732?).

21. *N.Y. Votes*, September 4, 1744, February 8, 1745-1746.

22. Ibid., April 25, 1746. For council disagreement, see ibid., February 21, 1745-1746. For the comparison of tax burdens on each county, see *N.Y. Laws*, vol. 3, pp. 404-405, 579. Table 4.3 is constructed from the 1745 census in O'Callaghan, *Documents*, vol. 6, p. 133, and the laws cited above.

23. Robert A. Becker, *Revolution, Reform, and the Politics of American Taxation, 1763-1783* (Baton Rouge: Louisiana State University Press, 1980), p. 43.

24. Governor Jonathan Belcher to the Lords of Trade, April 21, 1749, *New Jersey Archives*, vol. 7, pp. 245-246. The debate between the council and assembly can be followed in the *Council Journals*, March 14, 1748-1749, ibid., 16: 127; February 21, 1749-50, 213; February 8, 1750-1751, 248-249; and in *N.J. Votes*, March 16, 1748-1749, October 19, 1749; February 20, 22, 1750-1751. A newspaper piece in the New York *Gazette*, January 21, 1750-1751, depicted the proprietors on the council as willing to block the support of government for ten years rather than accept taxation of unimproved lands.

25. Kemmerer, *Path to Freedom*, pp. 230-231; *N.J. Votes*, October 12, 1751.

26. *N.J. Votes*, February 6 and 11, 1752.

Ranching and Speculation in Lynn County, Texas, 1876–1930

The Llano Estacado, the Staked Plains, and the High Plains are all synonyms for a geographical area of Texas. This area is one of vast, level expanses of land, most of which lie on an elevated plain which is bordered by the Caprock, an escarpment that divides the high, flat plains to its west from the lower, rolling, and broken prairies to its east. This Caprock, which forms the eastern boundary of the High Plains, ranges from just a slight hill of rocky debris in some areas to vertical cliffs of over 300 feet in other places. A similar escarpment marks the western edge of the High Plains in New Mexico and, along with the arbitrary Oklahoma border on the north, marks the bounds of the High Plains of Texas.

Within the High Plains of Texas are the South Plains, a local term describing a limited segment of the High Plains. Politically, the vague limits of the South Plains entail thirteen counties: Bailey, Lamb, Hale, Floyd, Cochran, Hockley, Lubbock, Crosby, Yoakum, Terry, Lynn, Gaines, and Dawson.[1] These counties all have a similar climate, history, and economic development which give them a certain similarity to each other and serve to unite them as a group.

Climatically, as well as geologically, the South Plains has all the characteristics of a Plains environment. The land is, for all practical purposes, level and treeless and has a subhumid or semiarid climate with an average rainfall of from fifteen to twenty inches annually.[2] These characteristics made this remote corner of Texas one of the last areas of the state to be settled. These same characteristics also dictated the historical and economic development of this particular region. Due to its hostile climate and geography, the South Plains was, initially, a barrier to settlers, but the region slowly developed into one of great economic opportunity.

In a historical and technical sense, the area was opened to settlement long before it was actually practical for settlement to begin. The land laws, passed by the Texas legislature over a thirty-year period, from 1876 to 1905, controlled and influenced the flow of people to the South Plains. In the early 1870s, all of the unappropriated lands in Texas were classified as public domain and therefore the property of the State of Texas. School lands were granted to individual counties and located in the unsettled public lands, to be used or sold by the individual counties at their discretion.

Inasmuch as land was its only asset, Texas bartered it for necessities such as railroads and other internal improvements and sold it whenever possible to settlers and land speculators. In 1873, a Texas state constitutional amendment permitted special grants of land in the public domain to railroads in order to encourage the building of railroads and other related internal improvements. This provision was also carried over into the Constitution of 1876.[3]

The land law of 1876 provided the railroads with sixteen sections of land per mile of track constructed and allowed the railroad to locate its land scrip in blocks, in specific reservations of the unoccupied public domain, and further made it the duty of the railroad to survey its lands and to transfer that land within eight years.

The railroads received only the alternate sections they had surveyed, in a checkerboard fashion, because the state reserved every alternate section of land for its public school fund in a law enacted in 1874. This 1874 law set the price for this land at $1.50 per acre.[4]

In 1879, the land law of Texas again changed. It provided for sales to actual settlers only, at a minimum price of one dollar per acre for most land, and set a limit of four sections as the maximum amount of land a settler could purchase. This was known as the Four Section Settler Act. At the same time, the unappropriated public domain in a large group of unorganized West Texas counties, including the South Plains counties, was offered for sale in unlimited quantities at fifty cents per acre.[5] This was called the Fifty Cent Act.

Following the election of John Ireland as governor of Texas in 1882, the land laws were radically altered. Further grants to railroads were prohibited and all of the public domain, with the exception of school land, was withdrawn from the market. A land board was created to classify the lands as agricultural, pastoral, or timbered. The board set prices of three dollars per acre for watered or agricultural lands and two dollars per acre for unwatered pastureland. The maximum amount any one person could purchase was eight sections of land, only three of which could be within five miles of the center of a county.[6] In 1887 the state expanded the terms of its sales to forty years at 5 percent interest, one-fortieth down, and also allowed for the leasing of school lands for a five-year period at four cents per acre.[7] In 1895, the price for land was lowered to one dollar per acre and 3 percent interest. By 1898, the unappropriated public domain was exhausted, when it was learned that the school land fund had not received its half of the lands granted since 1876. This ruling was reinforced in the case of *Hogue v. Baker* in 1898, when the Texas Supreme Court declared that there was no more vacant and unappropriated land in Texas.[8]

By 1900 the school fund had been balanced, all land appropriated, and the old days of homesteads and patents were ending. Only the leasing and buying of school lands remained to be carried out. In 1901, a land act made some changes in the leasing of school lands. Applications to lease land were to be sent to the land commissioner, and leases were not to be granted for periods longer than five years. The lessee had a sixty-day prior right to purchase the lands when the lease expired.[9] Also in 1901 the land law was amended to allow the sale of four sections of school land to a person who would be required to live on it for three years and make certain improvements.[10] In 1905, the highest bidder law was passed for the purchase of unsold school lands. Land was classified, and a price of $1.00 per acre was put on grazing land and $1.50 minimum per acre on agricultural land. On surveyed land, such as in Lynn County, as many as four sections could be bought by one person. On unsurveyed land, such as in far West Texas, up to eight sections could be bought by an individual. Land was sold to the highest bidder.[11] However, by 1907 and 1908, leasing of school lands was largely suspended so lands could be sold to actual settlers.[12]

Such were the many and varied ways that land could be acquired by the settlers on the South Plains after it had been made available and practical for settlers to come and to live. This short examination of the land laws of Texas is important because all of the South Plains counties, including Lynn County, were directly influenced by these various laws.

Lynn County, named for an Alamo defender, George Washington Lynn, was created in the legislative act of August 21, 1876. This act took land that had been either attached to Bexar or Young Territories in vague and meaningless terms and created a body of individual counties administered from specific areas.[13] As the population of Texas moved westward, the county of Lynn began to develop both a populace and an economic system based on liberal land policies and beef.

Lynn County, like most other South Plains counties, contained two types of land: railroad grants and school land. The predominating railroads that were granted land in Lynn County were the East Line and Red River Railroad Company; the Henderson and Overton Branch Railroad Company; the Tyler Tap Railroad Company; the Houston, East, and West Texas Railroad Company; the Gulf, Colorado, and Santa Fe Railroad Company; the Dallas and Wichita Railroad Company; and the Denison and Southeastern Railroad Company. The lion's share of land among these major railroad grants belonged to the East

Line and Red River Railroad Company, with the other railroads each holding substantial amounts of land. A small number of sections were held by the Indianola Railroad Company; the Gulf, West Texas, and Pacific Railroad Company; the Beaty, Seale, and Forwood Railroad Company; and the Adams, Beaty, and Moulton Railroad Company; but their holdings were a pittance compared to those of the major railroads.[14] School land, the other type of land in the county, occupied every alternate section of land in the railroad surveys, plus other specified tracts of land.[15] These various types of lands were taken up by the land companies, ranchers, and settlers from all over Texas and the nation. Lynn County land was patented under all the different land laws of Texas, and the changes in the laws influenced the type of person who bought land in the county. The evolution from the large land speculating companies to the cattle rancher to the farmer was thus wrought.

In its very early years, Lynn County was developed by two types of people or organizations. First came the absentee land speculator, individual or company, who bought land early and cheap to hold for a profit at a later time. Then, the pioneer rancher crept onto the South Plains and into Lynn County to use the land himself. Because the speculator acquired the land first, he will be examined first; but before land could be bought, it had to be surveyed.

The first survey party to come into Lynn County arrived in 1878. There were nine men in the party which was led by Jasper Hayes, a peg-legged ex-Confederate Army officer. This first survey of the South Plains established its beginning point at Double Lakes in northwestern Lynn County and worked outward from there. By the end of 1878, the first survey was completed and land in Lynn County was available to the purchaser.[16]

The first lands transferred in Lynn County were patented under the Constitution of 1876. These limited acquisitions were a prelude to the flood of patents issued to land speculators following the Fifty Cent Act of 1879. Between 1879 and 1882, when the Fifty Cent Act was revoked, almost 450 sections of land were patented in Lynn County, with a very large percentage of it going to land speculators. Although there were many individuals who patented small amounts of land for speculative purposes, there were several who collected large amounts in these formative years.[17]

Foremost among early Lynn County land speculators was the Lone Star Real Estate and Colonization Company. This company, although it had an office in Austin, was made up of men from Indiana and Ohio and did its business from these two states. The company was organized on March 22, 1877, chartered in Texas, and carried out its speculative endeavors until late 1904. Between 1878 and 1880, the Lone Star Real Estate and Colonization Company patented approximately 131 sections of school lands under the Fifty Cent Act in the name of both the company and its officers. The company even donated, laid out, and plotted a town in Lynn County, called Lynn City. It was laid out in 1880, and lots were sold. Lynn City was six miles west then six miles north of present Tahoka. Many people in the northern United States were sold lots in the town, although none ever came to settle. The land was eventually acquired by the T-Bar Ranch and was "populated" by cattle.[18]

Among the smaller speculators of the county, which were all individuals, were J. F. Frazier, who patented eleven sections of land in 1878; Oliver Loftin, who patented twenty-two sections of land between 1878 and 1880; Emma L. and Elisha P. Stout, who patented twenty-two sections of land between 1879 and 1880; James W. Barber, who patented seven sections in 1879; Charles M. Thornburgh, who patented twenty-one sections in 1880; Jasper Hayes, who as an individual and as a member of two ranches (the T-Bar and the Currycomb) patented at least fifteen sections between 1879 and 1880; and J. W. Goldsmith, who patented eleven sections of land in 1883. This small group of speculators, including Lone Star Real Estate and Colonization Company, patented almost 250 sections of land out of the less than 450 sections patented before 1883. The balance that was patented before 1883 was done so by a myriad of individuals, all but a very few for speculative purposes since only a handful of them ever actually saw their land and very few ever lived on it. This wave of speculative patenting came to an abrupt halt when the land laws of Texas were radically altered in 1883 in order to prevent such speculation and to promote the advancement of actual settlement into these newly created counties.[19]

With the changes in the land laws and the ending of large amounts of speculative purchasing of state lands, the South Plains and Lynn County settled down to a relatively peaceful period of almost twenty years spent building and maintaining a ranching economy. In the period between 1880 and 1900, six large ranches were either fully or partially located in Lynn County. A very small population, a stable and unchanging economy, and rural isolation evolved naturally from this ranching economy. The census of 1880 accentuated this small population, only nine people were found to be living in the county. Ed Ryan, a sheepherder, was found at Tahoka Lake, as was the McDonnill family of A.C., his wife Margaret, and five daughters. At Double Lakes, John Porter was running a one-man ranching operation.[20] From these meager beginnings a large ranching industry developed in Lynn County which eventually bridged the gap between the solitude and emptiness of the early settler period of the late nineteenth century and the bustling, prosperous farming communities of the twentieth century. Ranching made it possible for settlement to follow by bringing four important factors together: people, money, cattle, and very cheap land.

The first ranch to spread over into Lynn County came from the east. The Currycomb Ranch of the Llano Cattle Company of Fort Worth was owned by Colonel W. C. Young, president of the company. The company was chartered in 1880 with a capital of $400,000. The Currycomb Ranch took up a large portion of northwestern Garza County and overlapped about three miles into Lynn County's northeastern corner.[21] It was not very long until the Currycomb had a neighbor directly to the south, the Square and Compass Ranch.

The Square and Compass Ranch, owned by the Nave-McCord Cattle Company of St. Joseph, Missouri, was organized in 1882. Abraham Nave and James McCord, wealthy wholesale grocers in Missouri, took advantage of the cattle boom of the early 1880s to establish their own ranch. They bought the range rights of Jim and Finis Lindsey in southwestern Garza County in 1882 and started to build a ranch. They began by using the strange and unheard of policy of buying or leasing all the land they used. The ranch lapped over into Lynn County in its southeastern corner, north to the east central part of the county, then westward up to six miles into Lynn County.[22]

At Double Lakes in northwestern Lynn County, the largest and longest-lived ranch in Lynn County was headquartered. Cass O. Edwards came to Lynn County in 1883 to establish his T-Bar Ranch. From Fort Worth, he and his brother George had migrated to Crosby County in 1879 and ranched there until 1882. They ran cattle on the open range in Crosby and Dickens Counties along with John W. Slaughter. In 1883, Cass Edwards decided to move to Lynn County where he could obtain much more land. He did this after selling his Crosby County lands to C.C. Slaughter, older brother of John W., and by buying out Frank and Will Porter's small herd of 300 head and their ranch at Double Lakes.[23] In 1884, Edwards began to build up his herd and ranch with cattle he brought from Crosby County and land he obtained throughout western Lynn County. Immediately after his herds were established, in 1884, Cass Edwards began to buy and lease large tracts of Lynn County lands. Already a man of wealth from his Tarrant County ranching, he was willing and able to start big from the very beginning. In November of 1883 Edwards, along with W.C. Young, Jasper Hayes, and L.S. Gholson of Crosby County, formed the Tahoka Cattle Company with $200,000 capital and the T-Bar brand that was to become famous.[24] This organization enabled the ranch to begin immediate large scale operations and practically ensured its success. Within a very few years, the T-Bar Ranch had over 70,000 acres of land, either bought or leased, although they did not begin to patent land as Tahoka Cattle Company until 1895. By that time, its 87,000-odd acres, approximately 136 sections, ranked the T-Bar Ranch among the largest and best of South Plains ranches, particularly because it was all above the Caprock. The T-Bar was managed by W. T. "Bill" Petty, a cousin of Cass Edwards who moved to Lynn County in 1890. Edwards sweetened the deal for Petty with a bonus offer of fourteen sections of land to run the ranch. The ranch was a strong, healthy institution and the economic backbone of Lynn County.[25]

Other ranches followed Edward's T-Bar, the first being the Dixie Ranch in northern Lynn County. This was owned by Major W.V. Johnson, who moved to Lynn County in 1884 from Borden County to establish a new ranch and to escape the fence-cutting wars below the Caprock. Major Johnson was the first man to fence all of his ranch in Lynn County, and this set a trend that was never to be reversed. The Dixie Ranch was in north central Lynn County and encompassed about fifty thousand acres of land. The core of the ranch was thirty-six sections of Wilson County school lands. The school lands were those lands allocated to Wilson County under the land laws of 1840 and patented by the county in 1879. Major Johnson had purchased the block of land in 1884 as a single tract; thus, it was an integral unit of land, unbroken by any state-owned school lands.[26] The first post office in Lynn County was located at the headquarters of the Dixie Ranch, called Percheron, which was run by Major Johnson's son, George W. Johnson.[27]

In 1888, Enos Seeds, who had been with the Jasper Hayes surveying party in 1878, returned to Lynn County from Philadelphia and settled on land he had persuaded his father, Thomas Seeds, Sr., to patent in 1878. This land, near the present site of Grassland in eastern Lynn County was to become, for a while, the Diamond JO Ranch of Enos and his brother, Thomas Seeds, Jr. On January 12, 1889, the ranch house of the small Seeds establishment also called Grasslands, became the second post office in Lynn County. This post office served the county until May 7, 1900, and the Seeds ranch was a central point for travelers and social events of the whole area for over ten years.[28]

Due to the foreclosure of a loan by his Ft. Worth bank, C.C. Slaughter's interests came to encompass a ranch in Lynn County. In 1897, Slaughter foreclosed on a note which was backed by the ranch in Lynn County that F.G. Oxshire had been leasing from A.J. Harris since early 1886. This entire ranch comprised lands leased from the state, either by Slaughter or Harris. All 140,000 acres of it—between the T-Bar Ranch on the west, the Dixie Ranch on the north, and the Currycomb Ranch and Square and Compass on the east—was to become known as the Tahoka Lake, or the "Bull" Ranch, and was managed by an early Lynn County pioneer and friend of C.C. Slaughter, Jack Alley. Alley moved his headquarters to Tahoka Lakes and stayed there until the ranch dissolved.[29]

Closely following C.C. Slaughter into Lynn County was S.F. Singleton, who came to Lynn County in 1898. He began his Slash L Ranch on twenty-two sections of land leased from a Mr. Taylor, who had acquired it in 1880. The Slash L, located in southwestern Lynn County with its headquarters at the present site of New Moore, varied in size from 60 to 100 sections of land, as land laws changed and leases expired. The Slash L occupied most of the southwestern portion of Lynn County, with its open ranges and leased lands, and rounded out the matrix of the early ranch industry in the county.[30]

All of the ranches in Lynn County had one common denominator in their early days: leased lands on open ranges. Although the open ranges ended in the 1880s, the leased lands remained an integral part of ranching and an unforeseen trap for the rancher. Of all these large ranches, only the T-Bar Ranch was to survive. Cass Edwards did not want to sell his lands, but when forced to, he could afford to buy his leased lands and thus avoid the fate of his neighbors. In 1891, Cass Edwards began to buy and/or patent as much of his range as he could and continued the process until he could purchase no more land in 1907.[31] Other ranchers did not do this quickly enough and, when the leasing of state lands ended, they were forced either to end their ranching activity and let the land return to the state, as C.C. Slaughter did on his Tahoka Lakes Ranch, or buy land from newly arriving settlers at high prices, as S.F. Singleton eventually was forced to do to keep the Slash L intact.

The ranchers who continued to lease state school lands received a fatal jolt in 1902. In a suit brought by J.E. Ketner, a farmer and small stock-raiser in Lynn County, against Charles Rogan, Texas land commissioner, and C.C. Slaughter, who owned and leased large amounts of land in Lynn County, the Supreme Court of Texas ruled that under the Texas land laws of 1895, 1887, and 1901, no lease could be canceled and another substituted for it. The judges found this would violate the ideals of the land laws, that the school lands were eventually to be settled and bought by farmers. Henceforth, according to *Ketner v. Rogan*, no rancher could renew a lease on lands from the state until the land had first been offered to the public for settlement.[32] This decision ended the so-called lapse-lease practice whereby ranchers controlled the school land not only of Lynn County but of most of the South Plains. After the 1902 decision, a flood of farmers began to reach the South Plains; and ranch after ranch eventually had to give up its leased lands to the settlers as their individual leases expired. Lynn County was no exception.

As the farmers came to the area and took up previously leased lands, many times right in the middle of established ranch pastures, as Ketner had done, it was not long before the ranchers had to make a choice: obtain title to *all* of the land they used, or simply sell out. This choice was largely governed by the amount of land that was leased by the individual rancher. The more land leased, the more likely it would be that the ranch would succumb. Also, the fact that land prices were rapidly climbing influenced many ranch owners to "see the light" and sell out for a substantial profit.

The first large ranch to go under was that of C.C. Slaughter. His Tahoka Lake's Ranch of almost 200 sections was largely leased lands and, naturally, extremely vulnerable. After the

Ketner decision in 1902, Slaughter began to reduce his operation as the individual leases expired, and many of the leases were patented by his old friends and sympathizers. By 1906-1907, Slaughter had doled out his Bull Ranch as much as possible to people to whom he wanted to give land. Slaughter was able to select who was to get lands because he knew when his individual leases were to expire. He would tell his chosen beneficiary when the lease expired and what land it encompassed, giving the patentee an insurmountable advantage over other would-be homesteaders. The rest of his land was acquired by newly arriving farmers. Jack Alley, Slaughter's exforeman, handled this distribution chore, and in 1907 personally purchased four sections of land under the Four Section Settler Act, including Tahoka Lake, which he proceeded to build into a twenty-two section ranch encircling Tahoka Lake.[33]

Closely following on the heels of Slaughter's Tahoka Lakes Ranch closure were those of the Llano Livestock Company's Currycomb Ranch and the Square and Compass Ranch of the Nave-McCord Cattle Company and later of John B. Slaughter. The major factor in the ending of these two ranches was the Post Syndicate owned by the cereal magnate, C.W. Post. Although largely centered in Garza County, which adjoins Lynn County on the east, it had a strong effect on Lynn County. In 1906, C. W. Post began to buy up over 250,000 acres of land in Lynn, Garza, and Hockley counties.[34] In Lynn County he bought out the eastern portion of the Llano Ranch, while J.T. Lofton, its exmanager and part owner, kept the smaller western portion of the Lynn County part of the ranch for himself. John B. Slaughter, who had purchased the Square and Compass Ranch from the Nave-McCord Cattle Company in 1900, sold 50,000 acres of this land in 1907 to C.W. Post, keeping the remainder of the ranch and renaming it the U-Lazy-S. Parts of this ranch still overlapped into Lynn County, over twenty-five sections of it, but it was a small portion of what had comprised the Lynn County portion of the old Square and Compass Ranch.[35]

After these three old and large ranches had been broken up

for sale, along with the corresponding leases that each ranch lost through expiration, a lull in ranch closing existed for over a decade as the eastern and northern portions of the county were consolidated and established. The Dixie Ranch, although it was sold by Major Johnson to S.A. King of Waco in 1902 and lost its leased lands as did other ranches before 1910, kept its core of thirty-six sections of Wilson County school lands intact because all of it was privately owned land.[36] These lands were not opened to extensive settlement until 1923, when the Zappe Land Company acquired the Wilson County school lands and opened them up to settlers, finally ending the Dixie Ranch's history as a ranching unit and enterprise.[37]

Closely following the end of the Dixie Ranch came the demise of the Slash-L Ranch of southwestern Lynn County. The Slash-L Ranch, due to the expenses incurred in buying land from settlers coupled with the depressed cattle market from 1919 to 1921, closed out its books in 1921.[38] The ranch had finally succumbed to its two worst enemies: fluctuating prices and the land-hungry settler. In November 1923, the Slash-L Ranch lands were subdivided by the Newman Land and Development Company of Dallas and O'Donnell. The Newman company acquired these lands from the Singletons, and settlement of the old Slash-L lands began immediately, thus extending the farmer into southwest Lynn County. The Slash-L was sold out over a period of years, initially twenty-seven sections then the rest as demand called for it.[39] Thus, by 1923, only one of the old established ranches remained.

The T-Bar Ranch of Cass Edwards was one organization that was not to die, and as other ranches fell by the wayside the T-Bar grew stronger. Located from the central to the western portion of Lynn County, the T-Bar was one of most important institutions in the county. The T-Bar had three working divisions—the Three Lakes, the Double Lakes, and the Guthrie Lake division—each approximately one-third of the ranch's entire area. However, the T-Bar did suffer from the early incursions of farmers because of the *Ketner* decision. In the early 1900s (1902-1910), the T-Bar lost leases on approximately 17,000 acres in south central Lynn County.[40] This loss occurred even though the ranch owners had made every attempt to purchase all of its land, starting as early as 1891.[41] The T-Bar simply did not have enough employees to patent all of the lands used by the ranch, and naturally some land was lost when time and leases finally ran out. The ranch was at its peak in size before its leases were lost, prior to 1910. At one time, the T-Bar had approximately 136 sections of range leased and owned, plus land they had simply encircled and were using. By the 1930s, the ranch had decreased in size, through lost leases and limited sales to farmers, to around 70,000 acres, or approximately 110 sections.[42] Yet it remained economically healthy during all of the changes in the early decades of the twentieth century.

In 1919-1920, some changes were made during the estate settlement after Cass Edwards's first wife died. In this settlement, because Edwards soon remarried, the ranch was divided into approximately equal thirds. Cass Edwards provided that upon his death his son, Crawford Edwards, by his first wife, was to receive one-third of the ranch. Also, upon his death, his grandson, Cass Edwards II, son of Crawford, would receive another third of the ranch. The final third was to go to Edwards's second wife, Crawford's stepmother. However, the ranch continued to function as one unit, and this settlement did not cause any real problems until the 1940s. Thus, the T-Bar weathered the first decades of the 1900s intact.[43]

The ranching industry changed radically during the early twentieth century due to the influx of farmers and their families. As Lynn County entered the twentieth century, the rural ranching area with a minute population and an abbreviated political system inviting speculation was to be altered forever. The first third of the twentieth century, from 1900 to the mid-1930s, was to see a drastic and complete redesign of Lynn County in political, economic, and demographic terms. These changes encompassed the dissolution of most of the large-scale ranching in the county as a large farming population grew up around newly established urban areas. The changes in Lynn

County were sudden, but not boomlike as in other frontier areas. It was a rapid, yet steady, growth. Speculation in ranch lands had proven to be a rewarding enterprise though not without risks.

NOTES

1. Jean Alexandre Paul, "The Farmer's Frontier on the South Plains" (Master's thesis, Texas Technological College, Lubbock, 1959), p. 8.

2. Ibid., p. 9.

3. Seymour V. Connor, "Early Land Speculation in West Texas," *Southwestern Social Science Quarterly* 42 (March 1962):355.

4. Ibid., p. 357.

5. Ibid.

6. Ibid., p. 359.

7. Ibid., p. 360.

8. Thomas Lloyd Miller, *The Public Lands of Texas, 1519-1970* (Norman: University of Oklahoma Press, 1972), p. 114.

9. Ibid., p. 189.

10. Ibid., p. 200.

11. Ibid., p. 201.

12. Ibid., p. 189.

13. Seymour V. Connor, "The Founding of Lubbock," in *A History of Lubbock* ed. Lawrence Graves (Lubbock: West Texas Museum Association, 1962), p. 70; H.P.N. Gammel, comp., *The Laws of Texas*, vol. 9 (Austin: The Gammel Bookstore, 1898), p. 104.

14. State of Texas, General Land Office, *Abstract of All Original Texas Land Titles Comprising Grants and Locations to August 31, 1941*, vol. 6 (Austin, 1941), pp. 658-682.

15. Ibid., p. 654.

16. Lynn County *News* (Tahoka, Texas), December 3, 1930.

17. General Land Office *Abstract*, vol. 6, pp. 652-682.

18. Cass Edwards, "Abstract of the T-Bar Ranch" (manu-

script, Southwest Collection, Texas Tech University, Lubbock, Texas), pp. 639-640.

19. General Land Office *Abstract*, vol. 6, pp. 652-682.

20. U.S. Bureau of the Census, *Tenth Census of the United States, 1880, Population Schedules*, Lynn County, Southwest Collection, Texas Tech University, Lubbock, Texas. Hereafter U.S. census, 1880.

21. William Curry Holden, *Rollie Burns or an Account of the Ranching Industry on the South Plains* (Dallas: Southwest Press, 1932), pp. 106-110.

22. Ibid., pp. 125-126.

23. U.S. census, 1880. According to the census schedules, only John Porter lived at Double Lakes; but in 1883, Cass Edwards bought out two Porter brothers, Frank and Will. This conflict has many possible explanations, but no certain answer, so all the names from different sources have been included.

24. Edwards, "Abstract of the T-Bar Ranch," pp. 641-42.

25. Lynn County *News*, December 3, 1930.

26. Robert E. Abbe, Jr., "Abstract to Lots Number 9 and 10, Block 125, Wilson, Texas," 1974, pp. 2-7.

27. Lynn County *News*, December 3, 1930.

28. Ibid.

29. Jack Alley, "Fifty-Four Years of Pioneering on the Plains of Texas, as Told to Frank P. Hill," in ibid., April 28-August 4, 1932, p. 17.

30. Ibid., March 19, 1937.

31. Cass Edwards to David Murrah, November 5, 1973, interview, Oral History File, Southwest Collection, Texas Tech University, Lubbock, Texas. U.S., Bureau of the Census, *Compendium of the Eleventh Census, 1890*, vol. 1, p. 396. Although the manuscripts for the 1890 census are not available, research has isolated a portion of the twenty-four Lynn County residents. W.T. Petty and his wife lived at the T-Bar headquarters. Major W.V. Johnson, his wife, and at least one son lived on the Dixie Ranch. Enos Seeds, his wife, and a brother lived at

Grasslands. The majority of the remainder were in all probability ranch hands on the various Lynn County ranches.

32. *Ketner v. Rogan*, 68 S.W. 774 (1902).

33. Alley, "Pioneering on the Plains," p. 17.

34. Roy Sylvan Dunn, "Agriculture Builds a City," in Graves, *History of Lubbock*, pp. 254-255.

35. Alley, "Pioneering on the Plains," p. 13.

36. Abbe, "Abstract to Lots Number 9 and 10, Wilson," pp. 2-7.

37. Bobby Jolly, "Abstract of Lots Number 17-20, Block 15, Roberts Second Addition, Tahoka, Texas," 1974, pp. 25-26.

38. John A. Rickard, "The Ranching Industry on the Lower South Plains of Texas" (Master's thesis, University of Texas, Austin, 1927), p. 167.

39. Lynn County *News*, November 16, 1923.

40. Edwards to Murrah, November 5, 1973, interview.

41. Ibid.

42. Ibid.

43. Ibid.

A Rancher's Response to Revolution: Charles K. Warren's Investments in Mexico, 1909-1947

The story of the twentieth-century cattle industry in northern Mexico is complex. Torn by revolution, embargoes, invasion, and land confiscation, Mexican and American ranchers witnessed from 1910 to the 1970s the destruction and painfully slow reconstruction of what historically had been a vast and important industry.[1] The Mexican Revolution and its aftermath was especially difficult for American ranching investors; throughout the period, they faced problems unequaled in the annals of American ranching history. For one such investor, Charles K. Warren of Michigan, the lessons learned from his venture into the Mexican ranching industry proved to be difficult and expensive.

Charles Warren was the son of Edward K. Warren, an enterprising Michigan manufacturer and inventor of Featherbone. In 1883, the elder Warren had devised a method of producing from the quills of discarded turkey feathers an effective substitute for whalebone, which had been the principal supportive substance in ladies undergarments, particularly in corsets. Glued and stitched together, the quills, or Featherbone, assured the Warren family of a sizeable fortune.[2]

Young Charles Warren, much to his father's dismay, did not readily show interest in the family business. In late 1890, while selling his father's product in Texas, the 20-year-old

Warren suddenly abandoned his job and hired on to work as a cowboy on a large West Texas ranch near present-day Lubbock.[3] Although he worked on the ranch for only a few months, the venture persuaded young Warren that his future lay in cattle and in the Southwest. Upon his return to Michigan to manage his father's farm and subsequently to become vice-president of the Featherbone Company in 1903, he purchased a ranch in West Texas in partnership with his father and established the basis for what would become a small cattle empire.[4] Within twenty years, the Warrens had increased their Muleshoe Ranch—where present-day Muleshoe, Texas, is located—to encompass 250,000 acres.[5]

In 1909, Warren and his father expanded their operation into Mexico by purchasing the 100,000-acre Ojitos Ranch in northern Chihuahua. The next year they added at a cost of $100,000 the adjoining Palatada Ranch, which also included approximately 100,000 acres. Each of the two Mexican ranches was approximately fourteen miles square and lay thirty miles south of the southwestern New Mexico border near the tiny community of Janos. The Ojitos Ranch, for which the Warrens paid $175,000, boasted an elaborate hacienda headquarters, complete with its own church, lake, and community of buildings.[6] Although the Warrens hired foremen for each of the Mexican ranches, they managed the operations from Three Oaks, Michigan.

As in most of Mexico, Chihuahua on the eve of the Mexican Revolution was a haven for owners of large estates; seventeen persons owned two-fifths of the state.[7] General Luis Terrazas reportedly controlled more than 5 million acres, 1 million cattle, and employed 10,000 men. The American-owned Polomas Land and Cattle Company, which bordered the Warren ranches, encompassed 2 million acres and 28,000 head of cattle.[8]

The placid and prosperous ranching economy of northern Mexico was shattered with the outbreak of the Mexican Revolution in 1910. As the Revolution splintered among self-styled generals, the ranchers soon found their herds decimated from confiscation by both federal and rebel troops.[9] Cattle theft and scattered fighting quickly affected the Warren operation. By 1911, the fifteen Anglos who worked on the ranches resigned, leaving only two Americans as cowhands. For the duration of the Revolution, the ranches were maintained by Mexican employees.[10] And, as revolutionary bands began to frequent his ranches, Charles Warren gave thought to selling out: "I am not going to be worried to death with a revolution down there and a lease that is expiring within 30 days," he wrote in 1912. "I would rather pull down my money and take my cattle out at the expiration."[11]

Although military activity in Chihuahua increased sharply, Warren tried to placate every faction. During the battle of Ciudad Juárez in May 1911, he personally paid revolutionary leader Francisco Madero $2,000 to allow him to move a herd of cattle out of Mexico, a transaction Warren understood to be a loan which would be repaid by the Mexican government. When he could not recover the money, Warren claimed Madero simply pocketed the funds.[12]

As conditions worsened, and perhaps recognizing that his option to sell his interest would mean loss of his $275,000 investment, Warren appealed to the United States government for aid. However, the State Department exhibited little sympathy toward American property holders in Mexico. Its official policy, as proclaimed by President William Howard Taft on March 14, 1912, was for Americans to stay out of Mexican affairs.[13] Ambassador Henry Lane Wilson in Mexico City did demand that the Madero government bring about stability in order for American property to be protected.[14]

Ambassador Wilson's demand had little effect. In September, revolutionaries inflicted serious damage to Warren's holdings. Charles Warren immediately informed the State Department and asked for assistance to obtain protection and recover damages. On October 12, 1912, acting Secretary of State Huntington Wilson told Warren that the department had requested for his property "prompt and adequate protection by Federal [Mexican] soldiers."[15] In spite of the State Department's request, the situation worsened. In February 1913, following

General Victoriano Huerta's seizure of power and the subsequent murders of Madero and Vice President José Maria Pino Suárez, the Revolution spread and expanded. Pancho Villa immediately began raising an army in Chihuahua in opposition to Huerta. On March 26, Carranza published the Plan of Guadalupe calling for the restoration of a Constitutionalist government and the Revolution surged forward, often directly across Warren's ranches.

Warren was determined that his operation would survive the Revolution. With only a foreman and ten to twenty Mexican cowboys staffing the ranches, Warren ordered that branding be carried out on the open range rather than in a round-up. In September 1912, the Ojitos Ranch was looted of supplies and its mules were taken. In January 1913, the ranch lost 300 head of cattle to unnamed revolutionaries, then was forced to pay $7,500 to a local guerilla leader, José Ynés Salazar, so that the ranch could brand its calves.[16] In September the ranch paid to another local leader, Máximo Castillo, $2.50 per head so that it could export its cattle across the border. Because of the constant presence of undisciplined forces, ranch supplies were carefully rationed: "We have been buying just what we expected to use during the month and sending it to the people at Ojitos," reported Warren's ranch superintendent C.L. McDow in June 1913. "We don't care to keep much on hand a/c of Rebels may come along and take it."[17]

McDow's words were prophetic. In 1913, the ranches reported losses of fifty-five head of cattle killed by federal soldiers for food and thousands of others stolen by roving bands.[18] In addition, Warren was forced to pay taxes to each of the warring sides.[19] Dismayed, he hurried to Washington in July 1913, to see the newly appointed Secretary of State William Jennings Bryan, but returned to Michigan extremely disappointed: "All the sympathy I got out of them was to abandon our property and get out of Mexico. This Government is the biggest bluff that happened. Bryan said he would do nothing to protect American life or property in Mexico."[20] To his congressman Warren wrote, "If the U.S. government will do nothing more than it has done, do you think it will be possible to get a permit for 200 30-30 rifles and enough ammunition so that American citizens would have a chance of protecting themselves?"[21]

For the duration of 1913, Warren received no more assurances from the U.S. government. Woodrow Wilson's policy toward Mexico was similar to that of Taft. In August 1913, Wilson told Congress that the United States would remain neutral and urged all Americans to leave Mexico at once.[22] Charles Warren's only choice was to seek cover and wait out the storm. To protect his Mexican interests, he purchased the Alamo Hueco Ranch in southwestern New Mexico which lay immediately across the border from his Mexican ranches. The new ranch's location provided a convenient haven for Warren's cattle. However, lack of water on the Alamo Hueco allowed him to move only 3,000 of his 11,000 cattle from Mexico.

Meanwhile, in late 1913, Máximo Castillo and Pancho Villa began a systematic destruction of the Terrazas cattle empire which lay adjacent to the Warren ranches. For nearly two years, the revolutionaries raided the vast Terrazas prairies and drove the ruling family from Mexico.[23] During the pillaging, Warren's ranches were not spared. In November 1913, Villa's band crossed the Ojitos, destroyed the headquarters, and stole 4,000 cows and calves.[24] As a result, calf production, which had averaged nearly 4,000 head annually prior to the Revolution, dropped to 2,000 in 1914 and 1,100 in 1915.

Throughout 1914 and 1915, both Federal and Constitutionalist troops crisscrossed the ranches and fed themselves on Warren beef. As late as October 1915, although his army had been reduced to a guerilla band, Villa continued to harass the Warren operation by destroying the Ojitos Ranch's stock of corn and hay.[25] Dismayed Warren finally ordered the abandonment of the Ojitos in late 1915. Its cattle were moved to the Palatada, which lay closer to the American border.

Events in Mexico City and Columbus, New Mexico, helped to bring some stability to Warren's operation. Villa's San Ysabel massacre of several American engineers in January 1916, followed by the March raid of Columbus, prompted American military intervention. John J. Pershing and 6,000 troops, using Warren's Alamo Hueco Ranch as a staging area, rushed into Mexico in March. Pershing's first overnight encampment was at Warren's abandoned Ojitos Ranch.[26] With American troops in the area, Warren used the protection of American presence to withdraw temporarily the remainder of his Mexican cattle. Then in early 1917, as Mexico was preparing a new constitution and with the Revolution seemingly settled, Warren restocked his Mexican ranches.

Although he was able to resume his Mexican operation, Warren was forced to continue to pacify discontented elements in Chihuahua. In February 1917, José Ynés Salazar and 125 men visited the Ojitos and demanded of its foreman a payment of $5,000. Because the ranch had suffered considerable damage at the hands of Salazar's men, Warren offered Salazar only $3,000. Although Salazar's response to Warren was courteous and forthright, it reflected the cunning of the rancher's adversary:

I had absolutely no knowledge that depredations of the kind referred to had been committed against your interest, and against my express order to respect your properties in line with my promise to you.

I assure you that as soon as I can ascertain who were the authors of the outrage, they will be severely punished.

I, also, as well as yourself, am a man of my word, and like you consider it a sacred duty to keep my promises. I know that you keep your word, and will always believe it until I have reason to believe otherwise.

Taking into consideration all the reasons that you set forth, and in view of all the facts that you state have taken place, I consider your offer to pay $3,000 in place of five thousand as a sincere offer, made on your part in good faith, and for that reason I accept it; and if the amount of $3,000 gold is delivered to my messenger, who is the bearer of this, I promise you to respect, and to cause to be respected, your properties, with kindly consideration to the entent of my power.[27]

From 1915 to 1920, Warren's black foreman, Bunk Spencer, was captured six times and was twice held for ransom notes of

$5,000. Spencer ultimately was killed by bandits in 1921.[28] Two of Warren's men were killed in 1920 by a government force, provoking Warren's manager to inquire rhetorically of Warren, "Can you see the slightest difference between the new government and the rest of the real thieves that have been allowed to roam the Mexican ranges . . . ?"[29]

Although the Revolution left many of the large ranching estates devastated, Warren's operation survived and did so for several reasons. In spite of repeated raids on his ranches, Warren's men apparently never made enemies of the rebels, particularly Villa. Courted by Warren's superintendent, Villa visited the Alamo Hueco Ranch several times to dine.[30] Also, Warren's men generally remained loyal to their jobs. Until his death in 1921, Bunk Spencer maintained for the Warren operation a continuity of management on the ranches. Five men worked for Warren throughout the entire Revolution.

Warren was also careful to pay every cent of taxes levied, regardless of whoever was in power. Often he paid double taxes to accommodate the warring sides. When peace was finally restored, he witnessed a dramatic increase in legitimate taxes as the new federal government imposed a special $67,000 levy in 1919.[31]

Furthermore, in spite of cattle theft and high taxes, Warren was able to make the Mexican operation profitable. The reason was simple: cattle could be produced much more cheaply in Mexico than in the United States. For example, in 1915, average cost per head on Warren's Texas ranch was $9.08, in New Mexico it was $6.82, and in Mexico it was only $5.46. In 1918, his Texas cattle cost $9.08 and his Mexican, $6.63.[32] American county and school taxes more than offset Mexican export taxes and thievery.

By 1924, the Warren ranches in Mexico had been restocked to their 1912 levels. But two persistent questions remained: whether the Mexican Constitution of 1917, which stated that Mexico belonged to the Mexicans, would be enforced to the letter; and whether Warren's claims against the Mexican government would ever be settled.

For many years, Warren fought in the Mexican courts the provisions of the 1917 Constitution which provided which private property could be expropriated for utility, and that no foreigner could acquire direct land ownership within 100 kilometers of the border.[33] Initially, Warren's claim to outright land title was upheld by Mexican courts, but in 1926 Mexico's president Plutarco Elías Calles confiscated one of Warren's ranches for the benefit of the community of Janos. Warren protested vigorously to the U.S. State Department. His final reply from its diplomats was "Have you tried the Mexican Courts?"[34] Warren subsequently leased the confiscated ranch from the community for a number of years.

The claims question took more than twenty years to resolve. Negotiations between the Mexican and American governments dragged, halted, and resumed several times.[35] Finally, in 1940, of the original claim filed by Warren for $379,000 in damages, the Warren interests received $22,000 or 7 percent of the original amount. Average payment to American claimants was only 2.64 percent.[36]

Warren's Mexican venture finally began to pay dividends after 1920. In 1926, he considered acquiring additional holdings in Chihuahua, but the confiscation of his land halted additional purchases. Six years later, Charles Warren died at the age of 61. His death and a deepening economic depression influenced his heirs to curtail sharply the Mexican ranching operation.

Although the Warren company restocked its Mexican ranches in 1938, an outbreak of hoof and mouth disease in 1947 forced the United States to embargo shipments of Mexican cattle. As a result, the company decided to abandon its Chihuahua operation. It sold its Ojitos Ranch in late 1947 to the mayor of the city of Juárez for fifty cents per acre, less than one-third of the original purchase price.[37]

The sale ended thirty-eight years of Warren involvement in Mexico. In spite of the outright confiscation of one of the ranches and depressed sale of another, the Warren operation probably fared better than did other American ranches in Mexico.

Charles Warren's successful survival of the Mexican Revolution was due in part to his diplomacy with both the United States government and with warring factions in Mexico, in part to the isolation of his ranches and their close proximity to the American border, and in part to his relationship with his men on the ranches. The fact that he was able to survive the ravages of strife-torn Chihuahua was a remarkable accomplishment.

NOTES

1. Manuel A. Machado, Jr., *The North Mexican Cattle Industry, 1910-1975* (College Station: Texas A&M University Press, 1981), p. 7.

2. *Who Was Who*, vol. 1 (Chicago: A.N. Marquis Co., 1942), p. 1302.

3. Charles K. Warren to E.K. Warren, January 19, 1891. Records of E. K. Warren and Son, Southwest Collection, Texas Tech University, Lubbock. Hereafter Warren Records.

4. William H. Kramer to David Murrah, November 16, 1973, interview, Oral History File, Southwest Collection, Texas Tech University, Lubbock. Kramer began working for the Warren family as an office boy in 1902. In 1915, he became the bookkeeper for the Warren ranches, and later served as secretary-treasurer for E.K. Warren and Son. Until his death in 1978 at the age of 95, Kramer continued to serve as bookkeeper for the Warren interests in Three Oaks, Michigan.

5. David J. Murrah, "From Corset Stays to Cattle Ranching: Charles K. Warren and the Muleshoe Ranch," *West Texas Historical Association Year Book* 51 (1975):4-12.

6. C.K. Warren to Ladenburg, Thallman, and Co., February 19, 1910, Warren Records.

7. Florence C. and Robert H. Lister, *Chihuahua: Storehouse of Storms* (Albuquerque: University of New Mexico Press, 1966), p. 177; F. Warner Robinson, "The New Cattle Country," *Scribner's Magazine* 51 (February 1912): 177.

8. U.S. Senate, *Investigation of Mexican Affairs. Pre-*

liminary report and hearings of the Committee on Foreign Relations, U.S. Senate, pursuant to S. Res. 106, *directing the Committee on Foreign Relations to investigate the matter of outrages on citizens of the United States in Mexico,* Sen. Doc. 285, 66th Cong., 2d sess., 1912, p. 1102.

9. Lister and Lister, *Chihuahua,* p. 231; Machado, *North Mexican Cattle Industry,* p. 9.

10. Partnership Book, 1910-1924, Warren Records.

11. C.K. Warren to Mr. Cobb, February 24, 1912, ibid.

12. C. K. Warren to Edward Hamilton, February 2, 1912, ibid.

13. Howard F. Cline, *The United States and Mexico* (Cambridge: Harvard University Press, 1953), p. 13.

14. U.S. Department of State, *Foreign Relations of the United States* (Washington, D.C.: Government Printing Office, 1912), p. 842. Hereafter *Foreign Relations.*

15. Huntington Wilson to E.K. Warren and Son, October 11, 1912, Warren Records.

16. H.S. Stephenson to C.K. Warren, February 1, 1913, ibid.

17. Charles McDow to C.K. Warren, September 7, 1913, and Warren to McDow, September 12, 1913, ibid.

18. Monthly Payroll Report, June 1913, ibid.

19. C.K. Warren to E.L. Hamilton, November 5, 1913, ibid.

20. C.K. Warren to Ross M. Lynn, July 10, 1913, ibid.

21. C.K. Warren to William Alden Smith, May 7, 1913, ibid.

22. *Foreign Relations,* 1913, pp. 808-809.

23. Lister and Lister, *Chihuahua,* pp. 231-232.

24. C.K. Warren to E. L. Hamilton, November 5, 1913, Warren Records.

25. Monthly Payroll Report, October, 1915, ibid.

26. Frank Tompkins, *Chasing Villa* (Harrisburg, Pa.: Military Service Publishing Company, 1934), p. 77.

27. José Ynés Salazar to C. K. Warren, May 30, 1917, Warren Records.

28. Kramer to Murrah, November 16, 1973, interview.

29. R.V. Moorehead to C.K. Warren, June 24, 1920, Warren Records.

30. Kramer to Murrah, November 16, 1973, interview.

31. Tax records, 1919, Warren Records.

32. Profit and Loss Statements, 1914-1952, ibid.

33. "The Mexican Problem Solved," *North American Review* 220 (September 1924): 59-61.

34. U.S. National Archives, *Records of the Department of State Relating to Internal Affairs of Mexico 1910-1929* (National Archives Microfilm), "List of Papers," 5200/805. The actual correspondence between Warren and the State Department is not included in the microfilm. For unknown reasons, the letters were removed prior to filming or acquisition of the records by the National Archives. Probably the correspondence was used in the claims dispute and was never returned to its file. The information contained in the text is drawn from the indexed abstracts of the correspondence.

35. Ibid. See also Minute Book, 1927, Warren Records; Kramer to Murrah, November 16, 1973, interview.

36. Cline, *The United States and Mexico*, p. 209.

37. Kramer to Murrah, November 16, 1973, interview.

III

LAND POLICY AND ENTREPRENEURSHIP

"They have borne and forborne, and waited, and waited for something to be done to extinguish the Indian titles, until further forbearance ceases to be a virtue. . . . Hence hundreds have gone over, and thousands will soon follow, and make claims. . . .

"The country must be settled and improved and that speedily; Missouri is no longer to be on the borders of civilization. And woe be unto the man or the set of men who attempts to resist the onward march of the Anglosaxon race towards the setting sun, Nebraska! To Nebraska is now the rallying cry of thousands upon our borders. The cold steel of infantry' has no terrors for them. They are determined now to act, and take the country and settle it. Who'll prevent the people from settling on Uncle Sam's farm?"

Lucien J. Eastin, Editor,
St. Joseph (Missouri) *Gazette*,
April 26, 1854

The task of making the farmlands and ranchlands available efficiently and economically to the thousands who desired them was difficult. Demand frequently pressured the bureaucratic apparatus, forcing government to adopt and modify land policy. In turn, these land policies would satisfy in part only legitimate farming and ranching needs.

Land policy was formulated to encourage agricultural settlement. One of the most promising and eventually most workable statutes passed was the Town Site Preemption Act of 1844. Rita Napier argues that this law was the first of many preemption acts to benefit a multitude of settlers. With this act, the ranching and farming frontiers could be harnessed and tamed; prudent investments and urban amenities traveled westerly and joined agricultural needs. The Town Site Preemption Act of 1844 was to the town builder as the Homestead Act of 1862 was to the farmer; both were willing participants in the development of the agriculture frontier.

One man, according to Homer E. Socolofsky, was able to accrue a fortune in lands through the careful investment of his moneys and the skillful interpretation of federal land policies. That man, William Scully, a young Irish immigrant, successfully parlayed a small inheritance into title to thousands of agricultural acres through Mexican War military land warrants, railroad grants, and Morrill Land Grant acreage purchases from private landholders. Federal land policies allowed for the large and small farmer alike.

Another man, William L. Black, goat rancher and promoter, vastly shaped an industry rivaling cattle in its region. Paul H. Carlson documents the diversity of ranching with his discussion of the highly successful Angora goat industry of Texas. Begun in the United States in the 1850s, expanding throughout the Texas Edwards Plateau region by 1900, and becoming a multi-million-dollar business in the twentieth century, Angora goat ranching formed an important feature in American agriculture.

Land policy, then, proved to be essential to the orderly growth of agriculture. Entrepreneurship proved attractive to many such as Black and Scully. The furrowing of Lucien Eastin's "Uncle Sam's farm" and the building of Rita Napier's Uncle Sam, Louisiana, symbolized the combined efforts and mutuality of interests Americans had in federal land policy formulation.

Frontier Agricultural Settlements and Government Regulation: The Town Site Preemption Act of 1844

The Town Site Preemption Act initiated a new direction in land policy legislation. It was the first in a series of town site laws that encouraged and regulated the development of towns on the frontier for over half a century. While our view of land laws is of predominantly rural legislation governing the accessibility and cost of farm lands, this 1844 law indicates that Congress recognized the role of towns in westward expansion and sought to encourage their market role in the West. By making town land preemptible, the government lowered the initial cost of urban frontier lands and sought to ensure the development of actual towns rather than speculative sites. An analysis of the provisions of the law and of the process of town settlement will show, however, that the law was ambiguous and confusing. This precedent-setting legislation promised only partial success.[1]

Preemption was a hard-won right for frontier settlers. It gave a settler a "preferential right ... to buy his claim at a modest price...."[2] While the concept was known and used generally on the frontier fringe as early as the American Revolution, Congress did not agree to apply the principle to future settlement until 1841. Arguments against it included its encouragement of the control of western lands by a lawless rabble, its inclination to stimulate speculation and perjury, the desire to use public lands for revenue rather than giving land to settlers in small pieces for low prices, and the extra work it entailed for the General Land Office to administer. Vigorous agitation by frontiersmen who defied existing land laws by taking up land to which they had no legal right—and who petitioned for congressional protection of their improvements and for a right to buy the land they had developed at a low price—forced the government to recognize the necessity for such legislation.

As the interest in rapid expansion of the frontier grew, especially in the years following the War of 1812, policy makers came to see preemption as a method for encouraging settlers to risk frontier perils, create farms, and raise the value of land while pressing the line of settlement outward. Many also recognized that combinations of speculators and of settlers ordinarily prevented auctions at government land sales from bringing in more than the minimum price of $1.25 per acre. Indeed, preemption might actually stimulate the number of purchases. After a lengthy period of responding to squatter settlement by giving relief in the form of retroactive preemption laws, Congress finally passed the Preemption Act of 1841, thus giving squatters a preferential right to land they would claim in the future. Town sites were specifically exempted in the law, apparently because the government wished to continue producing revenue by auctioning such sites to the highest bidder.[3]

Certainly town sites had been objects of intense speculation and had brought high prices at auction. The cause of this interest was the greater possibilities for profit in the control of a trading or distributive site. In both the American and Canadian West, states W.L. Morton, "competition for [a] distributive site ... [was] even keener than that for [a] homestead site, for the potential gains, both from speculation and operation, were greater."[4] In the years before 1844, competitors at land sales bid up promising town sites to fantastic prices. Prior to the Panic of 1837, for example, there was a "rage for town sites." Most were laid out "on paper," and did not exist in reality. Uncle Sam, Louisiana, for example, sold for $500,000 at auction. Speculators laid out Cairo, Illinois, overnight and printed maps showing a thriving city. But Cairo did not exist, and after the spring flood, Roy Robbins notes, nothing could be found there but "a shanty, . . . a flock of geese, a lean pig, and a jackass."[5]

In the old Northwest, Morton continues, there was a "mad scramble for choice locations. . . . There was no fork, or falls, or bend in any river, no nook or bay on Lake Erie or Lake Michigan, no point along any imagined canal or railroad . . . but could be classed as a choice location for a flourishing metropolis—at least on paper!"[6] Perhaps sites for towns like Chicago and Toledo merited such speculation, but the instances where this was not true were many. And more consequential, if the promotor were to make his profit, the town lots would have to sell for enormous prices, out of the reach of the ordinary shopkeeper or craftsman. Often the lands were held, as were neighboring agricultural lands, until the surrounding regions were developed sufficiently to raise lot prices.[7]

Although those who describe the frontier settlement process seldom portray the relationship of town to country, their development was intimately related on the frontier. Farmers needed and desired towns near their farms where they could sell surplus produce and purchase manufactured goods or luxury items. Settlers moving from settled to frontier areas missed the comforts to which they had been accustomed: "Buckskin clothing, pineknot torches, and puncheon benches were not originally adopted through choice."[8] Before farm families could make purchases, they had to have a surplus and a market town in which to sell it. Indeed, some historians argue that a characteristic interest in the growing of cash crops was well-nigh universal.

Townsmen wished to reap the benefits from the settlement of new towns. There was money to be made in provisioning or housing travelers, catering to the desires and needs of soldiers at nearby forts, processing farmer's grain, acting as middlemen for agricultural produce, and providing goods and services to farm families in the hinterland. Where a ready source of income existed from overland or river travel, a fort, or a government outpost, towns often preceded or accompanied farms into a new area. Such towns acted as a powerful stimulus to the rapid development of the surrounding agricultural area. Other rural areas might wait longer for a market town to arise in response to agricultural development that would provide an economic base.[9] Ordinarily, town builders located frontier towns on river crossings, crossroads, good natural harbors and river ports, or near forts in order to obtain positions with control of avenues of trade and communication or domination of a productive countryside and raw materials. Whether towns pioneered settlement of an area or grew as a result of agricultural development, they provided a vital source of processing, services, manufactured goods, and markets and a focus for social and cultural institutions of the community.[10]

The first general town site legislation in 1844 evolved, in the wake of the triumph of prospective preemption for farmers, out of a plea from the inhabitants of Weston, a town in western Missouri. David Atchison, senator from Missouri, presented the petition which made an emotional appeal for the townspeople: "Town sites being exempted, by Congress from the operation of the Preemption laws your petitioners are without the shadow of a title to their homes. . . ."[11] The petition proposed that the town settlers be allowed to preempt their lands at the local land office. A trustee for the town would get a title for the site and then would give title to residents on individual lots. It was a request that Congress ratify, as it had in the past, the right of settlers, who had already established themselves and built a town, to their land and improvements. But it was a radical departure in that it requested preemption rights for a town. In addition, the petitioners sought to encourage community development by requiring that each lot owner contribute to a fund designed to make improvements that would benefit the town as a whole such as wharves, bridges, and grading of streets.[12]

The request for assistance to Weston citizens underwent a transformation into a general, prospective preemption bill for towns at the hands of the General Land Office, the Public Land Committee of the Senate, and senators and representatives in debate. After the petition was presented by Atchison, it went to the Public Land Committee which sought the opinion of Thomas Blake, commissioner of the General Land Office. The commissioner obviously favored a preemption policy for town settlers. Although the auction of town sites had been a source of revenue for the government in the past and so had been specifically exempted from the Great Preemption Act of 1841, Blake could see "no substantial reason . . . perceived for such exemption at the present time."[13]

Further, Blake saw danger in the granting of a single petition. Many towns were mushrooming on the public lands; inevitably a flood of petitions would follow if the Weston one were granted. Rather than respond to the plea of the Weston town settlers with a specific remedy, he proposed a general town site bill.[14]

Although the petition requested that the land office give titles to each lot in the town, Blake saw that approach as filled with potential difficulties. When Missouri, as part of the Louisiana Purchase, achieved territorial status, titles to lots in old towns established under the French and Spanish were unclear. Settling those titles involved extra surveying, hearings, and many additional reports and costs. The adjudication of claims was still unfinished as late as 1854.[15] "The experience of this office," wrote Blake, "is decidedly against the expediency of any legislation that would be likely to connect it administratively with the complicated questions and details growing out of the laying off of such towns, and the adjustment of titles to lots therein."[16]

Preemption, it seems, was a commendable public policy for towns that would promote expansion and settlement, but the past experience of the General Land Office and the paucity of staff and funds argued for leaving the essential processes of selecting sites, laying off towns, dividing up lots, and adjusting title to them to private initiative and private action. Thus Blake presented the committee and the Senate with a bill that provided for the first preemption of town lands on the frontier. Sites were limited to 320 acres and title would be given for the whole site, not individual lots. The cost to town settlers would be $1.25 per acre or $400 for an entire site.[17]

Blake craftily left the most difficult political question to Congress. Preemption, it would appear, was so well established a principle that extending it to town sites would raise few questions. Legislators and administrators did not limit their vision of expansion to the rural frontier but readily recognized the existence and positive function of towns and would willingly support their creation through a preemption policy. However, Blake carefully avoided defining whether the bill would offer retroactive or prospective preemption. Was the act to be for the relief only of towns that then existed on public lands without title, or was it to promise preemption right to future settlers who would be encouraged to settle towns as the frontier expanded? Prospective preemption, established as a principle of the land laws only three years before, was not so well entrenched that it would engender no debate.

The debate, though evidence on it is slim, indicated that the spirit of Henry Clay's silent opposition to squatters and preemption was present.[18] The bill that reached the Senate was worded inconclusively on the question of prospective preemption, but it seemed purely a relief measure. Debate flared over the issue on May 6 when Senator William Haywood of North Carolina moved that only towns begun "before the passage of this act" be given a prior right to buy. Western representatives sprang to the defense of prospective preemption immediately. The next day Haywood continued to press his attempt "to destroy the prospective preemption rights to lots in towns laid off on the public lands. . . ."[19] But Senator Spencer Jarnagin of Tennessee maintained there was

no good reason why those who located a quarter section of land, and laid off a town thereon, would not be as much entitled to the right of preemption to the lots in said towns as those who located a quarter section for agricultural purposes. If it was right and just in the one case, it was in the other. If the policy were wise as to the past, so it would be for the future.[20]

He believed that townsmen should share the privilege of preempting the public lands and the preemption should be both retroactive and prospective. He was joined in the fight by other westerners, and when Sidney Breese of Illinois moved that the bill be made prospective, his amendment passed without further debate.[21] Since the vote was not recorded, the nature of the coalition necessary to pass the bill is not clear, but westerners carried the fight on the floor. Preemption obviously still aroused opposition, but it was less vehement than that in 1841. Even though town sites were seen in previous years as a source of revenue to the government, the idea of the greater good of getting settlers in actual towns while promoting more rapid expansion of the frontier prevailed in 1844.

The only other issue to engender much debate was the question of whether the bill properly ensured that town sites would be acquired by actual settlers or by nonresident speculators. Actual settlers needed to be protected in their rights even though their use of the land was quite different from that of rural settlers. The bill was amended to protect their "several" interests. Whether the settlers were blacksmiths, shopkeepers, or doctors, they were assured of protection of their right to a title. Of greater significance was the insertion into the bill of the word "occupants." The legislators feared that vague wording would allow speculators to use this legislation. Requiring that only occupants of the town could make a claim ensured that those actually living on the site would be legal preemptors rather than nonresident speculators. The legislators also made special provision for Weston to guarantee that the town founders had adequate time—one year—to preempt their lands. In this form the bill readily passed both houses and became law in May of 1844.[22]

The careful attempts to prevent speculation in town sites

under the Town Site Preemption Act would prove fruitless. While faulty administration at the local level and the lack of a staff to investigate claims were causes of the failure of the legislation to prevent widespread speculation in town lands, much of the blame lay in the legislation itself.[23] Whether the wording was simply ambiguous or was deliberately vague is not clear, but the act was open to misinterpretation.

It is difficult to comprehend the way such legislation would operate by examining the provisions. Preemption involved legislative policy and principle, but it also defined a process of settlement. Preemption grew organically out of the practices of frontier squatters rather than out of the minds of legislators. Vast stretches of public land made up the public domain in 1844. This land was not unsettled, but was inhabited by Native Americans who would be removed from the land by treaty or warfare before white settlement could occur. The land was crossed by well-defined trade routes, usually laid out originally by natives for commerce or warfare. Most of the land west of the Mississippi, except for the tier of states immediately to the west of the river, was public domain in the 1840s.

Legislation, such as the Town Site Preemption Act of 1844 and the Great Preemption Act of 1841, was in itself, insufficient inducement for people to pack up their belongings, sell land or possessions, and trudge westward to begin a new serial in their lives. People moved in boom times when the price of grains was high and land values were rising. In such circumstances the prospect of land at $1.25 per acre was very tempting. Most people were less likely to take the journey to the West in bad times when prospects were less encouraging and when many could not afford to move.

However, if conditions were conducive to migration, townsite preemption offered generous inducements. Settlers squatting on unsettled frontier land could claim as many as 320 acres of land with the assurance of a purchase price of $1.25 per acre or $400 for the entire site. In the 1850s, when this legislation was applied the most, lots in towns were generally 25×125 feet.[24] There would be 13 or 14 lots per acre or approximately 4160 lots in each town site. The cost per lot to townsmen would be less than ten cents. The land to be disposed of under this act was quite cheap, and its cost would comprise a totally insignificant part of the cost of frontier town building. Compare this with the probable cost to town settlers on earlier frontiers: Bath, Louisiana, sold for $35,000 at government auction and nine months later was resold for $600,000; at auction, Harlem, Louisiana, brought $40,000 and was resold for $200,000. Lots in a site in Illinois where there was but one dwelling sold in the 1830s for $1,000 to $2,500 each.[25]

Low costs of town site preemption encouraged prospective settlers and speculators to seek out good sites and to attempt to build a town. It seems likely, though not certain, that settlers most attracted to such a venture would be those with town backgrounds and skills. If this law encouraged the development of towns in areas that would otherwise have had to wait until an agricultural surplus generated a fiscal surplus that seemed to justify building a town, then it could also play a role in a more rapid development of the surrounding agricultural region.

Settlers who wanted a town site on government lands first had to stake their claim, literally by driving stakes into the ground, as proof of their location.[26] Staking a claim gave visible proof of their choice of site, which could not exceed 320 acres. Next, the potential town builders had to record their claim to prevent others from choosing the same site. According to the Town Site Preemption Act, the corporate authorities or a judge of the county court would file a "declaratory statement" at the local land office. The land officers would record the claim and note it on a map in the land office. Administrators intended this to protect claims in several ways. By drawing the claim on a map, the local land officers made overlapping claims less likely, though it seldom entirely prevented conflict. The declaratory also gave the claimants sole use of the land—but not title to it—so they could fulfill the major requirement of preemption, the building of a town that would then give the claimants a preference in buying the site.

Next the proprietors were free to promote and build this town. In this developmental or formative period, the use of the public lands was solely a private matter. Here was the heart of the preemption process. On the one hand, settlers could earn a preferential right to buy before others at a low price by developing a town. Because they used the land for free while operating business enterprises of various sorts, town builders might also earn the money to purchase the site in the developmental period. In this way, public lands were used to subsidize private development. On the other hand, the nation benefited by the extension of the frontier and the value added to the land entirely by private action. During this period claimants were supposed to construct the basic essentials of a place of commerce: for example, dry goods shops, grocery stores, blacksmith shops, homes, churches, schools, perhaps a mill. Such a site had to be used "exclusively for the purposes of trade" and not for farming. This building enterprise was solely in private hands, even though the homes and businesses were on lands to which the builders had no title. Government officials made no checks on claims, on who controlled the site, or on what was built there. There were no specifications in the law for type or number of buildings or on the character or amount of improvements necessary to secure land. What control there was consisted primarily in the fact that the government could deny title to the proprietors when they attempted to preempt. This developmental period might last for as little as one year or as many as five.[27]

Finally, the town settlers would "prove-up" at the local land office, again through a judge or corporate authorities of the town or county, by offering testimony and witnesses, or proof, that they had built a town.[28] There had to be proof as well that those who wanted title to the town site were actually occupants, inhabitants in the town. The entry of the preemption claim by elected or appointed officials was to be another safeguard against speculators getting control of the site. The register, the official who recorded the claim, and the receiver, who took payment for the land, would decide if the evidence was sufficient. If it was, a patent, or title, would be issued for the entire town site. If not, an appeal could be made to the General Land Office in Washington, D.C. When a town did not actually exist on the site, the claim could be rejected and the land made available for farming.

The Town Site Preemption Act, by requiring that claimants build a town before they received title to the land, could ensure that town sites would not be acquired and then held off the market until an increase in value produced a speculative profit. The requirement that the government grant title only to people who were occupants of a site was a guarantee that the benefits of preemption went to actual settlers. As a prospective measure, the Town Site Preemption Act allowed, if not encouraged, settlers in the vanguard of migration to a newly opened area to select promising sites and develop them quickly as towns, thus creating marketplaces and encouraging the early developments of an agricultural surplus. Indeed, the prospective aspect of the law combined with the very low cost of the land might have promoted the rapid expansion of the town frontier.

However, there were flaws in the law that could undermine its effectiveness. Like much land legislation, the act contained ambiguous and confusing language that would necessitate much administrative interpretation and extensive litigation. The desire of Commissioner Blake to prevent the General Land Office from having responsibility for checking and granting title to each lot resulted in a provision that granted title for entire town sites only. This approach promised to be confusing in practice and detrimental to the larger goals of the legislation. How much land could an individual hold? If there were no instructions on how to divide the site, what would prevent one or a few people from monopolizing an entire site, while the majority of town settlers would have no access to land or the benefits of its low price?

Though the law called for improvements that would demonstrate a place of trade existed before the government could issue a title, it did not specify how much improvement was actually necessary to obtain the entire site nor how to divide the 320 acres if only a small portion of the site was settled. Could twenty people with one store and three dwellings qualify for a whole site? Or was it necessary to have a building on each lot? each block? each forty-acre subdivision? If a few scattered improvements sufficed, would not the major goal of ensuring the development of actual towns be undermined?

Another provision failed to take frontier conditions into consideration. The law required that corporate authorities make both declarations of intent to settle sites and preemption entries, but what if settlement, as it often did, preceded government? Could a settler enter a claim and have it protected by the law? Or might such a settler later find that, after developing a town, his application for title was rejected because the initial declaratory was not made by proper authorities?

This first town site law contained potentially beneficial provisions for encouraging and regulating the development of town sites on public lands. Most of its provisions indicate that the law was intended to transfer the land to actual occupants in towns which they built in the years between staking a claim and purchase. People were not to control town sites without living on them nor could they reserve sites, hoping for a rise in value, without building on them. However, the provisions did not offer sufficient and unambiguous protection for the goals of the legislation. One might even venture the view that a central aspect of preemption, that of leaving development in unsupervised, private hands, seemed likely to produce abuse of the law. Certainly the potentially beneficial principle voiced in the law was not underpinned by the provisions.

NOTES

1. Thomas Donaldson, *The Public Domain: Its History with Statistics* (Washington D.C.: Government Printing Office, 1884), has a brief discussion of the various town site acts on pp. 298-299. He also has a list of towns which preempted lands

under these acts on pp. 300–305 and 1278–1279; and U.S. *Statutes at Large* (1844): 657.

2. Paul W. Gates, *History of Public Land Law Development* (Washington, D.C.: Government Printing Office, 1968), p. 219.

3. Ibid. pp. 219-249; Malcolm Rohrbough, *The Land Office Business: The Settlement and Administration of American Public Lands, 1789-1837* (New York: Oxford University Press, 1968), pp. 200-221; Benjamin H. Hibbard, *A History of Public Land Policies* (New York: Macmillian, 1924); and Roy Robbins, *Our Landed Heritage: The Public Domain, 1776-1936* (Princeton, N.J.: Princeton University Press, 1942), each provide coverage of the changes in the land laws and the gradual adoption of preemption into law.

4. W.L. Morton, "The Significance of Site in the Settlement of the American and Canadian West," *Agricultural History* 25 (July 1951):97.

5. Robbins, *Our Landed Heritage*, p. 64.

6. Morton, "Significance of Site," p. 101.

7. Robbins, *Our Landed Heritage*, p. 64.

8. Fred Shannon, *Economic History of the People of the United States* (New York: Macmillan, 1934), p. 24.

9. Richard C. Wade, *The Urban Frontier* (Cambridge: Harvard University Press, 1959), pp. 1-35. Wade's thesis is that the town frontier preceded the agricultural. James Malin, in *The Community and the Grassland of North America: Prolegomena to its History* (Lawrence: James C. Malin, 1947), takes essentially the same position as Turner: the city was built economically upon the agricultural frontier as the latter developed a surplus that could be traded in the town for services or goods; F. J. Turner, *The Frontier in American History* (New York: Henry Holt and Company, 1921), p. 98.

10. Leroy Hafen and Carl C. Rister, *Western America* (New York: Prentice Hall, 1941), p. 383; H.U. Faulkner, *Economic History of the United States* (New York: Macmillan, 1929), pp. 76, 79.

11. "Petition of a number of citizens of the Town of Weston, Missouri, praying the adoption of measures to secure their ti-

tles to the holders of town lots therein," Senate Petition File 28a-G17.2, Committee on Public Lands, Record Group 56, National Archives, Washington, D.C.

12. Ibid.

13. U.S. Senate, Thomas Blake, Commissioner of the General Land Office to the Senate Public Land Committee, January 13, 1844, "Report of the Committee on Public Lands," 28th Cong., 1st sess., 1844, *Senate Documents*, no. 112.

14. Ibid.

15. U.S. Department of the Interior, Commissioner of the General Land Office, *Annual reports*, 1853-54.

16. Blake to the Senate Public Land Committee, January 13, 1844.

17. Ibid.; U.S. Senate, Bill 77, 28th Cong., 1st sess., 1844, Record Group 56, National Archives, Washington, D.C.

18. The discussion and passage of the act can be seen only through accumulated snatches of clues in the Senate *Journal*, the nearly illegible notations on the bill, or the selective reports in the *Congressional Globe*. Few newspapers throughout the winter and spring months when the Senate was considering the bill, or the few minutes when it was read quickly three times in the House and passed without hindrance, gave it even occasional reference. U.S. Senate, *Journal*, 28th Cong., 1st sess., 1844, pp. 111, 259, 264, 268, 274, 285, 286. For comparison, see Senate Bill 77 and U.S., *Statutes at Large* 5 (1944): 657; *Congressional Globe*, pp. 256, 605, 610-611; U.S., House of Representatives, *Journal*, 28th Cong., 1st sess., 1844, p. 918; and New York *Herald*, February 11, 1844. The small amount of interest in the bill can be accounted for—at least in part—by the importance of other issues before the Senate in this session: tariff, abolition, annexation, and various internal improvements.

19. *Congressional Globe*, pp. 610-611.

20. Ibid.

21. Ibid.

22. Senate Bill 77.

23. Rita G. Napier, "The Spirit of Speculation; A Study of Town Site Preemption and Land Use in Four Frontier Kansas Towns" (Master's thesis, American University, Washington, D.C., 1969).

24. Everett Dick, *The Sod-House Frontier* (New York: D. Appleton-Century Company, 1937), p. 41.

25. Robbins, *Our Landed Heritage*, p. 63.

26. There are no rules in the bill directing the staking of the claim in this specific fashion, but it was the practice on the frontier. Recording the claim was required by the land office within three months after settlement. See Donaldson, *Public Domain*, pp. 164-167, 688-695.

27. The length of time between settlement and preemption depended upon the completion of the government survey and the announcement of the public sale. Towns in territorial Kansas sometimes had as long as five years to build before entering the land for the title.

28. Senate Bill 77.

American Land Policies and William Scully

With the acquisition of a vast public domain in the late eighteenth century the infant United States began the evolution of a federal land policy. Potential purchasers were at first located along the coast, a great distance from these new land areas. Different states claimed fragments of the region to pay off Revolutionary War obligations. Even before the adoption of the Constitution, a system of rectangular survey of the public domain was begun which was followed, with minor alteration, into the thirty public land states.[1] There the man-made marks on the land reflected the north-south, east-west grid initiated in 1785.[2] Natives of those states, much more than other Americans, use cardinal directions for identifying locations or for providing information.

Of far greater diversity were the procedures employed by the federal government for transferring to private ownership that great national treasure of more than a billion acres of land. Two contradictory ideas surfaced for the evolving federal land policy. Strongest at first was the intention to dispose of land for cash to large-scale purchasers. This view, backed by political leaders such as Alexander Hamilton, looked on the land owned by the federal government as a significant source of revenue. Another pattern of public land disposal emphasized small-sized tracts to be made available to actual settlers at low cost or even at no cash outlay. Settler-oriented federal land laws developed slowly; the sale of land for gaining federal revenues was of far greater significance in the early years.[3]

To expect an important share of federal revenues to come from land sales is almost incomprehensible to late twentieth-century Americans. However, expenditures of the early federal government were modest, no greater in dollars than the amount spent by a present-day small American city. Land sales, as a consequence, produced revenues second only to tariff duties before the Civil War. Land disposal was encouraged by political leaders concerned with the perennial problem of balancing the federal budget.

Initial federal land sales in the 1790s were limited to tracts no smaller than 640 acres at a minimum price of $2.00 per acre. Even then it was the Congress's intention that half the land be disposed of in township-sized tracts (23,040 acres), but none of these larger offerings were ever sold. Moreover, the land office was some 400 miles from the offered land, handicapping buyers who wished to examine land before purchasing. Military land tracts, turned over to certain veterans of the Revolutionary War for unpaid services, mitigated to some extent the desire for small farms from the public domain.

By 1820 the clamor for sales of small units of land brought the minimum offering down to eighty acres, with a set price of $1.25 per acre.[4] The $1.25 cash price would remain in effect for more than 100 years. Federal land offices, by that time, were located conveniently to each area of surveyed and offered land; and the procedures for operating the General Land Office were refined and systematically followed.[5] Still land was not free, but a far greater number of land buyers were available for these small tracts than for the earlier offerings.

Even after 1820 the public domain was disposed of in a manner that profited the large speculator. Grants to states for canal construction, for reclamation of swamps, or for railroad corporations after 1851 generously feathered the speculator's nest. Eventually, though, most of this land would pass into the hands of small farmers.

The first truly settler-oriented land laws were the various preemption acts passed for specific land districts. Later a general law, the Preemption Act of 1841, applied to all offered land.[6] A settler could file a claim at a federal land office on as many as 160 acres of public domain. After at least six month's residence on the land and prior to its sale at public auction, the settler could buy the land at the minimum price of $1.25 per acre. Each settler had one preemption "right" and much of the choice midwestern farm land was purchased in this manner.

To federal land officers the disposal of quarter-section tracts was a booming operation, hence the term "land office business." Even more money could be gained for the government in the same period of time if the land could be sold in larger units—the price per acre was the same. Yet while sales of quarter sections were routine, disposal of larger portions of the public domain was unique. The small commissions provided to land officers built more quickly in large sales and these buyers received special attention.

Early arrivals in each new land district placed great value on a growing population. Thus businessmen, professionals, and politicians eagerly proclaimed the advantages of their new area. To them, a grave shortage was people for their new town and the labor they could provide. Capital to develop the unimproved lands also was in short supply. These private individuals advertised and "boomed" their new lands through correspondence and newly established newspapers. The public land states also sought population by publishing pamphlets and, at times, elaborate annual volumes to entice settlers into their area. Rarely did the federal government do the same; however, federal laws until the late nineteenth century placed no bar on movement of money or people. All of these interested groups advertised the economic possibilities for the man with capital. Optimistically, they described how a person could buy low cost land and build a fortune.

This was the message heard by William Scully in 1850 when the young Irish landlord was in his late twenties. As a member of a landed family of the lesser gentry, Scully had inherited about 1,000 acres of County Tipperary land in 1843. During the next seven years he was able to save £2,000 from the proceeds of his land, even though these years included the calamitous Potato Famine. The British Parliament also repealed the Corn Laws in 1846, ending an advantage for Irish farmers in the English market. Henceforth, low-priced grain from America and elsewhere would undercut the producers in the British Isles. These push and pull factors motivated William Scully to take his savings in 1850 and sail to America.[7]

After a summer of exploration Scully selected about 8,000 acres of government land in Logan County, Illinois. He visited many areas before he decided. He learned how to maximize his resources by buying the land with Mexican War military land warrants, which were issued to veterans soon after the war was over. When the bill providing for these veteran's benefits was debated in Congress there were discussions about restricting their use to the named military beneficiary, but the statute imposed no such limitation. Military land warrants could be sold and become assignable to someone else.[8] A national market existed for these documents; a former soldier could expect ninety cents to a dollar per acre if he sold. All of Scully's first purchases were made with this land scrip. Some accounts said that Scully advertised in Springfield, Illinois, newspapers offering to buy military land warrants.[9]

When Scully made his purchases at the federal land office in Springfield, the register and receiver—land office officials who recorded and took payment for the lands—treated him with every courtesy. But later accounts state that Scully did not wait in the line like others. Instead, he bought a place in line so his time could be used in looking for more land. The new landowner employed a Springfield merchant, John Williams, to oversee his land and to pay taxes when due. Scully then hurried back home to Ireland to describe to his brothers the significance of his action. He wanted them to return to the United States with him to acquire more low-cost land. None of his brothers were interested in leaving the secure position they occupied as a member of Ireland's lesser gentry. But one brother lent him £10,000 and Scully returned to Illinois for another land-buying expedition. Also, he married that year a young woman who brought him a £5,000 dowry. Presumably, this money was used in buying additional land in 1852. By that time, Scully's holdings in Illinois totaled more than 28,000 acres, all acquired from the federal government. Military land warrants were used for most of his land payments; cash was paid for only a few of these acres.[10]

Typically large-scale purchases of federal land were acquired by speculators and Scully may have had speculation in mind at first. In the meantime he brought his wife to Illinois where he built a large house near the center of his Logan County lands. Scully's land, low lying, rich, and water-logged, had been offered for sale soon after Illinois became a state in 1818. Many land seekers had passed it by. When seen in late summer and fall it seemed like ideal property but it rarely dried out before June—too late to plant corn. The swampy environment may have been responsible for Mrs. Scully's ill health in 1853 and Scully returned to his family in Ireland. A short time later he began selling his land at prices much higher than what he had paid. There were no government restraints on such action; a property owner had full title to land even if he was the first purchaser from the government. After obtaining sales contracts on about one-fourth of his land Scully stopped selling because of low prices brought on by the Panic of 1857. About one-half of the land buyers defaulted on payments and Scully used their down payment as rent. A long-time pattern of tenant operations was begun.

The Civil War dominated the next few years. Federal land legislation during the war included the Homestead Act, the Pacific Railway Act, and the Morrill Land Grant College Act, all passed in 1862.[11] The settler-oriented free land available under the Homestead Act was the culmination of federal land policy which made land available to farmer-settlers. However, the Pacific Railway Act and the Morrill Land Grant College Act served the interests of large-scale speculative land buyers.

One other Civil War feature which could have affected a

large-scale owner of real estate, such as Scully, was the war-imposed income tax. Scully figured his earnings from his Illinois tenant operations as basically a losing proposition when compared to the capital involved. His agent, John Williams, was directed to total his income and subtract his expenses. Consequently, Scully paid no personal income tax.

By 1870 the value of Scully's Illinois holdings had grown rapidly. He repurchased some of the land sold in the 1850s and other land was acquired. By his own estimate, his American property was valued at more than $1 million. His income was invested in corporate and government bonds. Also in 1870 Scully began purchasing parcels in Nebraska and Kansas. His acquisitions from the federal government in 1870 included more than 42,000 acres in Nuckolls County, Nebraska, and about 13,000 acres in Kansas, mostly in Marion County. This time the $1.25 price was paid in cash on these purchases. Additional land was acquired in Kansas, Nebraska, and Illinois from private sellers. In Kansas a considerable acreage was purchased from the Atchison, Topeka and Santa Fe Railroad, part of the land grant from the federal government. John Williams, Scully's first agent from Springfield, Illinois, also sold him thousands of acres. In Gage County, Nebraska, Scully acquired more than 20,000 acres from private sellers.[12] Some of this land had passed into private hands under the Morrill Land Grant College legislation.

By 1888 Scully's American holdings totaled more than 180,000 acres in three states. Local agitation in those and other states, however, brought restrictive legislation on alien-absentee land ownership. Such owners could not bequeath their holdings; instead, upon death, their lands were to be sold. All states where Scully owned lands developed these restraints. Congress also passed similar legislation applicable to the territories and the District of Columbia. During the hard times of the 1890s Scully added more than 43,000 acres of Bates County, Missouri, land to his estate and his land purchases came to an end.

To protect descent of his holdings for his family, he took out naturalization papers in 1895 and became an American citizen in 1900. During those years he moved his family to Washington, D.C., rather than to one of the states where he owned land. He believed federal action on incomes of District of Columbia residents was less restrictive than that of the states. But after gaining citizenship, London was again his home.[13]

Scully lived another six years, dying in 1906. His estate then passed to his wife. Because there were no federal estate taxes, the vast bulk of his holdings were transferred. In 1918 Mrs. Scully divided the American lands between her two sons. Since she lived another fourteen years, and no gift taxes existed in 1918, this transfer incurred no great expense. In 1942 and 1961, respectively, Scully's two sons died and death taxes were paid on portions of their inheritance and on land acquired in Louisiana during World War I. The Missouri land was sold during World War II before its owner died. Thus, the total amount of American farmland owned in 1983 by William Scully's heirs was in excess of 200,000 acres. Its value was reputed to exceed $400 million.

This immense wealth came to the family of William Scully in part because of nineteenth-century American land policy. Scully, like his brothers, had a moderate-sized Irish estate. But unlike his brothers he was willing to risk his savings to increase his wealth through acquisition of low-cost virgin American land. His early purchases in Illinois, enhanced through the use of military land warrants, laid the basis for his future wealth. Approximately 28,000 acres of government land was purchased there for about one dollar per acre. Since this land brought little revenue at first Scully paid the necessary expenses from his Irish income, enabling him to retain most of his land when many other large-scale purchasers were forced to sell. Scully usually relied on his Irish estate for his personal expenses. Net income from his American holdings went into more land or into bonds so his wealth grew rapidly. His subsequent purchases in Illinois from private sellers, government land in Nebraska and Kansas, and land there from private landowners were made from income coming from his initial

Illinois holdings. His cost for 55,000 acres of government land in Kansas and Nebraska was $1.25 per acre. His expenditure for more than 80,000 acres, purchased from the federal government in Illinois, Kansas, and Nebraska, was about $100,000. The 95,000 acres purchased from private sellers in the same three states amounted to about $900,000. His last big purchase, 43,000 acres in Missouri, cost him about $1 million. His American landed estate, acquired for an outlay of about $2 million over a period of forty-five years, was valued between $10 million and $15 million at the time of his death in 1906.

William Scully was able to use the intricacies of American land policy to his advantage so that his long-range goal of building a huge estate for his family was realized. American land policy in 1850 and even in the 1870s seemed to encourage this development. Thereafter, it would have been unlikely that a farming estate, such as the multi-state Scully operations, could be built through the use of various federal land laws.

NOTES

1. States not public land states included the original thirteen plus Vermont, Kentucky, Tennessee, Maine, West Virginia, Texas, and Hawaii.

2. Land Ordinance of 1785, *Journals of the American Congress*, vol. 4, May 20, 1785, p. 5207.

3. See Paul W. Gates, *History of Public Land Law Development* (Washington, D.C.: Government Printing Office, 1968), and Roy Robbins, *Our Landed Heritage: The Public Domain, 1776-1936* (Princeton: Princeton University Press, 1942).

4. Minimum offerings were eventually reduced to forty acres.

5. See Malcolm Rohrbough, *The Land Office Business* (New York: Oxford University Press, 1968).

6. U.S., *Statutes at Large* 5 (1841):453-458.

7. See Homer E. Socolofsky, *Landlord William Scully* (Lawrence: Regents Press of Kansas, 1979).

8. See Jerry A. O'Callaghan, "The War Veteran and the Public Lands," in *The Public Lands: Studies in the History of the Public Domain*, ed. Vernon Carstensen (Madison: University of Wisconsin Press, 1963), pp. 109-119.

9. Socolofsky, *Scully*.

10. Ibid.

11. U.S., *Statutes at Large* 12 (1862): Homestead Act of 1862, p. 392, Union Pacific Railroad Act, p. 489; and Morrill Act, p. 503.

12. Socolofsky, *Scully*.

13. Ibid.

9 PAUL H. CARLSON

The Development of the Angora Goat Industry in Texas

In 1980 Texas ranchers produced over 90 percent of all Angora goats in the United States and some 97 percent of all the country's mohair.[1] Ranchers in Texas, grazing nearly 1.5 million Angora goats that provided over 8 million pounds of mohair, produced nearly half of the world's mohair clip in that year.[2] The value of Angoras and their mohair in the state has been estimated at close to $150 million. Although these figures are impressive, the Texas Angora goat industry has not received much modern-day attention, and historians have virtually ignored the subject.[3]

A native of Asian Turkey, the Angora goat has spiral horns and a silky white fleece that hangs down in curly locks all over its body. Although most people prefer the meat of Angoras more than other goat species, the Angora is the most important breed for raising and selling goat hair. Its mohair makes a sleek cloth that is widely used for robes, capes, suits, and plush upholstery. Mohair goats today are crossbreeds between the delicate Angora and the Spanish goat—a cross that combines good mohair production with physical hardiness. Angora goats thrive best where there is a variety of brush and shrubbery which should include live oak and other evergreen browse to afford plenty of variety throughout the year. The vast Edwards

Plateau region of Texas offers the best Angora goat browse to be found in the United States and possibly in the world.

While there are conflicting reports concerning who brought the first Angoras to America, most authorities give credit to Dr. James B. Davis. A physician and a cotton expert from Columbia, South Carolina, Davis—a grand-looking man with large black eyes, black hair, florid complexion, and a high white forehead—brought a small flock of the goats to the United States in 1849. In 1844 President James K. Polk, in response to a request from the Sultan, had appointed Davis to introduce the cotton culture to Turkey. Upon completing his work there, Davis returned to the United States, bringing with him several Asiatic animals, including the Angora goats. After experimenting with them for ten years, Davis sold the purebred Angoras to Colonel Richard Peters of Atlanta, Georgia, who had been watching the work with great interest from the beginning. Many of the kids produced through Davis's breeding efforts were sold for good profit.[4]

There is conflicting information as to when the first Angoras arrived in Texas. F.O. Landrum, who lived on the Nueces River in Uvalde County, may have been the first, but in 1943 Professor John Ashton of Texas A&M University suggested that Colonel Robert A. Williamson of Gallatin, Tennessee, an agent for the Sumner Cashmere Company, took eight head of Angora to Austin in 1857.[5] Another account has Colonel W.W. Haupt, a powerful man who boasted that he never lived a day in town in his life, purchasing a farm in 1853 near Kyle in Hays County, where he ran the first steam cotton gin used in his area—"Western Texas" as it was called then. In 1858 he determined to herd goats and began raising some of the common stock. Quickly, however, he made arrangements with Colonel Peters to purchase for $100 eight head of Angora. The transaction marked the start of the "Haupt goats" which in later years became popular with Texas goat men.[6] Although others soon entered the goat business, Angora and mohair production for some time remained a secondary enterprise. Their numbers in Texas before the Civil War were so small as to be indeterminable.

After the war, as Texas sheep raising expanded, the Angora goat and mohair industry slowly picked up. Judge J. P. Devine introduced Angoras to his ranch near San Antonio in the 1860s. Devine, having acquired the goats from Colonel Peters in Georgia, took much pride in the animals. He maintained pure blooded stock, but also bred some of the billies to common Spanish does. He enjoyed surprising success at increasing mohair clips. In a letter to John L. Hayes, one of the first chroniclers of the mohair industry in America, Devine indicated that he had clipped much heavier fleeces in Texas from the same goats that had browsed in Georgia. The reasons for the good fortune, he explained, were the inexhaustible quantity of rich evergreen food throughout the winter and the dry atmosphere. His large fleeces, which averaged from four to five pounds on crossbred animals, encouraged many stockmen to adopt Angoras.[7]

Colonel W.D. Parish of Seguin purchased purebred Angoras in New England and shipped them to Texas. Like Devine, he bred them to Spanish goats with good results. Later Parish took his small band in wagons to Kendall County, where they could browse in the dry, brushy upland range of that region. George W. Baylor of Uvalde County wrote that in his opinion "Mr. Parish did as much towards starting the Angora goat industry in Texas as anyone."[8]

There were many other early breeders. The Arnold brothers and J. V. Abrams of Frio were among them. The Reverend D. S. Babb ran a flock near Sonora in Sutton County. R. H. Lowry of Camp San Saba was another of the first Angora raisers in Texas, who started with goats purchased from Haupt. William M. Landrum and his sons, W. E. and Frank raised Angoras in Uvalde County. Charles Schreiner of Kerrville, realizing the potential importance of the silky white goat, was instrumental in establishing Angoras in the hill country. He encouraged area ranchers to invest in mohair goats to diversify their ranch livestock.

Since it was soon found that Angoras thrived best in the rocky, rolling hills, the Edwards Plateau attracted most early breeders. There the number of Angoras slowly increased until after 1880 when expansion came more rapidly. Individual flocks remained small in the early stages of the business, seldom numbering more than 200 head. But Angora does, by often giving birth to twins, reproduced young at better than 100 percent of pregnancies; rapid flock expansion was common.

Mohair markets also improved. As early as 1863 textile manufacturers began installing proper machinery. But since it was expensive, New England mills were slow to incorporate the equipment. Nevertheless, when they found that mohair fibers attracted considerable attention among buyers of their goods, they moved to adapt it to their textile machinery. By 1880 mohair had become a popular fiber, used in a variety of fabrics. Railroad passenger car manufacturers found it especially attractive for plush upholstery.

The Angora industry developed along lines similar to the sheep industry. Indeed, from the beginning mohair growers were sheepmen, too. Only rarely in the early days did a rancher confine his livestock interests to goats. Mohair growers acquired purebred bucks to breed to common does in much the way sheepmen had upgraded Spanish *chaurro* breeds. Shearing goats was accomplished in much the same manner as shearing sheep, although it was the general practice to shear goats twice a year: in the spring and fall. Since cold, wet weather immediately following shearing could cause heavy losses, some ranchmen left a "cape," a strip of mohair three to four inches wide, down the back of each goat which offered some protection from bad weather. Others sheared with raised combs, leaving about one-quarter of an inch of hair on the goat. After it was shorn and packed, mohair was transported to warehouses to await inspection by buyers representing eastern mills. The processing of mohair into a finished fabric was similar to processing wool. Mohair was graded, scoured, combed, spun, woven or knitted, and washed just as wool.

While several prominent sheepmen entered the Angora industry in the 1880s, an even bigger spurt came in the next decade. Judge Bob Davis of Uvalde County became involved in 1893 when cattlemen gave him four calves. Davis traded the calves for forty Angora does. Over the next few years he set about building one of the finest Angora bands in that part of the state. His sons, Arthur and Bob Jr., carried on his work in the Uvalde area. The Davises were instrumental in having the headquarters for the American Angora Goat Breeder's Association moved to Sabinal, Texas, in 1924 from Kansas City. In 1926 the association headquarters was located at Rocksprings in Edwards County where it remains today. Claude Pepper, of Edwards County and son of J. D. Pepper, who had established a successful band in the 1880s, enjoyed one of the oldest continuing Angora lines in the country. James Prentice of Kimble County, who would win many prizes for his purebred Angoras at stock shows in the twentieth century, was another of the first men to run goats in West Texas. He was a charter member of the American Angora Goat Breeders Association.

Thus, by the mid-1890s Texas had become the center of an emerging Angora goat and mohair business. The industry needed only a promoter, and it found one in William Leslie Black. "Colonel" Black, as he was called in Texas, was a veteran of the Civil War. A charter member of the New York Cotton Exchange, he had acquired considerable wealth in the cotton trade, but in the 1870s he turned his attention to wool as a more profitable proposition than cotton. He toured West Texas, scouting the region for an ideal place to raise sheep. "In 1876," he wrote afterward, "I made a location of 30,000 acres of land at the headsprings of the San Saba River" in present Menard County.[9] Until 1884, when he moved to the Texas property with his family, Black hired a foreman to run the ranch, but he made a yearly trip from St. Louis to inspect his operation.

Black prospered in Texas. He raised sheep and cattle, watched market fluctuations carefully, and sold his cattle, sheep, and wool at good profits. In the meantime, he entered the Angora goat business. As early as 1876 when he bought the West Texas property, he learned that Mexican herders preferred to eat goat. Since goats were cheaper than sheep, he purchased a small flock to supply his herders with fresh meat.

By 1884 he had discovered that Angoras, gaining popularity farther east, were a superior breed and possessed greater commercial value than the common Mexican (Spanish) species he owned. Knowing that he could upgrade his common stock by introducing full-blooded Angora sires, he bought from Colonel Richard Peters of Atlanta, Georgia, eight males and four females, paying $750, including delivery to his ranch. Although he considered it an enormous price for goats, the investment proved a solid one. In a few years Black increased his flock enough to justify shearing the animals to sell the mohair. Within eight years of purchasing the purebreds he counted nearly 8,000 head of well-graded Angoras.[10]

Black found the animal perfectly adapted to his San Saba River country. The altitude and climate were ideal, and the region held an abundance of fresh, clear water. The hilly range along the breaks of the San Saba provided year-round browse, and the Angoras helped to clear the brush from his cattle pastures. His nannies produced young at a rate of nearly 125 percent per year. Neither disease nor scarcity of grass depleted the flock, for the animals lived on the leaves and shoots of the scrub oak, mesquite, and other shrubs of the region. Nor did the crossbreds require close watching. They took care of themselves, regularly came home with a herder to the pens at night, but did not require close stables. Black's crossbred flock doubled in size each year and after eight generations of breeding he had difficulty distinguishing between his purebred and crossbred Angoras. Moreover, he experienced no problem in selling the mohair. Wool warehouse men welcomed it as they did wool. Textile manufacturers liked its silky luster, its great affinity for dyestuffs, and its strength and durability. They used it extensively in the manufacture of drapery, portiere cloth, linings, cloaking, knitted garments, rugs, and numerous other fabrics. Railroad passenger car manufacturers preferred mohair to wool for upholstery.

In 1893 when a devastating panic and depression struck the United States, Black suffered financial losses. He sold his cattle and sheep and he dumped his wool on the market for only seven cents per pound. He also mortgaged the greater part of his land. Yet he still browsed eight thousand Angoras. These, he figured, would need to be thinned out or in a couple of years they would overrun his ranch.

Accordingly, Black contacted a personal acquaintance with Armour & Co., a Chicago meat packing firm, offering to sell 1,000 fat wethers at Armour's price, if the company would return the hides. Declining, the friend informed Black that goat meat was not popular among Armour's customers and did not sell. Nor would the company venture to buy the animals in large numbers until people had overcome their prejudice against it. His friend advised slaughtering the goats for their hides and tallow and packing the meat in cans labeled "roast mutton." Deciding there was money to be made in such a dubious proposition, Black concluded that he would butcher the animals himself.[11]

Thus, the Range Canning Company was born, one of West Texas's first meat packing firms. It was also a rendering plant and a tannery. Black, after returning from New York where he went to obtain investors and money from old friends in the cotton trade, dammed up the San Saba River and built a water wheel to provide power. He constructed a large combination slaughter house and cannery with a rendering plant nearby, bought machinery, purchased thousands of two-pound cans, and ordered beautiful four-color labels. He hired W. G. Tobin from a Chicago meat packing company to oversee the work. He built the tannery on a low bluff overlooking the dam, brought in an experienced tanner, and employed about twenty-five people, mostly Mexican-Americans, to carry on the canning, tanning, and rendering operations. To house his employees, Black erected a row of small homes and established a two-story store for workmen and their families. The ranch now resembled a small factory town.[12]

Black slaughtered 3,000 old nannies and wethers in 1893 and the following year 4,000 other animals. In 1895 he slaughtered hogs in addition to Angoras. The canning operation went smoothly, but Black found difficulty selling his so-called roast mutton. When new labels, calling his meat "boiled mutton," did not help, he changed the labels again. This time he printed them as "W.G. Tobin's Chili Con Carne." That spurious scheme worked. He contracted to sell his product to a Chicago packer who, perhaps typical of some meat packers of that era, disposed of the mislabeled product in Europe. Black apparently thought well of the deception. He made some money on the venture. As for the tallow, not only did he find a market for it, but also the broker with whom he placed it asked for more, reporting that it was of a superior character and would command a premium for making fine candles. In January 1895, Black shipped 20,000 pounds of tallow to Chicago. Altogether, he realized from the sale of canned meat, lard, and tallow a profit of almost three dollars per animal.[13] The tanning operations were also profitable. Black experienced little trouble in finding a ready sale for his dressed skins, selling as many as 1,000 to a single wholesale house, Marshall Field's, in Chicago.[14]

By 1896 his goats had again increased to a large number. But Black determined that rather than continue his slaughtering operation, he would sell his surplus animals to area stockmen interested in grazing Angoras. That was not hard to do. The Edwards Plateau was a natural habitat for goats, and ranchers there were realizing that Angoras were easy to raise and that mohair production was an attractive proposition. Accordingly, Black promoted the sale of his goats. In response, ranchers invested heavily in Angoras. Black sold thousands of goats in some two dozen area counties. For a brief time, as he labored to cut his flocks, his ranch became a busy auction mart and trading center. As a result of all this activity, Black's goats became the foundation of many West Texas flocks.

Several people from outside the state visited him. One man, Dr. J. R. Standley of Taylor County, Iowa, wanted to ship goats northward to sell at public auction. Indicating that he had cleared about 500 acres of his farm by running goats, Standley offered to buy all the goats Black would ship. Caught up in Standley's enthusiasm, but not willing to ship all his goats,

Black entered into an agreement in 1897 to deliver 1,000 goats for sale on Standley's farm. At the sale, occurring in July, farmers bought them all. That fall Black sent a second shipment of 1,000 head. The following year he delayed shipping until buyers of his goats had sufficient time to test the value of the animals. But when demand increased, he and Standley resumed the enterprise. In fact, sales were so brisk that Black found it necessary to buy from area raisers additional Angoras for shipment north. By 1900 he had sold more than 15,000 Angoras in the Midwest and was selling them elsewhere as well.[15]

The Angora goat industry spread. With few exceptions every state in the country had Angoras at one time or another, but in 1900 Texas led the nation, producing over one-third of all Angoras in the United States. Its farmers and ranchers grazed some 627,000 goats. Of these, approximately 100,000 were Angoras that when clipped produced an estimated 275,000 pounds or more of mohair classified as "mostly short, six months' staple, but very clean and light fleeces, fluffy, and cottony."[16] Twenty years later Texas counted nearly 2 million goats and accounted for over 75 percent of the country's total mohair clip. In Texas the Edwards Plateau became the center of the industry, completely dominating the state's output.

Because Texas not only assumed the lead among states raising goats and mohair but also far outdistanced the others, Angora goat and mohair production trends in the state compared closely with year-to-year changes in the United States. As early as 1910 Texas ranchers produced 71.2 percent of the mohair clip and nearly as large a percentage of goats. In 1920 the Texas mohair clip represented 79.2 percent of the total U.S. production. Ten years later the figure was 84.2 percent. In Texas from 1900 to 1942, rapid growth, with the exception of breaks in 1922, 1932, and 1942, characterized the production of mohair. This steady increase was not as evident in the production figures of other states; a cyclical movement characterized them rather than a trend. The period of most rapid growth came after 1922 when Texas contributed a large increasing proportion of the mohair clipped in America. Indeed, for nearly half a century after 1930 Texas produced more mohair than either Turkey or South Africa, the two leading countries, next to the United States, in the production of mohair.[17]

In the twentieth century the industry has changed from an adventure to a settled business. Farmers and ranchers have introduced modern methods for range management, erected mesh-wire fences to eliminate the need for herders, and used Angoras to supplement cattle and sheep operations. On the Edwards Plateau a Texas livestock triumvirate of cattle, sheep, and goats has developed. Ranchers graze all three species in the same pasture. The cattle eat long grasses, the sheep eat short grasses, and the goats browse on leaves, brush, and many weeds that cattle and sheep ignore.

After rapid expansion in the 1920s, goat and mohair production suffered through three years of decline in the early 1930s. In 1932 mohair prices dropped to only nine cents per pound. from a high of sixty-nine cents in the mid-1920s. When prices recovered somewhat in 1935 mohair production expanded once again.[18]

In its early stages World War II proved a boon for the mohair trade. Angora and mohair production jumped sharply. But by 1942 it had leveled off and declined. Demand for fabrics for furniture and apparel, high initially, had dropped as decreases in automobile production—for which 40 percent of the mohair was used—occurred in 1942. Mohair production on Texas ranches dropped correspondingly. Later mohair became a supplement for wool and entered in woven and knitted garments. However, when ties, socks, sweaters, pile fabrics for cold-climate clothing, officers' summer uniforms, and other mohair outlets were found, manufacturers turned from domestic to cheaper foreign sources, especially South Africa, for the raw material. Nevertheless, the Texas mohair trade enjoyed several good years.

One goat man who prospered was Adolf Stieler. Nearly ruined financially by problems of the Great Depression, Stieler said that he "had nothing but a good credit rating left in the

1930s."[19] Using that credit he bought tens of thousands of goats at "rock bottom" prices. During World War II, Stieler, known as the "king of the goat men," ran some 50,000 goats on his extensive holdings in the hill country. He made Comfort in Kendall County his headquarters, but the Stieler holdings reportedly encompassed some 90,000 acres in Gillespie, Llano, Kerr, Edwards, Blanco, and Bexar Counties.[20] Afterward, realizing that he was overgrazing his land, he cut his bands back to 18,000 head. He continued to make money off his land, however. As he displaced the goats, the land attracted deer and turkey. Stieler leased that land to hunters at good profit, he claimed. He also continued to sell his mohair at war-inflated prices.[21]

After 1945 mohair was somewhat neglected in America in favor of wool and the new synthetic fibers that attracted consumer attention. Some manufacturers produced new fabrics from mohair, but despite widespread promotional activities, the American consumer lost interest in the material for several years. About 1950, after a temporary embargo on Argentine wool sent wool prices up, mohair revived briefly. In addition new cloth, especially blends of mohair with wool, created new demand. Soon other blends for tropical garments followed. Research by the U.S. Department of Agriculture and other groups, which advertised many of mohair's unique properties, gave mohair a new identity among textiles. Despite such efforts, however, American manufacturers found it increasingly difficult to compete with a postwar rejuvenated British industry. Consequently British manufacturers with their novel fabrics and yarns sought raw American mohair, and they, as well as the Japanese, Dutch, and Italians, successfully sold finished mohair goods in the United States. By 1959, 75 percent of the annual American mohair clip was sold abroad, mostly in Britain. The situation has continued to the present.[22]

Such foreign buying helped to encourage mohair production. Production continued upward to reach a peak in 1965 when output in the seven leading states reached 32,464,000 pounds,

97 percent of which came from Texas. The number of Texas goats and kids clipped during 1965, the largest yearly clip on record, totaled 4,612,000 head. The average clip per goat was nearly seven pounds. The average price received for mohair, however, dropped to sixty-six cents per pound, forcing the total value of mohair to Texas growers to fall 24 percent from 1964's record $27,428,000.[23]

In recent years mohair production has lost more ground. Until 1971 the United States remained the world's leading producer of mohair, but the country has since fallen to second rank behind Turkey. The 1965 figure of nearly 5 million Angora goats browsing on American farms and ranches fell to about 2 million in 1973 and to less than 1 million two years later. Recently because of unprecedented high mohair prices, the number of Angoras has increased slightly. Among the states Texas continues to graze the largest number, producing more than 90 percent of all Angora goats in the country.[24] In 1980 the ten leading counties in Angora goats were Edwards, Val Verde, Upton, Sutton, Kimble, Terrell, Crockett, Mason, Mills, and Gillespie.

As the mohair branch of the industry struggled through the 1950s and afterward, the goat meat market improved.[25] The outlet for goat meat became well established in the post-World War II era, with its center at the Union Stock Yards of San Antonio. There workers handled 200,000 to 400,000 or more head of goats per year in the 1950s, receiving shipments from as far away as Kingman, Arizona. Practically all meat from adult goats sold through regular marketing channels and was handled in one simple process called "boning out." Packers used or sold the boneless meat for mixed meat formulas for packages, such as fresh or smoked breakfast sausage, frankfurters, and bologna sausage. The milk-fed kids, or *cabritos*, were processed in whole or half carcasses and sold to retail markets, chain stores, cafes, and hotels. In 1975, however, Texas slaughtered only 67,000 goats, down from 447,800 slaughtered in 1970.[26]

While marketing trends fluctuated downward, the handling

of goats on the ranch changed only slightly, although the sheep wagon, a home on wheels for herders, has all but disappeared. Ranchers raise their goats within fenced pastures rather than with herders, though an unrelenting labor shortage encouraged a spurt in the 1950s of importing Basque herders from Europe. Peak work periods on the ranch occur in the spring of each year when the kids are born and castrated and the adult goats sheared. Most shearing crews, still mainly Mexicans, move from ranch to ranch by truck and use electric shears, but otherwise the process has not changed since the 1920s or earlier.

Rocksprings, in Edwards County, is called the "Angora goat capital of the world." It houses the headquarters and museum of the American Angora Goat Breeders Association. San Angelo, in Tom Green County in the heart of the Texas sheep country, is one of the world's leading centers for producing, processing, and shipping of mohair. There are warehouses, scouring plants, and slaughterhouses in the city that serves as the headquarters for the Texas Sheep and Goat Raisers Association.

In the early 1980s, after more than a decade of retrenchment, there was renewed optimism among industry leaders. The long-depressed business seemed to be on the mend. Some freshly shorn mohair, stimulated by the turn of American fashion to a natural fiber look, brought prices of more than six dollars per pound in 1981. There also was a small demand for breeding stock as farmers and ranchers considered moving back into the Texas Angora goat and mohair industry. It is well they should, for the Angora goat, providing both food and fiber, represents nearly $150 million to the Texas economy each year.

NOTES

1. Research for this article was made possible in part by a grant from the Food and Fiber National Institute of Achievement and by a grant from the Faculty Research Committee at

Texas Lutheran College. I am also indebted to Charles Wood who encouraged me in my research on the Texas sheep and goat industry.

2. *Texas Almanac*, 1980-1981, p. 577; Paul H. Carlson, interview with Elmer Kelton, June 6, 1981. Also see Natural Fibers Economic Research, *Texas Sheep and Goat Wool and Mohair Industry* (Austin: University of Texas, 1974), pp. 8-14.

3. The best general histories of Texas have a combined total of less than two pages on the state's Angora goat industry, and few historians have dealt with the subject in either professional journals or monographs. See Paul H. Carlson, "William L. Black and the Beginning of the West Texas Angora Goat Industry," *West Texas Historical Association Year Book*, 55 (1980):3-14.

4. "History of Mohair," typewritten report in the records of the Mohair Council of America, Southwest Collection, Texas Tech University, Lubbock, hereafter referred to as MCA Records; "The Report of the Association," printed report of the American Angora Goat Breeders Association, n.d., in records of the American Angora Goat Breeders Association, Southwest Collection, Texas Tech University, Lubbock; George T. Willingmyre et al., *The Angora Goat and Mohair Industry*, Misc. circular no. 50, U.S. Department of Agriculture, 1929, pp. 13-20.

5. John Ashton, "The Golden Fleece of Early Days," *Southwestern Sheep and Goat Raisers Magazine, S and G Raiser,* 24 (December, 1943):15-16; hereafter Jno. A. Black, "The Cashmere Shawl Goat," *Texas Almanac*, 1860, pp. 197-198.

6. Ervin Hickman, "Texas Has Twenty-five Million Dollar Angora Goat Industry," *S and G Raiser,* 16 (July 1946):20.

7. Quoted in William Leslie Black, *A New Industry, or Raising the Angora Goat* (Fort Worth: Keystone, 1900), p. 77.

8. Ibid. p. 78.

9. William L. Black, "Ranching on 10¢ Land in Texas," *The Cattleman* 114 (July 1927):31.

10. Black, *A New Industry*, pp. 12-13.

11. Ibid; San Angelo *Standard-Times*, August 29, 1954; *Texas Livestock Journal* (Fort Worth), October 28, 1982.

12. Newspaper clipping, in Morgue Files, records of the Texas Sheep and Goat Raiser Association, Southwest Collection, Texas Tech University, Lubbock, hereafter TSGRA Records. Edith Black Winslow, *In Those Days, Memories of the Edwards Plateau* (San Antonio: Naylor, 1950), pp. 40-41.

13. Black, "Ranching on 10¢ Land in Texas," p. 12-13 Black, *A New Industry*, pp. 13-15; San Angelo *Standard*, January 12, 1895.

14. Winslow, *In Those Days*, pp. 40-41.

15. Black, *A New Industry*, p. 15.

16. Ibid., p. 104; Texas Department of Agriculture, *Texas Historic Livestock Statistics*, Bulletin 131, 1903, pp. 35-39; Willingmyre et al., *The Angora Goat and Mohair Industry*, pp. 11-19; and U.S. Department of Agriculture, Division of Crop and Livestock Estimates, typewritten report, May 5, 1923, Southwest Collection, Texas Tech University, Lubbock.

17. T.R. Hamilton, "Trends in Production, Use and Prices of Texas Mohair," *S and G Raiser* 25 (July 1945):14.

18. Texas Crop and Livestock Reporting Service, *Texas Historic Livestock Statistics*, Bulletin 131, p. 38.

19. Newspaper clipping, Morgue Files, TSGRA Records.

20. Ibid.; C.W. Towne and Edward N. Wentworth, *Shepherd's Empire* (Norman: University of Oklahoma Press, 1946), p. 325.

21. Newspaper clipping, Morgue Files, TSGRA Records; "Life Visits the Goat King," *Life Magazine*, May 1942.

22. V. M. Pritchell, "The Mohair Industry in the Southwest," *Monthly Business Review* 35 (December 1950): 193-195; Mohair Advisory Board Mission to Britain and Europe, "The Promotion of South African Mohair," n.d., pp. 19, 41, MCA Records.

23. Texas Crop and Livestock Reporting Service, *Texas Historic Livestock Statistics*, Bulletin 131, p. 38.

24. Ibid.; "Mohair Clip Sets New Record," *S and G Raiser* 156 (March 1966):2B-3.

25. The term "chevon," the name for goat meat widely used before World War II, has virtually been discontinued.

26. Texas Crop and Livestock Reporting Service, *1975 Texas Livestock Statistics*, Bulletin 135, Austin, Texas, June 1976, pp. 11-13; Pritchett, "The Mohair Industry in the Southwest," p. 201.

IV

ENVIRONMENT AND LAND MANAGEMENT

"I find the longer we live in these valleys that the range is becoming more and more destitute of grass; . . . where grass once grew luxuriantly there is now nothing but the desert weed. . . . There is not profit in this, neither is it pleasing in the sight of God."

Orson Hyde, Mormon apostle addressing
the General Conference of Saints,
Salt Lake City,
Utah Territory, 1865

For an agriculturalist the land is a majestic gift, a special resource that gives of itself bountifully. It is to be cherished, nourished, and worshiped. And yet the land has not always been carefully respected. The farmer and the rancher have a reasonable record of regarding the environment, but if they have erred it is on the side of mistaken management and supplication of the environment.

Orson Hyde, for one, recognized the twin responsibilities of the agriculturalist with reference to the land. Environmentally the farmer and the rancher seek a balance. The land must be renewed, and it must be agriculturally productive. To discover the middle ground was often a complicated and difficult task, sometimes resulting in environmental disaster.

Spring 1983 and 1984 were nightmares for many Utahans. Their beautiful mountains turned into cascades of dangerous flooding streams and mud slides. Scores of highways, homes, farms, and ranches will be altered forever. Dan L. Flores documents the origins of this modern-day ecological crisis. He finds that early Mormon efforts to settle the mountain sides of Utah caused irrevocable damage to grasslands and timberlands. Farmers and ranchers alike neglected to heed the delicate balance of the environment.

Political considerations have also entered the history of agricultural land usage. One of the most valuable regions in terms of agricultural production today is California's Central Valley, so it is not surprising that control of these lands produced a struggle of national proportion. Stephen P. Sayles writes of what appeared to be an innocuous amendment—the Straus-Boke Rider of 1948-1949—that caused political and environmental disruption in the nation. The Bureau of Reclamation sought to protect the lands of the Central Valley for small farmers; other Californians saw these policies as restrictive and oppressive and as retarding the advance of agriculture. A brief victory was achieved for the family farmer.

Frequently agriculturalists have tried to improve the capabilities of their lands. These efforts have taken many forms, but none have been more colorful or romantic than those of altering the weather. Delmar Hayter describes that process for Texas. Early experiments were confined to crude cloud seeding by nineteenth-century entrepreneurs such as C.W. Post who desired increased precipitation for his dry West Texas utopian community. In the twentieth century the federal government has sought to explore the possibilities of rainfall augmentation, lightning suppression, hail limitation, and snowpack supplication scientifically through its HIPLEX project with one such experimental station located at Big Spring, Texas. All of the experimenters have simply wanted to modify nature, thereby providing water for a thirsty land.

Weather modification on the High Plains of Texas, reclamation of valuable croplands in California's Central Valley, and abuse of Utah's mountain grasslands and timberlands are but three examples of attempts of American agriculturalists and their supporters to grapple with the balancing factor. Land, its environment and management, has been and will remain at the center of the struggle for survival of the farmer and the rancher.

Agriculture, Mountain Ecology, and the Land Ethic: Phases of the Environmental History of Utah

In seeking to discover the causes of modern ecological dilemmas, the environmental movement of the 1970s and 1980s has developed a penetrating critique of a number of mainstream American institutions. Historians Lynn White, Jr., and Roderick Nash, for example, have credited the Judeo-Christian religious ethic, which places man at the center of a subservient biosphere, as central to the development of environmental callousness and mismanagement.[1] Philosopher Eugene Hargrove has argued that Western, Lockean property concepts are too exclusive to permit the emergence of an ecologically sound society.[2] Yet another historian, Donald Worster, in a recent award-winning study, lays the responsibility for this nation's greatest environmental disaster, the Dust Bowl of the 1930s, on capitalism's relentless drive for profit.[3]

Environmental historians have looked for documentation to the example of the American West. Initially settled between 1865 and 1900, the West appears to offer in its history a portentous example of unplanned, wasteful, disruptive, and undemocratic natural resource exploitation. Indeed, long before the contemporary interest in ecology, Stuart Chase in his seminal study *Rich Land, Poor Land* and Roy Robbins with *Our Landed Heritage* wrote eloquently of the abuses inherent in the age Vernon Parrington had called "the Great Barbecue."[4] Awareness of the potential for environmental disruption combined with the Progressive desire for efficiency to provide the rationale for the federal conservation movement, which was aimed initially at the ecologically sensitive western lands. Public land ownership, regulated natural resource use, and empirical rather than spiritual knowledge about ecological balancing were introduced, with varying degrees of success, to America by the early twentieth century.

Many questions remain unanswered, however, with respect to the environmental history of western America. For example, given the institutional complex and cultural trends, was it actually possible to have had an egalitarian, planned, nonexploitive society on the American frontier of the nineteenth century? Necessarily lacking today's environmental grasp, how successful would such a society have been in modern ecological terms? Finally, has the federal policy of attempting to educate westerners to the ecological realities of the region, with its arid plains and deserts tenuously held together by humid mountain oases, been the most successful approach to creating a stable, agriculturally based civilization?

While contemporary trends in the West enable us to address the last of these questions only tentatively, it is possible given the present state of research to explore the two former questions more fully. For such a society did exist in the nineteenth-century American West, and for nearly half a century it brought to bear upon one of the most ecologically sensitive regions of North America a set of values much in line with modern environmental philosophy. This society was created by members of the Church of Jesus Christ of the Latter-day Saints, a religious sect known as the Mormons, who in 1847 initiated a series of settlements along the western edge of the Rocky Mountains, centering in present Utah.

Founded by Joseph Smith of upstate New York in the 1820s, the Mormon church emerged in America at a time when utopian, communal, and socialistic experimentation was widespread, and state involvement in economic matters was considered neither unusual nor threatening. These influences on

Smith's pronouncements have been well documented; one of his close collaborators in the early years of the church, Sidney Rigdon, was an intellectual reformer who had been involved in several communal experiments in the Midwest.[5] The societal plan that emerged from Smith's 112 "revelations" (some of which were institutionalized in *The Doctrine and Covenants*) featured the essence of liberal thought of the time. The Law of Consecration and Stewardship, later known as the United Order, attempted to establish a socialism for the Saints by conferring all individual wealth to the church, which would then redistribute it according to need.[6] After an initial experimentation with this doctrine in Ohio Mormon communities it was abandoned, although in the guise of the United Order it was tried sparingly in the West on a trial basis. But its existence in the early doctrines did pave the way for a number of radical doctrines that were widely utilized in Utah. The two most important of these were church stewardship over natural resources and the communalism practiced by Mormon pioneers in preparing for the millennium by creating a society, Zion, which would cleanse and beautify a "cursed earth" through a "pragmatic mastery of the forces of nature."[7]

It has been argued, by historian Leonard J. Arrington among others, that Mormonism, with its Calvinist stress on temporal rather than worldly concerns and its incorporation of the most utopian and egalitarian ideas of early nineteenth-century America, developed one of the most thoroughly indigenous religious philosophies to come out of the New World experience. The Puritan origins of these ideas are apparent. Yet, even while the Mormons preserved intact the Judeo-Christian stewardship ethic, the responsibilities thus implied had a communal rather than an individualistic application. It was this centralized planning, regulation, and cooperation that was most in line with twentieth-century environmental philosophy.

The opportunity to try these ideas in a virgin setting did not come before Smith's death. But he was ably succeeded by Brigham Young, a pragmatist who nonetheless shared Smith's utopian dreams. Hounded and persecuted in Missouri and Illinois, by 1846 the Mormons were considering an emigration to Texas, Oregon, California, and even Vancouver Island. But in May of 1844, explorer John C. Fremont returned from an expedition to California by way of the Great Basin, and at the foot of the Wasatch Front had found "a region of great pastoral promise abounding with fine streams . . . [and] soil that would produce wheat," although "this fertility of soil and vegetation does not extend far into the Great Basin."[8] Before his death, Smith had written in his diary that he had dreamed that "the Saints . . . would be driven to . . . [and] become a mighty people in the midst of the Rocky Mountains."[9] Given that prophecy and the desired isolation of the Wasatch Front, when Fremont's report was read to the assembled Mormon Quorum the issue was settled. The American "Great Trek" was about to begin.

In order to understand the environmental history that follows, it is essential to re-establish, with as much scientific precision as possible, the ecological outlines of the setting which the Mormon pioneers entered when they emerged from Emigration Canyon in the late summer of 1847. Fortunately, a number of accurate first-hand accounts, as well as subsequent studies by ecologists, exist to make this possible.

The environment of the region settled by the Mormons was the result of both natural and human forces which had been at work for tens of thousands of years. The setting was dominated by the massive Wasatch Range, the product of nearly 300 million years of uplift, erosion, faulting, and sedimentation.[10] Stretching like a wall more than 200 miles north and south, and rising to elevations exceeding 12,000 feet, the Wasatch was rent by a series of structural troughs that had been carved into steep canyons by water and glaciers. Westward through these mountains tumbled sparkling rivers—which the Anglo-Americans would name Bear, Ogden, Weber, Provo, Jordan, and Sevier—as well as dozens of smaller streams.

Rivaling the mountains in importance were the contours of the basin floor which abutted them. Nearly perfectly flat out away from the mountains, the basin was the legacy of ancient Lake Bonneville, a gigantic freshwater lake produced from the melt of the Wisconsonian Period glaciers. Over thousands of years Lake Bonneville had alternately risen and fallen to create a series of lakeshore terraces on the Wasatch (and on the smaller Oquirrh Range twenty-five miles to the west) as well as numerous deltas and benches where the rivers had spilled their sediments into the lake. As the climate had become warmer and drier, Lake Bonneville had shrunk to a salty remnant without drainage, thereby creating the Great Salt Lake. But it had left deposited along the Transition Zone of the Wasatch a narrow, rich, alluvial piedmont of fans, deltas, and terraces, through which meandered the sweet, clear water of the mountains.[11]

The hydrography was somewhat unique. A rain shadow cast by the Sierra Nevadas to the west produced desert conditions in the basin itself, with less than five inches of precipitation annually. But the Wasatch, thrusting up at right angles to prevailing winds, formed an orographic barrier to induce precipitation, so that the narrow Transition Zone at their base received thirteen to eighteen inches and the high mountains up to fifty inches most years. The great bulk of the precipitation on the highlands fell as snow, and its melting annually sent from 8 to 10 million acre-feet of water surging through the drainage in late spring and early summer.[12] Local convectional cells formed over the mountains in summer to produce often violent rainstorms at intensities of up to eight inches per hour for short periods. Yet the thickly vegetated watersheds handled these without problems in the virgin setting. Thermal inversions caused by the great altitude differences between mountains and basin played some climatic tricks, making the lowest valleys the coldest, but also producing chinook winds which left the canyon mouths surprisingly frost free—an unexpected boon to later agriculture.[13]

The east-west altitude and precipitation zones effected a corresponding zonation of soils, and hence biological life. In the high mountains were chernozem soils, which were dark and humus-rich but often rocky, while on the flats below, where the drainage had brought the salts down, alkaline soils prevailed. Between these, however, the deltas and fans of the Transition Zone featured sandy, porous chestnut soils, fertile and rich in lime.[14]

Combined with the diversity of altitudes and precipitation, these soils grew a remarkable array of vegetation which, from the reports of early observers, ecologists are now able to reconstruct. On the tops of the mountains, the elevation and short growing season produced an alpine tundra featuring short sedges, particularly *Carex albonigra* and *C. pseudo-scripoidea* and dwarf bluegrass (*Poa rupicola*) and wheatgrass (*Agropyron trachycaulum*). Below the tundra lay the narrow Hudsonian Zone, occupied by elfinwood timber where Engelmann spruce (*Picea engelmanni*) was the chief dominant. Lower down there existed the montane forest of the Canadian Zone, where ponderosa pine (*Pinus ponderosa*), lodgepole pine (*P. contorta* var. *latifolia*), and Douglas firs (*Pseudotsuga menziesii*) predominated, with interspersed meadows of tall grasses such as Letterman needlegrass (*Stipa lattermani*) and beardless wheatgrass (*Agropyron inerme*). In the canyons and on the lower slopes there existed a diversified understory, of which the Utah juniper (*Juniperus osteosperma*) was most important. The Transition Zone benches and valleys were largely carpeted with tall, waving wheatgrasses (*Agropyron* spp.) and bluegrasses (*Poa* spp.) and a variety of forbs. Less than 20 percent of the Transition Zone, one ecologist believes, was vegitated with shrubs such as big sagebrush (*Artemesia tridentata*) and rabbitbrush (*Chysothamnus* supp.) in the virgin setting. Salt-tolerant halogetens such as greasewood (*Sarcobatus vermiculatus*) were the principal flora of the desert basin.[15]

Most of the principal native fauna of the region, including the bighorn sheep (*Ovis canadensis canandensis*), the wapiti (*Cervus canadensis nelsoni*), the mule deer (*Dama hemionus hemionus*), the pronghorn antelope (*Antilocapra americana americana*), and the white-tailed jackrabbit (*Lepus townsendii townsendii*), ranged over the entire region, the larger ungulates often migrating from one biome zone to another with the changing seasons. In contrast, the black-tailed jackrabbit (*Lepus californicus deserticola*) was confined to the desert floor, while the Utah grizzly (*Ursus utahensis*), black bear (*Ursus americanus cinnamomum*), moose (*Alces alces gigas*), and mountain bison (*Bison bison athabascae*) ranged only in the mountains and high valley meadows.[16]

A question of increasing ecological interest is the role American Indians played in modifying the environment of North America. The evidence is clear that men and women had lived on the flanks of the Wasatch for at least 10,000 years prior to the coming of the Mormons. At first, it is now conjectured, they were Paleo-hunters who stalked and killed the megafauna of the Pleistocene Epoch; later these were replaced by the Basket Makers, predominantly hunters and gatherers who practiced an archaic lifeway; and by 1000 A.D. by the Puebloid group of agriculturalists known as the Anasazi. These peoples were ultimately replaced by Shoshonean peoples, ancestors of the Utes and Paiutes encountered by the Mormons.[17]

All of these peoples utilized fire as a basic practice of hunting and to produce more succulent pasturage for game, thus leading perhaps to far-reaching ecological implications along the Wasatch Front. The highly respected Utah ecologist, Walter Cottam, has argued in fact that through the use of fire, Indians were able to maintain, against the true bench and foothill climax of shrubs and junipers, a postclimax grassland which was actually a relic of an earlier, wetter age.[18]

Into this centuries-old environment, with its delicate balance of water, slope, vegetation, and fire, stepped more than 1,600 Anglo-American farmers, with 30,000 cattle and "an immense number of sheep," and armed with the cultural baggage of Mormonism.[19] "The Lord has done his share of the work," Young told his followers, "he has surrounded us with the elements . . . with which to build up, beautify and glorify . . . Zion."[20] To people used to the verdant countryside of Illinois and Missouri, it must have seemed a strange country, but under Young's leadership the Mormon pioneers threw themselves zealously into the task to transform the Utah earth into a garden, and thereby to prove that in communal action there existed an alternative to the capitalistic order which worked, as Young put it, "to make a few rich, and to sink the masses of the people in poverty and degradation."[21]

With their centralized leadership and their belief that the earth and all its products were the property of a divine entity,[22] the Mormon brand of stewardship was at once less theoretical than Christian stewardship. Individual Mormons, for example, dedicated land and projects to the divinity. Additionally, the doctrine of continuing revelation was not only a boon for coping with a new environment, but endowed church decrees on natural resources with the power of supernatural sanction. The Mormons thus provide the closest American example of the Judeo-Christian stewardship ethic, or the "Abrahamic Land Concept," in action on a pristine frontier.

Mormon stewardship modified the Lockean view of private property use. The earth could not be "owned," but it could be occupied temporarily provided the occupant "improved" it, or used it "beneficially." To Mormon thinking this meant changing the natural order to make it more productive of the things most useful to themselves. Above all the land must be distributed democratically; members were even expected to give over part of their land if a project or a new arrival needed it. Between 1847 and 1869 the church assigned titles, of usually no more than twenty acres, by drawing and petition.[23] These small plots were a clear recognition that arable lands were limited in Zion, although such Jeffersonianism was also encouraged by the irrigation which made their mountain benchland farming possible.

The mountain topography of the country they now inhabited had left the areas receiving the most adequate rainfall too high and rocky to farm. To combine the water of the highlands with the fertile land below, the Mormons followed the lead of both Indians and Spaniards in North America. In this way the Wasatch environment reinforced their yen for communal action; irrigation was an intimidating undertaking for even the most rugged of individualists. The church leaders also borrowed certain features of Hispanic water law, specifically public ownership combined with a priority right of diversion for users. It planned and controlled the collective construction of canals and laterals and the allotment of water. An early historian of institutions called these projects "one of the greatest and most successful community or cooperative undertakings in the history of America."[24]

Centralized control over land and water also extended to other major resources, notably timber and grass, and even minerals. As Young told a band of new arrivals in 1847: "There shall be no private ownership of the streams that come out of the canyons, nor the timber that grows on the hills. These belong to the people; all the people."[25] Timber was obviously sparse relative to the eastern humid conditions the Mormons had known, and it was much more difficult to access. Using it sensibly necessitated restraint. After a brief experiment with unfettered use, the church decided to grant monopolies, or concessions, to responsible persons who would open roads into the mountains and then regulate timber cutting on designated slopes. The extent of this regulation went beyond the mere charge of a toll for road use, for in 1851 a territorial ordinance established the rather stupendous fine of $1,000 for anyone convicted of wasting or burning timber. Yet full use was implied, and since there were no attempts at reseeding, the stands of lodgepole and ponderosa pine and Douglas fir were drawn down quickly by the steady increase in population.[26]

The approach with grass was similar and oriented more toward democratic distribution than conservation, although there were cases where the church regulated grazing by requiring a grant-of-use permit.[27] The herding of stock communally did eliminate competitive use of the range as long as the Mormons had only themselves for competition. Yet Mormon stockmen, possibly somewhat bewildered by the strangeness of the Mountain West, with its complicated life and water zonation, appear to have overgrazed much of their country rather quickly. The Indians first voiced concern over the decline of grass for game herds in the 1850s. By the 1860s the Mormons themselves were uneasy over its scarcity.[28]

Mormon communities, unlike those which sprang up elsewhere in the Mountain West, were not organized around exploitation of only one resource but instead made use of a variety of natural products. Parley P. Pratt's scouting parties ranged up and down the Wasatch Front in search of suitable Transition Zone sites where later farm-villages (or "stakes") could be begun. This farm-village community was particularly suited to the mountain frontier, although the idea predated the move West, coming from Joseph Smith's "Plat of the City of Zion" which itself evolved from utopianist experimentation with the New England village. Church policies respecting natural resources were handled locally by stake bishops and councils, a necessary delegation of powers given the distances and transportation facilities. Far from being independent and self-sufficient city-states, the farm-villages were cogs in a societal economic network. By 1900 nearly 500 of them had been established along the western slope of the Rockies, extending into Nevada, Arizona, and Idaho.[29]

Out of step with the spirit of laissez-faire political economic doctrine which came to characterize American society during the post-Civil War years, the Mormons struggled against outsiders, and themselves, to remain uncontaminated. Brigham Young seems to have remained unyielding. During the 1870s he resurrected the communism of Smith's early theories by starting several United Order colonies—small, self-sufficient, entirely communal villages—and as late as 1868 held before the Saints this vision of collectivism:

> I have looked upon the community of Saints in vision and beheld them organized as one great family of heaven ... working for the good of the whole more than for individual aggrandizement; and in this I have beheld the most beautiful order that the mind of man can contemplate.[30]

For a variety of reasons, however, the communal, egalitarian society advocated by the early church leaders began to crumble during the 1870s. Gentiles who found Mormon ways authoritarian and un-American began passing through Utah regularly as early as 1849, and with the completion of the transcontinental railroad in 1869 they arrived in numbers that soon challenged the Mormon presence. Forced increasingly to compete for resources with them, many Mormons—such as the Godbeite organization of Mormon businessmen—lost their affection for egalitarianism. When Young's death in 1877 removed the major advocate of the old order, Mormons in Utah began a process of Americanization, which one author has compared to Southern Reconstruction, that ended in 1896 with Utah's statehood and an almost complete incorporation into the laissez-faire American mainstream. Although separation of church and state and abandonment of plural marriage were the most symbolic reforms required to "bring the territory into conformity with national standards," Americanization in process had meant a tacit recognition that resource use was a matter of competition rather than "state" planning.[31] By that time, the first steps had been taken to implement a land-use plan in Utah which left to state and science what church and religion had once attempted.

Although Leonard J. Arrington, the dean of Utah historians, has asserted that Mormon resource policy "seems to have protected Utah from the abuses and wastes which characterized many frontier communities in the West," as early as the 1860s Utah's very landscape, read as a historical document, indicated otherwise. Even before the rush of individualistic Gentiles into the territory, Utah's environment was showing signs of deterioration. In its efforts to provide for the growing numbers of converts by making "the desert bloom as the rose," the Mormons decidedly overstrained the fragile Wasatch environment.[32] Accustomed to eastern conditions and lacking scientific knowledge of plant succession, or of the relationship between water, vegetation, and slope, and forced increasingly both to provide for larger numbers and compete for resources with non-Mormons, the church could not develop a land ethic. Its doctrines provided for egalitarian resource distribution, but by its own definition it was no longer using Zion beneficially, for Zion land was becoming less productive yearly and more unstable. Rather than blooming as the rose, it was in danger of being overgrown with pigweed and inundated with flood debris.

The consequences of disrupting the natural stability seem not to have occurred to many Mormons, but one who did worry was Orson Hyde. Addressing the General Conference of Saints in 1865, Hyde invoked both profit and stewardship as reasons why the Mormons should promote the conservation of their grass. "I find the longer we live in these valleys that the range is becoming more destitute of grass; the grass," lamented Hyde, "is eaten up by the great amount of stock."[33] Although Hyde did not mention it, timber also was beginning to come under heavy assault by the 1860s. At the beginning of that decade, there were 28 sawmills operating in the Wasatch. Twenty years later they had increased to 100, and by 1900 the entire western slope of the mountains had been denuded to such an extent that surveyor Albert Potter reported "it would be difficult to find a seedling big enough to make a club to kill a snake."[34]

Because of traffic over the Mormon Cutoff, Gentiles were obviously in Utah with their herds during much of the 1850s and 1860s, an exception being in 1857, during the Utah War. According to the Works Progress Administration grazing researchers, the "chief injustice" done to Utah grasslands was done by these transient operators rather than the Mormon herders. Utah's cattle population peaked before 1880, and soon cattle were giving way to sheep, many of them herded around the West wherever forage could be found. By 1889 a million sheep and 350,000 cattle were in Utah; by 1899 the cattle population had stabilized, but the sheep count had increased fourfold. Like the wild grazers they replaced, these stock animals grazed the valleys in winter and followed the melting snows into the high mountains during spring and summer. With supplemental winter feeding breaking the old natural balance by keeping alive thousands of animals which would have died had they been wild, the enormous herds tramped and gouged the water-logged spring soils and ate the meadows down until individual bands could be spotted from the valleys below by the dust clouds they raised.[35]

Another barometer of change set into motion by the Mormons and accelerated with the coming of non-Mormons was an almost complete change in the vegetation patterns of the western front. By comparing the records kept by very early observers such as Peter Skene Ogden and Howard Stansbury with those of later scientific and survey expeditions, it becomes obvious that as early as the 1870s an unexpected transformation was taking place. For almost two decades the grasslands of the valleys and lower slopes managed to recover from the grazing of Mormon stock. But serious overcropping combined with the control of Indian fires led by the 1870s to the unfolding of a new succession pattern in Utah which erased forever that of the virgin setting. Gradually the grasses gave way to sagebrush, rabbitbrush, and shadscale *(Atriplex confertifolia)*, followed by a rapid invasion of juniper, which in a century would expand its range sixfold. After 1900, exotic invading annual weeds such a cheatgrass *(Bromus tectorum)* and the tumbleweed, Russian thistle *(Salsola kali)* began overspreading the range to take the place of the native grasses.[36] Utah ecologist Walter D. Cottam's assertion that the original grasslands were a relic climax preserved by the fire ecology only explains why the Utah grasslands were so fragile. It does not exonerate the foolish overuse which led to their disappearance.

In 1878, emerging from the scientific study of the Mountain West which had begun with Ferdinand Hayden's geological and geographical survey of the territories, John Wesley Powell's landmark "Report on the lands of the Arid Region of the United States, With Special Reference to Utah" was published, arguing that the cooperative nature of early Mormon society ought to be adopted as a general plan of settlement in the West.[37] Although not adopted (fortunately, given its serious flaws), the Powell monograph reflected the growing belief among American scientists that a land-use plan for the

West had become a critical necessity. Many within American scientific circles—among them Chief Forester B.E. Fernow and Franklin B. Hough of the American Association for the Advancement of Science—were beginning to agree with George Perkins Marsh, author of *Man and Nature* (1864), that the high mountains of the West must be retained in public ownership and their use regulated in order to protect the watersheds upon which the entire region was dependent.[38]

Public ownership of the mountains, perhaps the most critical legislation ever passed for the perpetuation of civilization in the American West, came about with astonishingly little fanfare. In 1891 a section was attached to the end of a twenty-four-part land revision bill which empowered the president to set aside "forest reserves" in the West. It passed both Senate and House virtually without comment.[39] Within fifteen years, aided by the ideas and support of Forester Gifford Pinchot and President Theodore Roosevelt, the principles of federal ownership and regulated multiple use (with fees and permits for some uses) had been established for the National Forest system. With the passage of the Taylor Grazing Act in 1934, these principles were extended to desert and valley lands, first regulated by the Grazing Service, and then the Bureau of Land Management.

One year following statehood Utah got its first Forest Reserve (Uinta); by 1910 there were ten more, now called National Forests, that covered nearly all of the mountainous areas, or about 14 percent of Utah land. Perhaps because early church regulation of resources had established a precedent of control, the people of Utah were more solidly in favor of the National Forest plan than was generally the case in the West. It was supported by the Mormon church, and Senator Reed Smoot of Utah was one of the few western legislators who championed its cause.[40] Yet for users, immediate economics still outweighed "theories" such as conservation. Their constant pressure on the Forest Service for more freedom was indirectly aided by a number of scientists and scientific bureaus, such as the Corps of Engineers and the U.S. Weather Service, which openly began to doubt the postulated relationship between vegetation and runoff that had provided the rationale for the creation of the system.[41]

Ironically, the very land of the Mormon experiment provided the ultimate proof for that hypothesis. Beginning in 1881 and continuing thereafter with mounting fury and frequency, the now deteriorated mountain watersheds, which geologic evidence proved had not flooded since Lake Bonneville had receded 25,000 years before, began periodically sending tons of water, soil, and boulders broiling into the streets and irrigation works of the towns below them. The Manti area of southeastern Utah, settled by Mormons in 1862, began flooding in 1888, and although local petitions closed the Manti National Forest to grazing in 1904, nine devastating floods struck the area between 1888 and 1909. By 1930 thirteen Mormon communities in southern Utah had been abandoned because of flooding.[42]

Even with Forest Service regulation and the Manti lesson, grazing and logging pressures continued to be too intense on the Wasatch. By the 1920s a widespread land collapse had begun. Between 1923 and 1930, sixteen Utah counties suffered devastating floods, finally leading Governor George Dern to appoint a flood commission to study the causes of the phenomenon. After two years of study the commission concluded that the mountain topography of Utah was incapable of absorbing heavy rains with the watersheds so critically depleted by overgrazing, fires, and overcutting of timber, and warned of continuing catastrophe if large-scale mitigation was not undertaken.[43] Although a few watersheds were cross-terraced, at considerable expense, to break up the gullying and then replanted and closed to grazing, no widespread reforms ensued. In 1945 Salt Lake City suffered a flood that caused nearly $500,000 in damage. Its first flood in ninety-eight years of occupation was directly the result of the burning of a single square-mile of the highly flammable alien, cheatgrass, which had left the ground exposed. By 1950, after only one century of white occupation, twenty watersheds, from one end of the Wasatch Mountains to the the other, were open to flooding.[44]

In the mid-1930s it had become apparent in Utah that floods

and altered plant succession were only two manifestations of the widespread environmental deterioration. During that decade, the area at the north end of the Oquirrh Range, specifically Tooele, Skull, Cedar, and Rush Valleys—only sixty years before praised as an excellent grassland of waving native species—became the only dust bowl in Rocky Mountain history. Eventually 46,000 acres lay bare to the winds, and in 1935 the Department of Agriculture anticipated that the town of Grantsville would have to be abandoned. The Soil Conservation Service closed the area to use and made it a demonstration plot in revegetation, but Utah's battle with surface wind erosion and dust bowls did not abate. After particularly severe problems struck again in 1955 and 1960-1961, ecologist Cottam began to predict that Utah was, as he put it, "Sahara-Bound."[45]

Contributing to the general ecological degradation was the twentieth-century transformation of Utah's agriculture. Portended-by government reservoir development and an increase in average farm size from 30 acres in 1870 to 212 in 1900 (and 1,032 in 1977), commercial agriculture and its techniques now held sway. When the Office of Foreign Seed and Plant Introduction imported strains of strong, red winter wheat from Siberia, a flurry of dry farming began, pushing the fields up mountain slopes as steep as 20 percent. Yet even the booms in wheat, sugar beets, and horticulture could not submerge the serious problems in soil erosion, malaccumulations of water and salt from irrigation and canal seepage losses of up to 50 percent of their precious water. By mid-century half the arable lands in Utah had been exhausted to the point of requiring artificial fertilization. And while one of the legendary events of early Mormon history had established a precedent for biological pest control, commerical monoculture built up harmful insect populations to the point that first DDT, and later 2,4-D, malathion, endrin, and other pesticides were sprayed on crops with malevolent effects for the food chain.[46]

Strangely, in view of its environmental history, contemporary Utah seems less open to environmentalism than almost any other part of the Mountain West. Utah ecologists such as J. H. Paul, Ray Becraft, C. L. Forsling, Reed Bailey, and Walter Cottam, ably assisted by native literary sons Bernard DeVoto and Wallace Stegner, appear to have been far less convincing with their empirical data than the early Mormon leadership was with its religious pronouncements. Their conclusive documentation of detrimental vegetation changes since settlement, as well as of the critical relationship between abused watersheds and floods, have been unsuccessful in convincing a clear majority in Utah. Although a Utah Conservation Association was formed in the 1930s, and the Utah Academy of Arts, Science and Letters promoted an omnibus State Department of Conservation to consolidate and centralize resource use planning in 1948 (and, in the process, invoking images of China's mountain lands collapse if nothing was done), sportsmen's groups defeated the movement.[47]

During the "environmental decade" (1965-1975), Utah did pass a Land and Water Conservation Fund Act (1965) to stimulate conservation, but it did not make participation mandatory. Three years later a Conference on the Future of Utah's Environment, held in Salt Lake City, resurrected the ecologist's fears for the state once again, but to little avail.[48] Modern Mormons have not only embraced capitalism and state's rights, but most are rather hostile to environmental concerns of any kind. Utah senator Orin Hatch, who in 1980 introduced Bill S.1680 calling for the "return" to Utah of all National Forest and Bureau of Land Management (BLM) lands within the state, a beginning for what he has termed "the second American Revolution," is a major spokesman for the Sagebrush Rebellion who regards ecologists as "toadstool and dandelion worshippers." A Rocky Mountain poll taken in late 1979 indicated that nearly half of Utahans agree with his sentiments. Even the classic Mormon concept of stewardship is now convoluted. "In the [modern] Mormon mind," environmental researcher Don Snow has written, "the earth as we know it is a temporary state of affairs, soon to be cleansed 'in the twinkling of an eye' by the redeemer. If industry makes a mess of air and watersheds, that's of little consequence."[49] Only those who know Utah's early history would understand the appropriate irony of representing a Mormon bishop as the anti-environmental antagonist in Edward Abbey's novel *The Monkey Wrench Gang* (1975).

The federal government, consequently, remains the major force of environmental sensitivity in Utah. Since 1925 the Department of Agriculture has attempted to reverse watershed deterioration by cutting back on both permits and grazing seasons. In the 1970s Environmental Impact Statements on grazing in BLM lands and the Wasatch National Forest concluded that "the declining condition of millions of acres of rangelands caused by overgrazing" was still so widespread that a massive reduction would be necessary to show a reversal by the year 2000.[50] Helped by the passage of the BLM Organic Act in 1976, this reduction is now underway in Utah.

For environmental philosophy, the lessons of the Utah experience may be difficult to accept. The Mormon experiment is useful in testing some of the hypotheses of the environmental movement's critique of American institutions, although it is complicated by the relic nature of Utah grasslands and the relatively early presence of Gentiles whose free abuse of resources was beyond the pale of the church. Early Mormonism, it is clear, did possess the democratic and communal impulses valued by environmentalists and the centralization and support necessary to carry out a land ethic agricultural program, even while "remaking" the Wasatch Front. But without an empirical understanding of how mountain land worked, even practical stewardship of the Mormon variety was unsuccessful.

NOTES

1. Lynn White, Jr., "The Historical Roots of Our Ecologic Crisis," *Science* 155 (March 1967): 1203-1207; Roderick Nash, *Wilderness and the American Mind*, rev. ed. (New Haven: Yale University Press, 1973), pp. 13-20. See also essays by James Barr, "Man and Nature: The Ecological Controversy and the

Old Testament", René Dubois, "Franciscan Conservation versus Benedictine Stewardship"; and Arnold Toynbee, "The Religious Background of the Present Environmental Crisis," in *Ecology and Religion in History*, ed. David and Eileen Spring (New York: Harper and Row, 1974).

2. Eugene Hargrove, "Anglo-American Land-Use Attitudes," *Environmental Ethics* 2 (Summer 1980): 121-148.

3. Donald Worster, *Dust Bowl: The Southern Plains in the 1930s* (New York: Oxford University Press, 1979). Worster's book won the Bancroft Price as the most important book published on American history in 1979.

4. Stuart Chase, *Rich Land, Poor Land: A Study of Waste in the Natural Resources of America* (New York: McGraw-Hill, 1936); Roy Robbins, *Our Landed Heritage: The Public Domain, 1776-1970*, (Lincoln: University of Nebraska Press, 1976).

5. Leonard J. Arrington, "Mormon Economic Policies and Their Implementation on the Western Frontier, 1947-1900" (Ph.D dissertation, University of North Carolina, Chapel Hill, 1952), pp. 96-97.

6. "If ye are not equal in earthly things ye cannot be equal in obtaining heavenly things." *The Doctrine and Covenants of the Church of Jesus Christ of Latter-day Saints*, vol. 76 (Salt Lake City, 1921 edition), p. 6.

7. It is not clear whether the Mormons saw themselves, and Utah, in Old Testament terms before the migration, but they certainly did afterward. In this they emulated the ancient Hebrews, who had viewed the arid deserts of the Middle East as cursed wilderness (Gen. 3:17, 18), the antithesis of the green, lush garden from which man had been expelled (Gen. 2:9). Both the name and the promise that Brigham Young offered the Saints came from the Book of Isaiah (51:3): "For the Lord shall comfort Zion; he will comfort all her waste places; and he will make her wilderness like Eden, and her desert like the garden of the Lord." In time Young invoked an identical image: "We had to leave our homes and possessions on the fertile plains of Illinois to make our dwelling places in these desert wilds, on barren, sterile plains amid lofty, rugged moun-

tains." And later: "We were the first to plant out orchards and to improve the desert country, making it like the Garden of Eden." And finally this clear link: " . . . we wanted to get to a strange land, like Abraham." *Journal of Discourses* (Liverpool, England: Albert Carrington, 1852-1886), vol. 20., p. 223; vol. 19, p. 60; and vol. 14 p. 208.

8. Donald Jackson and Mary Spence, eds., *The Expeditions of John Charles Fremont* vol. 1 (Urbana: University of Illinois Press, 1970-1973), p. 695.

9. Quoted in W. Eugene Hollon, *The Great American Desert* (New York: Oxford University Press, 1966), p. 91. This was corroborated by Young, who remembers it in less visionary terms: "In the days of Joseph we have sat many hours at a time conversing about this very country. Joseph has often said, 'If I were only in the Rocky Mountains with a hundred faithful men, I would then be happy, and ask no odds of mobocrats.'" *Journal of Discourses*, vol. 11, p. 16.

10. For the geologic history of the central Rockies, see Philip King, *Evolution of North America* (Princeton: Princeton University Press, 1959), pp. 90-128.

11. W. E. Coffman, "The Geography of the Utah Valley Crescent" (Ph.D. dissertation, Ohio State University, Columbus, 1944), pp. 10, 24; Wasatch Front Regional Council, *Historical Settlement and Population Patterns along the Wasatch Front* (Bountiful, Utah, 1976), pp. 1-2; Wallace Stegner, "Dead Heart of the West: Reflections on the Great Salt Lake," *Rocky Mountain Magazine* 3 (November 1981): 56-59.

12. Elmo Coffman, "Our Resources"; Ralph Woolley, "Our Resources: Water"; and Reed Bailey, "Utah's Watersheds" in *Proceedings, Utah Academy of Sciences, Arts and Letters* 25 (1947-1948): 24-25, 36.

13. Wasatch Front Regional Council, *Historical Settlement*, p. 4; Coffman, "Geography of the Utah Valley Crescent," pp. 34-35, 40.

14. Wasatch Front Regional Council, *Historical Settlement*, pp. 76-77; James Carley et al., "A Soil Survey and Soil Interpretations of Ogden Valley," *Utah Agricultural Experiment*

Station Research Reports, No. 14 (1973); U.S., House of Representatives, "Report of the Secretary of the Interior," *House Exec. Doc. 1*, 34th Cong., 3d sess., 1857, pp. 546-547.

15. Although the primary documents exist to do it here and elsewhere in the Mountain West, excellent work by Utah scientists on historical ecology has made it unnecessary for the author to re-create the presettlement ecology from the original sources. See, for example, Earl M. Christensen and Myrtis A. Hutchinson, "Historical Observations on the Ecology of Rush and Tooele Valleys, Utah," *Utah Academy Proceedings* 42 (1965):90-105; A. C. Hull, Jr., and Mary Kay Hull, "Presettlement Vegetation of Cache Valley, Utah and Idaho," *Journal of Range Management* 27 (January 1974): 27-29; Walter P. Cottam, "An Ecological Study of the Flora of Utah Lake, Utah" (Ph.D. dissertation, University of Chicago, Chicago, 1926); Richard D. Guymon, "Ecological History and Biological Resources of San Juan County, Utah" (Master's thesis, University of Utah, Salt Lake City, 1964); Heber H. Hall, "The Impact of Man on the Vegetation and Soil of the Upper Valley Allotment, Garfield County, Utah" (Master's thesis, University of Utah, Salt Lake City, 1954); and John H. Wakefield, "A Study of the Plant Ecology of Salt Lake and Utah Valleys before the Mormon Immigration" (Master's thesis, Brigham Young University, Provo, 1933).

16. See Christensen and Hutchinson, "Historical Observations," pp. 99-103. For original ranges of the faunal subspecies herein indicated, see E. Raymond Hall and Keith R. Kelson, *The Mammals of North America*, 2 vols. (New York: Ronald Press, 1959). For both floral and faunal climax dominants, see Victor E. Shelford, *The Ecology of North America* (Urbana: University of Illinois Press, 1963), pp. 152-168.

17. Jesse D. Jennings, *Prehistory of North America* (New York: Harper and Row, 1968), pp. 183, 264, 274-276; Jesse D. Jennings and Edward Norbeck, eds., *Prehistoric Man in the New World* (Chicago: University of Chicago Press, 1964), p. 162; James H. Gunnerson, "Plateau Shoshonean Prehistory: A Suggested Reconstruction," *American Antiquity* 28 (July

1962):44; David Madsen et al., "Man, Mammoth, and Lake Fluctuations in Utah," *University of Utah Antiquities Section, Selected Papers No. 5* (1977); Ross T. Christensen, "On The Prehistory of Utah Valley," *Proceedings, Utah Academy of Sciences, Arts and Letters* 25 (1947-1948): 101-109; Ralph V. Chamberlain, "Man and Nature in Early Utah," *Proceedings, Utah Academy of Sciences, Arts and Letters* 24 (1946-1947): 3-22.

18. Walter P. Cottam, "The Impact of Man on the Flora of the Bonneville Basin" (Salt Lake City, 1961). This pamphlet is housed in Special Collections, Milton R. Merrill Library, Utah State University, Logan, Utah. Cottam cites primary documents on the Indian use of fire in the area and points out that both big sagebrush and Utah juniper are fire intolerant.

19. Leonard J. Arrington, *Great Basin Kingdom: An Economic History of the Latter-day Saints, 1830-1900* (Cambridge: Harvard University Press, 1958), p. 18.

20. *Journal of Discourses*, vol. 9, pp. 282-283.

21. Ibid., vol. 2, p. 348. Mere subsistence obviously was not the goal of this cooperation: "If we will work unitedly, we can work ourselves into wealth, health, prosperity and power." Ibid., vol. 12, p. 376.

22. See *The Doctrine and Covenants*, 104:13-18, 55-56. Young's pronouncements were consistent with those of Smith on stewardship and cooperation: "There is any amount of property, and gold and silver in the earth . . . and the Lord gives to this one and that one . . . but it all belongs to him. . . . No person on earth can truly call anything his own. . . ." And on cooperation: "This co-operative movement in only a stepping stone to what is called the Order of Enoch, but which is in reality the Order of Heaven." *Journal of Discourses*, vol. 16, p. 10, vol. 9, p. 106, vol. 13, p. 2.

23. Leonard J. Arrington, "Property among the Mormons," *Rural Sociology* 18 (December 1951):345; and Feremorz Y. Fox, "The Mormon Land System: A Study of the Settlement and Utilization of Land under the Direction of the Mormon

Church" (Ph.D. dissertation, Northwestern University, Evanston, Ill., 1937).

24. Gordon Thomas, *Development of Institutions under Irrigation with Special Reference to Early Utah Conditions* (New York: Macmillan, 1920), p. 27.

25. B. H. Roberts, *A Comprehensive History of the Church of Jesus Christ of Latter-day Saints*, vol. 3 (Provo, Utah: Brigham Young University Press, 1930), p. 269.

26. Arrington, "Property among the Mormons," p. 348. The Territorial Ordinance of 1850, signed by Governor Brigham Young, is reprinted in George Steward, "Utah's Biological Heritage and the Need for Its Conservation," *Proceedings, Utah Academy of Science, Arts and Letters* 25 (1947-1948):7-8. See also Ezra C. Knowlton, *History of Highway Development in Utah* (Salt Lake City: Utah State Road Commission, 1967), p. 24. At first Young also determined that his constituency should use "Dead wood" for fuel so as "to foster the growth of timber." Roberts, *A Comprehensive History*, vol. 3, p. 269. This must have become impractical rather early.

27. Arrington, "Mormon Economic Policies," p. 178.

28. Works Progress Administration, History of Grazing Collection, 1690-1941, Special Collections, Milton R. Merrill Library, Utah State University, Logan, Utah, Box 15, Folder 2. Hereafter WPA Grazing Collection.

29. Lowery Nelson, *The Mormon Village: A Pattern and Technique of Land Settlement* (Salt Lake City: University of Utah Press, 1962), pp. xv, 11, 26-27, 38-40, 53; Joel E. Ricks, *Forms and Methods of Early Mormon Settlement in Utah and the Surrounding Region, 1847 to 1877* (Logan: Utah State Univeristy Press, 1964); Lynn A. Rosenvall, "Defunct Mormon Settlements: 1830-1930," in *The Mormon Role in the Settlement of the West*, ed. Richard Jackson (Provo: Brigham Young University Press, 1978), p. 60.

30. *Journal of Discourses*, vol. 12, p. 153. On United Order settlements, see Leonard J. Arrington, *Orderville, Utah: A Pioneer Mormon Experiment in Economic Organization*

(Logan: Utah State University Press, 1954); and Feremorz Y. Fox, *Experiments in Cooperation and Social Security among the Mormons: A Study of Joseph Smith's Order of Stewardship and Consecration, and Brigham Young's United Order* (Salt Lake City: Deseret News, 1937).

31. Gustave O. Larson, *The 'Americanization' of Utah for Statehood* (San Marino, Calif.: Huntington Library, 1971), introduction, p. 35.

32. Arrington, "Mormon Economic Policies," p. 178. Wayne L. Wahlquist, "Population Growth in the Mormon Core Area: 1847-1890," in Jackson, *The Mormon Role in the Settlement of the West*, has worked out a population schedule for Utah which he believes to be more accurate than the census reports. According to figures in his Table 2, the population in Utah increased from 1,637 in 1847 to 97,229 by 1870, with 55 percent of these residing along the Wasatch Front. Between 1848 and 1883, he estimates (his Table 5) that the Mormons had to provide homes for some 72,551 who emigrated to Zion from abroad.

33. *Deseret News* (Salt Lake City), November 16, 1865.

34. Charles S. Peterson, "Albert F. Potter's Wasatch Survey, 1902: A Beginning for Public Management of Natural Resources in Utah," *Utah Historical Quarterly* 39 (Summer 1971):249. See also "Forest Reserves," *19th Annual Report of the U.S. Geological Survey* (Washington, D.C., 1898), p. 22; U.S. House of Representatives, "Report on the Forests," *House Misc. Doc. 1*, 47th Cong., 2d sess., 1883, vol. 13, pt. 9, pp. 567-569.

35. Will C. Barnes, "The Story of the Range," in the WPA Grazing Collection, Box 6, Folder 11; see also Box 15, Folder 2; Box 7, Folder 3. In addition, Don Walker, "The Cattle Industry of Utah, 1850-1900: An Historical Profile," *Utah Historical Quarterly* 32 (Summer 1964): 34; Leonard J. Arrington and Thomas G. Alexander, *A Dependent Commonwealth: Utah's Economy from Statehood to the Great Depression*, Dean May, ed. (Provo: Brigham Young University Press, 1974), p. 16; N. Keith Roberts and B. Delworth Gardner, "Livestock and the Public Lands," *Utah Historical Quarterly* 32 (Summer 1964):

286; *U.S. Census Report* 1880, volume on Agriculture, pp. 144-176. For a fuller discussion of altitudinal grazing migrations and the mountain environment, see Dan L. Flores, "Islands in the Desert: An Environmental Interpretation of the Rocky Mountain Frontier" (Ph.D. dissertation, Texas A&M University, College Station, 1978), pp. 404-410.

36. Christensen and Hutchinson, "Historical Observations," p. 98; Cottam, "The Impact of Man," p. 9. Respecting the area of what is now the Manti/La Sal National Forest in southeastern Utah, Cottam says: "Local history and ecological data regarding Mountain Meadows establish a record of almost complete change in vegetation since settlement in 1862." Walter Cottam and George Steward, "Plant Succession as a Result of Grazing and of Meadow Dessication by Erosion since Settlement in 1862," *Journal of Forestry* 38 (August 1940): 31. For a species and habits breakdown of the *Chenopodianceae*, or pigweeds, which have replaced the native grasses in many areas of Utah and the West, see Harold W. Rickett, *The Central Plains and Mountains*, vol. 6 *Wild Flowers of the United States* (New York: McGraw-Hill, 1966), p. 110.

37. John Wesley Powell, *Report on the Lands of the Arid Region of the United States, With a More Detailed Account of the Lands of Utah* (Washington, D.C., 1878). For a laudatory assessment of Powell's plan, based on local and collectivist "grazing and water districts" and (later) legal rights and institutional lines conforming with natural drainage, consult Wallace Stegner, *Beyond the Hundredth Meridian: John Wesley Powell and the Second Opening of the West* (Lincoln: University of Nebraska Press, 1954). In light of subsequent scientific findings, the major flaw of Powell's plan was his stream flow. His plan would have turned the mountain watersheds over to the lumber companies for clearing. See Flores, "Islands in the Desert," pp. 283-289, for a more critical analysis of Powell's land-use plan.

38. "Every civilized government," Fernow wrote, "must in time own or control the forest cover of the mountains in order to secure desirable water conditions." B. E. Fernow, "Report upon the Forestry Investigations of the U.S. Department of

Agriculture, 1877-1898," *House Doc. 181*, 55th Cong., 3d sess., 1898, p. 316. Marsh had opened this debate in America with his *Man and Nature*, now recognized as a work of major significance to American environmental history. He spoke of the disasters which had befallen China and areas of the French Alps when mountainous areas were stripped of their trees. By 1891, eight European nations already had moved to public ownership of their mountains, among them Germany, Fernow's homeland.

39. Lands committee chairman Lewis E. Payson of Illinois implied in the House that the reserves might be "temporary," but were necessary for "conserving the general good by preserving the watersheds. . . ." Congressman Thomas C. McRae of Arkansas noted prophetically that "we shall hear from it [the reservation clause] in the future." *Congressional Record*, 51st Cong., 2d sess., 1891, vol. 22, pp. 3613-3616. Bills to establish such a mountain reserve system in the West had been introduced in every session of Congress beginning in 1882. In 1890 both the American Association for the Advancement of Science and the National Academy opined that "no other problem confronting the government of the United Stated is equal in importance to that offered by the present condition and future fate of the forests of western North America." Quoted in Robbins, *Our Landed Heritage*, p. 312.

40. Thomas G. Alexander, "Senator Reed Smoot and Western Land Policy, 1905-1920," *Arizona and the West* 13 (Autumn 1971): 245-264; Peterson, "Albert F. Potter's Wasatch Survey, 1902," pp. 249-253. Smoot was one of the few western legislators who also supported the Pettigrew Amendment, which opened the Reserves to multiple use, and the fee and permit system later implemented by Pinchot. The question of support for the National Forest system was not the clear-cut "people vs. special interests" confrontation of Progressive rhetoric, but subsequent research has not erased the suspicions that the opponents were motivated by greed. Generally speaking, farmers and urban dwellers in the West were supportive of the system, as was the National Forestry Association and some of the individual timbermen and cattlemen. The most vehe-

ment opponents were (and still are) the sheepmen, the mining industry, and the majority of cattlemen. See Lawrence Rakestraw, "Uncle Sam's Forest Reserves," *Pacific Northwest Quarterly* 44 (October 1953): 145-146; and Lawrence Rakestraw, "The West, States' Rights, and Conservation: A Study of Six Public Land Conferences," *Pacific Northwest Quarterly* 47 (July 1957): 89-99.

41. Again contrary to popular impression, not all eastern government scientists supported the rationale of the forest system. In addition to the two entities mentioned, Hiram M. Chittenden of the reservoir survey also expressed doubts regarding the beneficial effects of vegetation upon stream flow. The science of "oekologie" was then in its infancy. For a discussion of their arguments, see Gordon B. Dodds, "The Streamflow Controversy: A Conservation Turning Point," *Journal of American History* 56 (June 1969):56-69.

42. Robert V. R. Reynolds, "Grazing And Floods: A Study Of Conditions in the Manti National Forest, Utah," *U.S. Department of Agriculture Forest Service Bulletin 91* (Washington, D.C., 1911). Of a total of forty-three Mormon settlements which were abandoned because of environmental factors, the highest number of failures (sixteen) was due to flooding. All but three of these were located in southern Utah, in the Colorado Plateau country. Rosenvall, "Defunct Mormon Settlements," pp. 60-61, Table 2. At this time, it cannot be said whether environmental disruption caused by overgrazing or cutting was responsible, but since all but two were abandoned after more than a decade of occupation, it appears likely that this was the cause. Rosenvall, who is unfamiliar with the techniques of historical ecology, assumes the rivers were simply unpredictable.

43. The position of the Weather Service that bared slopes yield more runoff than vegetated ones was ably documented in Utah, where some studies indicated that as much as sixty-two times the amount of water came from bared slopes. But the Utah experiences made the further point that without vegetation, mountains shed their soil, boulders, and other debris along with the water, in destructive and erosive floods. Where

vegetated slopes normally lose *no* soil from rainfall, bare slopes averaged 110 cubic feet per acre soil loss during heavy storms. Further, the rapid runoff of degraded mountain slopes interfered with water percolation, causing streams to dry up prematurely. In one of the 1920s floods, gullies were cut seventy-five feet deep to bedrock, rock and debris covered the ground to a depth of eight feet at the mouths of the canyons, and 300-ton boulders rolled through towns and irrigation systems. Sixty years later, these gullies are still etched into the slopes. Utah ecologists proved that they could revegetate a slope and stop floods in no more than a decade, but when flood fears subsided they found the public apathetic to their arguments that use ought to be severely curtailed. For several score high quality black-and-white photographs which graphically illustrate the seriousness of this mountain lands collapse, see Utah Land Board, Intermountain Forest and Range Experiment Station, U.S. Forest Service; and the Utah Agricultural Experiment Station, *Report of Utah Flood Survey, 1931, 1932*, Special Collections, Milton R. Merrill Library, Utah State University, Logan, Utah. Other major studies documenting the relationship between watershed abuse and ecological collapse in Utah include C. L. Forsling, "A Study of Herbaceous Plant Cover and Soil Erosion in Relation to Grazing on the Wasatch Plateau in Utah," *U.S. Department of Agriculture Bulletin 220* (Washington, D.C., 1931); Report of the Flood Commission, "Torrential Floods in Northern Utah," *Utah Agricultural Experiment Station Circular 92* (Logan, 1931); Reed Bailey, C. L. Forsling, and R. J. Becraft, "Floods And Accelerated Erosion in Northern Utah," *U.S. Department of Agriculture Misc. Publication 196* (Washington, D.C., 1934); Richard Marston, "Effect of Vegetation on Rainstorm Runoff," *Proceedings, Utah Academy of Science, Arts and Letters* 26 (1948-1949); Ernest O. Butler, "Forest and Watershed Fires in Utah," *Utah Agricultural Experiment Station Circular 115* (Logan, 1940); Raphel Zon, "Forests and Water in Light of Scientific Evidence," *Sen. Doc. 469*, 62d Cong., 2d sess., 1913.

44. Steward, "Utah's Biological Heritage," p. 14; George W.

Craddock, "Salt Lake City Flood, 1945," *Proceedings, Utah Academy of Science, Arts and Letters* 23 (1945-1946): 51-61.

45. Cottam, "The Influence of Man," p. 10; Christensen and Hutchinson, "Historical Observations."

46. *U. S. Census Report*, 1900, Volume on Agriculture; Steward, "Utah's Biological Heritage," p. 7; George F. Knowlton, "Our Resources: Beneficial Insects," *Proceedings, Utah Academy of Science, Arts and Letters* 25 (1947-1948):39; Charles S. Peterson, "The 'Americanization' of Utah's Agriculture," *Utah Historical Quarterly* 42 (Spring 1974):109-125; John E. Lamborn, "A History of the Development of Dry Farming in Utah and Southern Idaho" (Master's thesis, Utah State University, Logan, 1978). For early reservoir development, see Thomas G. Alexander, "An Investment in Progress: Utah's First Federal Reclamation Project, The Strawberry Valley Project" *Utah Historical Quarterly* 39 (Summer 1971):286-304. Although not considered in this article, mining also had an adverse impact on the Utah agricultural environment. Silting and pollution of streams used for irrigation, and sulphur poisoning of stock and crops, emerged as a major problem around 1900. See John A. Widtsoe, "The Relation of Smelter Smoke to Utah Agriculture," *Utah State Agricultural College Experiment Station Bulletin No. 88* (Logan, 1903). The author also wishes to thank John Lamborn of the Special Collections Library at Utah State University for allowing him to peruse Lamborn's unpublished paper, "The Smelter Cases of 1904 and 1906."

47. Walter Cottam, "General Plan for Conservation," and Ross Hardy, "Our Program for Action," both in *Proceedings, Utah Academy of Science, Arts and Letters* 25 (1947-1948):69-70, 77, respectively. Paul was professor of natural science at the University of Utah, as was Cottam. Becraft was professor of range management at Utah State, Bailey for years was the director of the Intermountain Forest and Range Experiment Station at Ogden, and Forsling was research ecologist in the U.S. Forest Service. Bernard DeVoto, a well-known historian and literary figure who died in 1955, spent years trying "to

save the West from itself" through his *Harper's* columns. See Peter Wild, *Pioneer Conservationists of Western North America* (Missoula, Mont.: Mountain Press, 1979), chapter 9, for a good sketch of DeVoto. Wallace Stegner has become an able replacement for DeVoto and is a widely acclaimed writer and environmentalist.

48. Michael Treshow and C. M. Gilmour, eds., *Proceedings, Conference on the Future of Utah's Environment* (Salt Lake City: University of Utah Press, 1968); Lyle Blair, "An Analysis of Counties and Municipalities Which Did Not Participate in the Land and Water Conservation Fund Act of 1965, Utah: 1965-1970," (Master's thesis, Utah State University, Logan, 1974).

49. Don Snow, "Squeezing the Daylights out of Zion," *High Country News*, July 25, 1980, pp. 5-6; Wallace Stegner, "If the Sagebrush Rebels Win, Everybody Loses," *The Living Wilderness* 45 (Summer 1981): 30-35. Stegner points out that the permit owners are the most vocal members of the "rebellion." Some 70 percent of land within the boundaries of the state is federally owned, with 45 percent in Bureau of Land Management lands and 14 percent in National Forest. Only 13 percent is privately owned, while 5 percent is in state hands.

50. Arthur H. Roth, Jr., "A Graphic Summary of Grazing on the Public Lands of the Intermountain Region," *U.S. Department of Agriculture, U.S. Forest Service, and Intermountain Forest and Range Experiment Station Project 3298* pt. 1 (Washington, D.C., 1940), pp. 1-6; U.S. Forest Service, Intermountain Region, *Draft Environmental Impact Statement and Proposed Land Management Plan: Wasatch National Forest, Utah* (Ogden, 1977); U.S. Bureau of Land Management, *Final Environmental Impact Statement: Livestock Grazing Management on National Resource Lands* (Washington, D.C., 1974), I-1 through I-10; Deevon Bailey, "Economic Impacts of Public Grazing Reductions in the Livestock Industry with Emphasis on Utah," (Master's thesis, Utah State University, Logan, 1980).

11

STEPHEN P. SAYLES

The Politics of Reclamation: California's Central Valley and the Straus-Boke Rider of 1948-1949

On June 20, 1948, the 80th Congress enacted the Department of the Interior appropriations bill which appropriated $407 million to fund departmental operations for fiscal year 1949. Attached to this appropriation measure was a House-sponsored rider specifying that after January 31, 1949, the posts of commissioner, assistant commissioner, and regional director of the Bureau of Reclamation were to be filled with engineers having a minimum of five years experience. This rider was directed against the current commissioner, Michael Wolf Straus, and his director of Region II, Richard Lathrop Boke, of Sacramento. On June 30, President Harry Truman signed with great distaste the legislation into law in order to continue Interior Department funding for 1949. He declared that the rider was "an attempt to destroy the national power policy" and that it violated constitutional separation of powers by removing two executive officials charged with enforcement of reclamation law. The president concluded that "the consequences of the rider would serve land monopolies and private power interests in the West."[1]

What became known as the Straus-Boke rider was not only a constitutional issue but also reflected the politics of a decade-long jurisdictional dispute in the Central Valley of California between the Bureau of Reclamation and the Army Corps of

Engineers. Ostensibly a struggle over the development of the Kings and Kern River watersheds, Table Mountain, and the American River, it had the potential to undermine federal reclamation policy in the Central Valley Project area and in the West. Part of the problem was bureaucratic in nature and concept. The Corps constructed single-purpose flood control and navigation works and reported to congressional committee. The Bureau was an agency of the Interior Department and responsible for the enforcement of federal reclamation law. It answered to the secretary of the interior and to the president. "The engineers pride themselves in their lack of philosophy, in the best Army tradition," chided author Robert deRoos. "They simply want to build dams."[2] The Bureau possessed a social philosophy. Central to its concept of the general welfare was the protection of the family farm and low-cost public power to farms and cities. The family farm, believed the Bureau, was the backbone of American democracy while large landholdings created social castes and class conflict.[3]

An important issue went to the heart of this jurisdictional battle. The Central Valley Project, hailed as the largest project of its kind in the world, was scheduled to be completed by the Bureau in July 1951, when water from the Sacramento Valley watershed would be shifted to the arid lands of the San Joaquin Valley. In contention, wrote Senator Sheridan Downey, Democrat of California, was whether or not the 160-acre limitation feature of the Reclamation Act of 1902 ought to be enforced in the project area. This provision would limit the amount of water to a landholder on a federal reclamation project to 160 acres, or in such community property states as California, to 320 acres. "That sounds rather unimportant and a bit dull," noted the senator. But, "that little clause in the Reclamation Act is about as harmless as an atomic bomb."[4]

To put it another way, who was to benefit from the Central Valley Project? Large landed interests in the San Joaquin Valley, the California Chamber of Commerce, private power utilities, the California Farm Bureau Federation, and the Irrigation District Association supported the Corps of Engineers to avoid the acre limitation and public power policies of the Bureau of Reclamation. Returning veterans, religious organizations, organized labor, and the California Grange backed the Bureau and its rigid enforcement of reclamation law. Each looked forward to control of an agricultural bonanza. The former group initiated a conflict over the Kings River development and caught the Bureau's Sacramento office unprepared. During World War II, Charles L. Carey took over the Bureau's Region II, brought in a new team, and prepared his people for a long, bitter contest for dominance in the Central Valley.

Carey's emergence in Sacramento came at an opportune time. Senator Downey and his allies, notably Congressman Alfred J. Elliott, Democrat of Tulare, California, had launched a crusade to eliminate acre limitation from federal law, or failing that, to exempt the Central Valley from its enforcement. Downey, who rose to power on the "Ham 'n' Eggs" movement in 1938, became convinced that land ownership patterns in the valley and easily available ground water supplies made the 160-acre limitation unenforceable. This point was driven home, said Downey, in 1944 when he conducted hearings on farm problems relating to national defense. What he had learned shocked him: a federal agency was determined to "rule the valley" and conduct social engineering.[5]

In 1944, anti-Bureau forces made their move. Congressman Elliott attached a rider to the Rivers and Harbors bill calling for repeal of acreage limitation which nearly cleared Congress until liberal senators threatened a filibuster. In that same year, Senator Downey attached an amendment to the Flood Control Act authorizing the Corps to construct a 335,000 acre-foot Folsom Dam and Reservoir facility on the American River. Bureau leadership, however, refused to accept this congressional mandate and persisted in an effort to wrest Folsom Dam from the engineers. By late 1947, Downey found the Bureau's campaign "so shocking" that he launched a determined movement to fire Bureau Commissioner Straus and Regional Director Boke, who had succeeded the late Carey in 1945. He was aided in this endeavor by Republican senator

William F. Knowland of California and Congressman Leroy S. Johnson of Stockton who feared that attaching Folsom Dam to the Central Valley Project might delay the dam's construction for years.[6]

In January 1948 California congressmen Clair Engle and George P. Miller coauthored legislation to have Folsom Dam built as proposed by the Bureau of Reclamation. President Truman, tiring of the conflict in the Central Basin, decided to use the Engle-Miller bill as a vehicle to resolve the Bureau-Corps dispute. He recommended that the Corps be authorized to build and operate a power plant in coordination with similar installations at Shasta and Keswick Dams. "To achieve such coordinated operation the Folsom Dam and Reservoir, once constructed," he said, "should be transferred to the Bureau of Reclamation for operation and maintenance."[7]

Downey and the Corps immediately attempted to undermine presidential policy. The Corps argued that the president's message conflicted with congressional policy established under the 1944 Flood Control Act and would be "detrimental to the flood control program and the cause of water resource development generally."[8] Downey used the issue as a means to rid the valley of Straus and Boke and their enforcement of acreage limitation. He had support in the Republican party and among southern Democrats who were restive against the burgeoning bureaucracy of the New Deal and the erosion of legislative powers to the executive branch. And, to these people, the Bureau of Reclamation and its policies under Straus and Boke symbolized all that was wrong in the reclamation field.

"Big" Mike Straus, called "the most arrogant bureaucrat in Washington," ruled an empire supplying 9 million westerners with water and power from ninety-six dams, 16,000 miles of canals, and over 3,000 miles of transmission lines. He had come from a progressive political background at home, in the University of Wisconsin, and in his association with Harold L. Ickes in Chicago. As a reporter and editor of Chicago and New York newspapers, Straus became a fervent New Dealer and served as Ickes's information chief for the Public Works Administration and the Interior Department during the 1930s. During World War II he served on the War Production Board and organized some 7,000 labor-management committees. He returned to Ickes in 1943 as assistant Interior secretary in charge of liaison with Congress and supervision over personnel. On December 12, 1945, Straus became Bureau commissioner succeeding Harry W. Bashore. Throughout his tenure under Ickes, he was an enthusiastic supporter of federal reclamation programs and enforcement of reclamation law.[9]

While Commissioner Straus created a bureaucratic empire for himself in the Interior Department, another ambitious bureaucrat caught his attention. Richard L. Boke was born in California and attended Antioch College where he majored in economics, biology, and literature. During the New Deal he served in the Soil Conservation Service in the Southwest and became its regional director in Albuquerque. During World War II he acquired valuable administrative experience in Nelson Rockefeller's Inter-American Affairs Committee and in the Foreign Economic Administration. In 1945 Straus moved him to Sacramento as chief of operations and maintenance in Region II. His greatest accomplishment was to negotiate a water service contract with the South San Joaquin Municipal Utility District which included an excess acreage limitation provision. This contract broke a solid front in the Central Valley against such negotiations for Central Valley Project water and power services and was the basis for future contractual negotiations. Late in 1945 Boke became director of Region II. He "is not one of our regulation reliable, non-crusading Reclamation engineers," wrote Straus to Ickes, and he could be relied upon to enforce reclamation law and public power policies.[10]

Between 1946 and 1948 the Straus-Boke control of the Central Valley came under serious challenge. Downey and Elliott led the attack citing the reclamationists' lack of engineering degrees, their social philosophies as they intruded upon existing land ownership patterns, the barrage of Bureau propaganda upholding acreage limitation and public power policies, and their failure to inform Congress on various problems. One problem was the "carry-over" issue of funds from one fiscal year to the next, and a Boke memorandum exhorting his engineers to spend all their money during the fiscal year. Another issue plaguing the Bureau was a temporary shortage of funds that caused a "shut-down" on Central Valley Project construction on November 30, 1947. Not only were 1,500 workers laid off just before Christmas, alleged their critics, but the funds actually had been available for construction until early 1948.[11]

All of these charges related to the management of the Bureau and acreage limitation in Region II. Representative Forest A. Harness, Republican of Indiana and chairman of the Subcommittee on Publicity and Propaganda of the Committee on Expenditures in the Executive Departments, became so concerned late in 1947 that he resolved to investigate the Bureau's Sacramento office. Six investigators searched for information from Bureau offices in Denver, Sacramento, and Washington, D.C. In late 1948 committee counsel Franklin T. Bow returned from Sacramento with what he considered to be enough evidence to warrant public hearings. Held during spring 1948, these hearings were so "one-sided," noted Harold Ickes, that they were designed "to accomplish the political strangulation of Boke and Straus without giving them . . . a chance to be heard."[12]

On May 14, Harness requested that the Subcommittee on Appropriations for the Interior Department, chaired by Ben F. Jensen, Republican of Iowa, amend the Interior Department appropriations bill to include language that top Bureau positions be filled with qualified engineers. Although Jensen was sympathetic to the proposed amendment, his subcommittee did not include it in the legislation. On May 27, as the legislation reached the House floor for debate, Congressman Elliott offered an amendment that required the positions of commissioner, assistant commissioner, and regional director be filled by engineers with at least ten years of experience. He submitted a letter from Harness in support of his amendment and pointed to the recent Central Valley Project "shut-down" and rising costs of project construction as examples of "incompetent" leadership of Straus and Boke. "They are not engineers, they are not capable, they are not qualified," declared Elliott. Worse, they "have lied to Congress. They lied to the Senate, and they have lied to my people back home many, many times." In spite of sharp opposition, the Elliott amendment carried 59-32, indicating that less than a quarter of the full House was present.[13]

The Straus-Boke rider was amended by the Senate during May and June. Republican Kenneth M. Wherry of Nebraska played a key role in lessening the punitive aspects of the rider as well as establishing January 31, 1949, as the date of enforcement. During an evening session in early June, whatever hopes the administration may have had of defeating the rider faded. No senator moved to delete the rider from the appropriations bill because Sheridan Downey displayed readiness to filibuster the subject. Eager to get on the campaign trail for the November elections, the Senate adopted the rider on June 14 and adjourned,[14] leaving the president with the option of accepting an obnoxious rider or veto the entire bill and leave the Interior Department without funds after July 1. The president signed it on June 30.

Reaction to the Straus-Boke rider was immediate. Interior Secretary Julius A. Krug, having succeeded Ickes in 1946, denounced the House action and declared that it had violated its own rules and the Constitution, invaded the prerogatives of the executive branch, and undermined the reclamation program. He added that the rider was a new kind of "financial and political pressure" to force the Interior Department to ease up on 160-acre limitation enforcement.[15] The *Washington Post* offered that the only offense of Straus and Boke "was that they were advancing power distribution and irrigation in the rich Central Valley of California according to the letter and spirit of reclamation instead of according to the wishes of the power and corporate farming interests of the region."[16] The liberal San Francisco Labor Council pointed out that the positions delineated in the rider were "primarily administrative, [and thus] engineering training and experience are totally beside the point."[17]

That was precisely the point for Downey, Harness, and Elliott. Recent history demonstrated that legislative ouster of executive officials was a feasible course by which to alter federal policies. In 1923, for instance, John Davis had been ousted on the ironical ground that "he was an engineer rather than an administrator."[18] In 1943, attempts to remove Robert M. Lovett from the Interior Department and Goodwin B. Watson and William E. Dodd, Jr., from the Federal Communications Commission failed because an appropriations rider had specifically mentioned their names.[19] Congressman Elliott had evaded this problem by imposing new qualifications for Bureau officers without specifically mentioning names. Even so, Senators Joseph C. O'Mahoney of Wyoming and Carl T. Hayden of Arizona, veterans of the Lovett et al. controversy, thought the rider to be unconstitutional because it "prescribes qualifications solely for the purpose of inflicting punishment" on Boke and Straus.[20]

In the face of this criticism, proponents of the rider presented their case on August 4. The Harness Committee made public its findings and conclusions. This report charged that "propagandists" in the Bureau had "prostituted" the agency "for their own selfish bureaucratic ends." It listed a series of charges illustrating lies and misstatements on the part of Straus and Boke relating to "carry-overs" for Central Valley Project funding, the project "shut-down" of November 30, 1947, and contempt for Congress in various public statements. Special criticism was reserved for the Bureau's "propaganda machine" in which articles and pamphlets "would influence class against class, liberal against conservative, and inject into the mind of readers ideologies sponsored by some of the planners."[21]

The rider became inextricably tied to presidential politics. President Truman, campaigning for re-election against a "do-nothing Congress," pledged to call the legislature into special session in early August. Paul S. Taylor of Berkeley, an authority on reclamation law, urged the president to *"include a re-*

quest for repeal of the Straus-Boke rider" in his address to the special session. This request, he advised, should be a demand not so much "for eliminating injustice" as to revoke "skull-duggery" against the people by "interests" dominating the 80th Congress. The real issue was between veterans who wanted to farm with government purchasing of excess land-holdings and acreage limitation and excess landholders who wanted to monopolize government reclamation water.[22]

On August 7, President Truman urged Congress to repeal the Straus-Boke rider. He argued that the rider aimed at the removal of two men whose only crime was to enforce federal reclamation law and public power policies. He continued, "That they should be legislated out of office is diametrically opposed to the principle on which this Government is founded." Their lack of engineering expertise had no validity: "The positions which they occupy are primarily administrative in character and do not necessarily require a professional engineering background."[23] Republican leaders seemed unimpressed. Senator Wherry called the presidential request "another political maneuver" and indicated that the Senate would not act without prior House action. The House showed little inclination to change its mind. Congressman Jensen noted that "the people of the West are well pleased with the restriction."[24]

As Truman anticipated, Congress did not act on the Straus-Boke rider. He campaigned in the West during August, hammering on the benefits of federal reclamation in the region, and Straus wrote an encouraging note on potential western support in November. "I relish the privilege of going all the way down the line with you in this contest to the final payoff," he wrote.[25] The president scored an upset victory on November 2 and brought Democratic control over both houses of Congress as well. The mood of the Straus-Boke rider repeal forces was jubilant. Their old tormentor Harness had been defeated in Indiana, and Elliott had declined to stand for re-election in California. A Washington State reclamation leader predicted that "the wrong will be righted immediately."[26] Western politicians and newspapers sympathetic to the Bureau took up the call, and California labor leaders declared that Straus and Boke "deserve full support, not condemnation."[27]

As expected, repeal of the Straus-Boke rider ranked high on the list of administration priorities in the 81st Congress. On January 7, 1949, Truman urged Congress to repeal the rider, and the presidential request was sent on to the House Appropriations Committee. On February 1, the rider went into effect, but both Straus and Boke continued at their jobs at the request of Secretary Krug and the president. At the most they would not receive salaries until July 1 when fiscal year 1949 terminated. In the meantime, Congress would be pressured to repeal the rider and vindicate the stand of the executive department.

On February 14, 1949, the House Appropriations Committee, chaired by Clarence Cannon of Missouri, inserted a clause repealing the rider into the First Deficiency Appropriations Act. Two days later a brief skirmish erupted on the House floor when Republican congressman James W. Wadsworth of New York, formerly of the Harness Committee, failed to attach a rider to the appropriations bill to prevent the repeal of the Straus-Boke rider. The Wadsworth amendment lost by a 136 to 87 vote.[28]

It was a much tougher proposition on the Senate side. Senator Downey exhibited no intention of backing down on the issue. Testifying before the Subcommittee on Appropriations for the Interior Department in late February 1949, he portrayed Straus as a power-hungry bureaucrat who ruthlessly hounded his predecessor, Harry W. Bashore, out of office. According to Downey, Bashore "found himself, though nominally the Chief of the Reclamation Bureau, in reality the captive of ideologists in the Interior Department. Seeking to live with his conscience, under men who had none, he ended stripped of all authority, and, to escape a position that had become intolerable, he resigned."[29]

That was not exactly the way Bashore remembered his association with Straus. Visiting the nation's capital a couple of weeks later on an unrelated matter, Bashore informed Secretary Krug that he had come to Washington "somewhat reluctantly" and had no intention to serve there for more than five years. During this period, he continued, "I made considerable efforts to find a man of high calibre to succeed me." Impatient with his lack of success, he was dissuaded from resigning several times by Assistant Secretary Straus. Finally, said Bashore, "Mr. Straus intimated to me that unless I had someone else in mind he would be interested in the job of Commissioner." Bashore then recommended Straus to Ickes, and "nothing has transpired since to cause me to regret that recommendation."[30]

Also testifying before the Senate subcommittee in late February was Secretary Krug who was queried about the status of Boke and Straus. Chairman Kenneth M. McKellar of Tennessee wondered if the secretary had evaded the intent of Congress by retaining these officials in their posts beyond the January 31, 1949, deadline. Krug thought not, declaring that he had strictly complied with the law by cutting off their salaries since February 1. The law did not abolish the positions to which they had been appointed by the president and approved by the Senate. "Moreover," Krug said, "that appropriations act will expire as of July 1, and they can be put back on the payroll. I am in strict compliance with the law and I hope that you will repeal that rider right now."[31]

To the secretary's dismay, however, disturbing rumors appeared that the rider repeal effort was not going well in the appropriations committee. Committee members had received information relating to the loyalty status of Straus and Boke. The House Un-American Activities Committee (HUAC) had turned over information concerning Straus's associations with persons outside his office. Included were such examples as his lunch with representatives of the Soviet Tass News Agency and the Communist New York *Daily Worker* in 1942, his $63 contribution to the Spanish loyalists late in the 1930s, and his wife's supposed "liberal views" on black civil rights. To clear up the matter, Chairman McKellar appointed a subcommittee—composed of Senator Joseph C. O'Mahoney as chairman, Pat McCarran of Nevada, and Guy Cordon of Oregon—to visit with Attorney General Tom C. Clark and the president to obtain permission to view FBI files on these officials.[32]

Additional charges came in from the Central Valley. One was from consulting engineer Frank Crampton of Nevada City who telegraphed Senator McKellar on March 22 with an urgent request that the Senate probe subversive activities, engineering conclusions, cost estimates, and economic studies of all projects authorized during the Straus-Boke era. Crampton alleged that Boke had suppressed reports not confirming Bureau planning and that towns, cities, and farmers were "intimidated on threats no water will be made available unless Boke's plans [are] agreed upon."[33]

McKellar immediately sent this information to O'Mahoney. Also, later that day, receiving word that Attorney General Clark had refused to grant the O'Mahoney subcommittee access to FBI files, McKellar and his appropriations committee refused to restore Straus and Boke to the federal payroll. The committee further instructed the Senate, in conference with House members over the First Deficiency Appropriations Act, to take a firm stand in support of its refusal to repeal the rider.[34]

Reaction from the Interior Department was swift and angry. Secretary Krug declared that this loyalty issue was "a complete phony" and "instigated by Senator Downey because his fight to give vast federal benefits to large landholders in California has failed in every other instance."[35] Straus informed O'Mahoney that he wanted to appear before his subcommittee "at any public meeting you may hold." He pointed to the decision of the Interior Department Loyalty Board as confirming his patriotism and reminded the senator that neither the FBI nor HUAC "has questioned me or accused me in any way of any improper or illegal actions." The central issue remained whether or not the 160-acre limitation should be applied to the Central Valley Project area. Senator Downey and others "failed to change the law," wrote the commissioner, and they now "undertake to change the management and thus change the policy laid down by the Congress."[36]

On March 29, O'Mahoney sent a written report of his subcommittee's work to Senator McKellar. His subcommittee had interviewed Attorney General Clark in mid-March, and Clark assured them that he had read the Straus file, along with data provided by the FBI, HUAC, and the Interior Department Loyalty Board. He "found nothing of substance therein affecting either [Straus or Boke]."[37] On April 3, O'Mahoney reported publicly that the Interior Department Loyalty Board and Attorney General Clark had given Straus and Boke a "clean bill of health." Even so, the senator made it clear that he would not use these results to reverse the action of the appropriations committee against the repeal of the rider. The issue, he said, could be resolved in another money bill, referring to the Second Deficiency Appropriations Act just passed by the House.[38]

While the First Deficiency Appropriations Act remained in conference between House and Senate managers, H. J. 226 passed the House on April 14, and the Senate followed on May 5, containing the Straus-Boke rider. This resolution was a temporary federal pay measure designed to get federal paychecks to government employees while Congress continued to wrangle over the rider in conference. The president was reported to be inclined toward a veto in which he had the support of Secretary Krug.[39] However, the Bureau of the Budget encouraged the president to sign the resolution and emphasized that it was a temporary measure to provide salaries for some 20,000 employees until the deficiency appropriations bill became law.[40] Truman complied with the Bureau of the Budget "with regret." He wanted "to make it clear," he said, "that I am signing the present joint resolution only as a means of making funds available for carrying on the Government's work while the principle involved . . . is given further consideration."[41]

On May 16, 1949, Congress made up its mind on the rider question. The House-Senate conference report indicated that the House receded on the issue,[42] and the First Deficiency Act was sent on to the president for signature. The president signed it on May 24. The Second Deficiency Appropriations Act passed slowl through Congress and was signed into law on June 23, again without language repealing the rider. On June 30, fiscal year 1949 terminated; the Straus-Boke rider was without effect, and the two officials returned to the federal payroll. The administration then turned to the matter of back pay accrued between February 1 and June 30, 1949, as a means of vindicating its stand on the controversy.

The issue dragged through the summer, highlighted by Downey's unusual testimony of July 21, 1949, before O'Mahoney's Committee on Interior and Insular Affairs. He returned to his theme of Straus as a power-driven bureaucrat and portrayed former Commissioner Bashore as a victim of Straus's ruthless ambition: "Mr. Bashore sat in a big chair in my room with tears in his eyes, told me that he was a beaten and defeated man, that he loved his job, he thought he could do a great one, but he could no longer endure the political pressure and the manipulations from Mr. Straus and his associate, and he did resign."[43]

In mid-October 1949 Senator O'Mahoney scheduled hearings to investigate national water resource problems. Preliminary to this general investigation, O'Mahoney intended to give the Interior Department an opportunity to reply to Downey's broadsides issued during the summer. Straus denied "each and every one of the charges" of corruption and mismanagement. He admitted to being human, of having made mistakes, but he never intentionally violated his oath of office. He declared that he would "not be intimidated . . . no matter how many times false charges are reiterated or trumped up."[44]

Harry Bashore protested Downey's portrait of him being a "beaten and defeated man" in his relations with unscrupulous superiors in the Bureau. If anyone had pressured him to resign, he said, it was his wife. He acknowledged that he had been reluctant to hire Boke as regional director, but he did recommend him "as the best man available" for the position. The chief criticism against Boke, he observed, was his successful campaign to get landowners to sign water service contracts that included 160-acre limitation provisions. To avoid this provision, Bashore suggested that large landholders pay construction charges in full.[45]

The Senate hearings were highlighted on October 13 during a dramatic confrontation between Senator Downey and former Interior Secretary Ickes. Ickes accused the senator of "unabashed perjury" in his depiction of Bashore's resignation on July 21 and suggested that the Justice Department take "appropriate action." Continued Ickes,

One would wish that the passion and eloquence and restless assuidity shown by the distinguished Senator from California, in hounding, with sadistic perseverance, two faithful public servants had been employed in a worthier cause . . . . What a tender scene Senator Downey presented of himself wiping the tears from the Bashore peepers as the two sat together that never-to-be-forgotten day in the Senator's office.[46]

On October 15, the Senate hearings abruptly concluded as Congress neared adjournment. Among the last items to be handled by Congress was the Supplemental Appropriations Act for fiscal year 1950 which included $3 million for the Interior Department for various purposes. On October 14, the House passed the measure with a provision appropriating $8,581.68 to be used to pay the salaries of Straus and Boke between February 1 and June 30, 1949. The Senate Appropriations Committee struck that pay provision out upon learning that Senator Downey would discuss at length the abuses of the Straus-Boke regime in the Central Valley. During the House-Senate conference negotiations, House managers held firm on the pay proviso. On October 19 their firmness was rewarded with amendment 17 of the conference report which reinserted the $8,581.68 appropriation in the Supplemental Appropriations Act. That afternoon, Congress accepted the conference report and enacted the appropriations measure.[47] Upon the president's signature, Senator Downey lost his battle to influence reclamation policy in the Central Valley of California by legislative ouster of the officials charged with the enforcement of that policy.

The first session of the 81st Congress ended badly for Senator Downey. Not only did he ultimately lose the Straus-Boke rider issue, but the authority of the Bureau of Reclamation in the Central Valley was strengthened materially as well. Moreover, the senator and the Corps of Engineers lost their battle over Folsom Dam on the American River as President Truman applied the "Folsom formula" to the Central Valley Project. The Corps would be responsible for single-purpose projects providing flood control and navigation improvements while multiple-purpose projects were to be developed by the Bureau. Such a policy, said the president, would provide "a sound comprehensive plan without duplication of effort and overlapping of jurisdiction" and "provide for unified administration and operation of the completed works."[48] The president signed the "Folsom formula" into law on October 15, 1949.

Senator Downey paid a high political price for his opposition to the Bureau and reclamation law in the Central Valley. He had isolated himself from organizational Democratic support since 1944, and in the primary campaign of 1950 he faced a serious challenge from Congresswoman Helen Gahagan Douglas who made the 160-acre limitation the centerpiece of her campaign.[49] Calling for the dismissal of Straus and Boke from the Bureau to the end, Senator Downey retired in 1950 for reasons of health and, thus, set the stage for the controversial contest between Douglas and Representative Richard M. Nixon in the November election.

The use of the legislative rider is as ancient as parliamentary government. Critics of the rider complain that it "is designed to blackjack the president into approving legislation which he otherwise might veto."[50] During the same congressional session in which Congressman Elliott successfully attached his rider to an appropriations bill, Congress beat down other riders which would have prohibited the use of power revenue from the Central Valley Project to defray irrigation costs to farmers, monopolized the sale of project power to the

Pacific Gas & Electric Company, and forbade distribution of project power outside California—all of which noted the San Francisco *Chronicle*, "are admirable examples of the rule that there are no good riders."[51]

The irony of the Straus-Boke controversy was that the means to compel their removal existed in the very nature of the electoral system. In 1952 the Fair Deal of the Truman administration was repudiated by the American electorate, and a new team took over the Interior Department under Interior Secretary Douglas McKay of Oregon and Under Secretary Ralph A. Tudor. Senator Downey must have marveled over the breath-taking speed of the departure of Straus and Boke and their replacement by officials sympathetic to the new philosophies guiding the administration. Their immediate purpose, said Tudor, was to eliminate "the philosophers, the public relations people and some others, exclusive of engineers."[52] Within a year Tudor removed from the Sacramento office nearly 800 workers of the total 2,100 workers under Richard Boke. The Straus-Boke era in the Central Valley of California had finally come to a conclusion.

NOTES

1. *New York Times*, July 1, 1948.

2. San Francisco *Chronicle*, November 25, 1945. For more information on this struggle, see Robert de Roos, *The Thirsty Land: The Story of the Central Valley Project* (Stanford: Stanford University Press, 1948), and Arthur Mass, *Muddy Waters: The Army Engineers and the Nation's Rivers* (Cambridge: Harvard University Press, 1951).

3. U.S. Department of the Interior, Bureau of Reclamation, *The Effect of the Central Valley Project on the Agriculture and Industrial Economy and on the Social Character of California*, Central Valley Project Studies, Problem 24 (Washington, D.C.: Government Printing Office, 1949), p. 13; Walter R. Goldschmidt, "Large Farms or Small: The Social Side," *Western Farm Economic Association Proceedings*, 1944, pp. 216-227.

4. Sheridan Downey, *They Would Rule the Valley* (San Francisco: Sheridan Downey, 1947), p. 5.

5. Ibid., pp. 5-11.

6. Sheridan Downey to the president, December 5, 1947, and Leroy S. Johnson to Harry S Truman, December 3, 1947, *Papers of Harry S. Truman*, File 620, Harry S Truman Library, Independence, Missouri. Hereafter, HST Papers.

7. Harry S Truman to the Congress of the United States, January 13, 1948, ibid.

8. Kenneth C. Royall to the president, February 27, 1948, ibid.

9. Paul F. Healy, "Our Most Arrogant Bureaucrat," *Saturday Evening Post* 224 (April 19, 1952): 46-47.

10. Downey, pp. 21-24; *Congressional Record*, 80th Cong., 2d sess., April 13, 1948, p. 4489; Michael W. Straus to Harold L. Ickes, August 31, 1945, *Joseph C. O'Mahoney Collection*, Archive of Contemporary History, University of Wyoming, Laramie. Hereafter O'Mahoney Collection.

11. U.S. House of Representatives, *Hearings before the Subcommittee on Appropriations on Interior Department Appropriations for 1949*, 80th Cong., 2nd sess. (Washington, D.C.: Government Printing Office, 1949), pp. 520-521, 571-575, and 584-595.

12. Harold L. Ickes, "Man to Man," New York *Post*, June 18, 1948.

13. Forest A. Harness to Ben F. Jensen, May 14, 1948, *Harry W. Bashore Collection*, Archive of Contemporary History, University of Wyoming, Laramie, hereafter Bashore Collection; *Congressional Record*, 80th Cong., 2d sess., May 27, 1948, pp. 6630-6632.

14. J. A. Krug, Press Release, May 14, 1948, Bashore Collection; *Congressional Record*, 80th Cong., 2d sess. June 14, 1948, p. 8113.

15. *New York Times*, May 28, 1948.

16. *Washington Post*, January 21, 1949.

17. San Francisco Labor Council, May 28, 1948, O'Mahoney Collection.

18. Sacramento *Bee*, October 8, 1948.
19. Roland Young, *Congressional Politics in the Second World War* (New York: Columbia University Press, 1956), pp. 49-53.
20. *Washington Post*, June 6, 1948.
21. *Congressional Record*, 80th Cong., 2d sess., August 4, 1948, pp. 9747-9751.
22. Paul S. Taylor to Harry S Truman, July 21, 1948, HST Papers, Official File.
23. Excerpts from "President's Message to Congress," August 7, 1948, O'Mahoney Collection.
24. *New York Times*, August 8, 1948.
25. Michael W. Straus to Harry S Truman, August 17, 1948, HST Papers, Official File.
26. Kirby Billingsley to Michael W. Straus, November 5, 1948, O'Mahoney Collection.
27. C. J. Haggerty to Harry S Truman, November 18, 1948, ibid.
28. *Congressional Record*, 81st Cong., 1st sess., (February 16, 1949), pp. 1263-1264.
29. Harry W. Bashore to Julius A. Krug, March 11, 1949, O'Mahoney Collection; Harry W. Bashore to Julius A. Krug, March 18, 1949, Bashore Collection.
30. Harry W. Bashore to Julius A. Krug, March 11, 1949, O'Mahoney Collection.
31. *New York Times*, February 25, 1949.
32. Ibid., March 23, 1949.
33. Frank Crampton to Kenneth M. McKellar, March 22, 1949, O'Mahoney Collection.
34. *New York Times*, March 23, 1948.
35. Julius A. Krug to Joseph C. O'Mahoney, March 23, 1949, O'Mahoney Collection.
36. Michael W. Straus to Joseph C. O'Mahoney, March 23, 1949, ibid.
37. Joseph C. O'Mahoney to Kenneth M. McKellar, March 29, 1949, ibid.
38. New York Times, April 4, 1949; *Congressional Record*, 81st Cong., 1st sess., April 11, 1949, p. 4284.

39. Julius A. Krug to Harry S Truman, May 6, 1949, HST Papers, Bureau of the Budget Bill File.

40. Roger W. Jones to William J. Hopkins, May 12, 1949, ibid.

41. Harry S Truman, "Statement by the President," May 12, 1949, ibid.

42. *Congressional Record*, 81st Cong., 1st sess. (May 16, 1949), p. 6293.

43. *New York Times*, October 14, 1949.

44. Visalia *Times*, October 12, 1949.

45. Ibid.

46. "Investigation of Administration of the Bureau of Reclamation," October 13, 1949, pp. 1 and 16, O'Mahoney Collection.

47. *Congressional Record*, 81st Cong., 1st sess., October 19, 1949, p. 15086.

48. U.S Department of the Interior, Bureau of Reclamation, *Central Valley Basin: A Comprehensive Report on the Development of the Water and Related Resources of the Central Valley Basin* (Washington, D.C.: Government Printing Office, 1949), p. 5.

49. Letter to author from Matthew O. Tobriner, April 11, 1977.

50. Sacramento *Bee*, June 19, 1948.

51. San Francisco *Chronicle*, June 1, 1948.

52. Ralph A. Tudor, *Notes Recorded While Under Secretary, Department of the Interior, March 1953-September 1954* (M. Lucile Tudor, 1964), July 6, 1953, and May 10, 1953.

Finding Water for a Thirsty Land: Weather Modification in Texas

Controlling the immediate environment has interested most Texans throughout time. This is caused in part by their close association with many different forms of agriculture and the great weather differences that are experienced in most years, particularly in the necessary amounts of rainfall. It has been said that everybody talks about the weather, but that no one does anything about it. This has certainly not been true for Texans. They have been especially active in rainfall augmentation and to a lesser degree in lightning suppression, hail limitation, and snowpack supplication.

The earliest humans were aware of environmental variations and appealed to supernatural forces to deal with these problems. Many of the early attempts at rainmaking were tied in with religious observances.[1] One of the earliest recorded attempts at rainmaking was that of Elijah.[2] Conditions on that occasion convinced observers there could be no doubt that rain was caused by the cloud inducer; and that it did not rain until a cloud appeared.

Many other attempts have been made since then to modify the weather. Some were reported as failures, some as successes, but the subject has always attracted interest to try anything that promised results. The possible reasons for rainfall— such as the conclusions of battles, threats against religious deities, supplications to the heavens, certain other weather phenomena, and volcanic activity—were all taken into consideration at various times.[3] The explanations that were popular in the late nineteenth century, for example, were believed by many: precipitation occurred because "rain follows the plow"; "rainfall can be increased by tree planting"; "concussions can induce rain"; and "fires cause air to rise."[4]

The first recorded efforts at rainmaking in Texas were those of Robert Dyrenforth in 1891 and 1892. He had previously conducted weather modification tests in Utica, New York, and Washington, D.C. The Department of Agriculture authorized $9,000 to be spent for experiments in Texas, which was influenced in part by a congressman from Illinois, Senator Charles B. Farwell, who had an interest in the XIT Ranch. Experiments were conducted on the C Ranch near Midland, Texas, and later on the King Ranch in South Texas. An additional appropriation was secured for work near San Antonio in 1892. These results were negative and finished the work of Dyrenforth.[5]

C. W. Post, of Post cereals' fame, purchased large tracts of land in the vicinity of Post, Texas, for the purpose of development and resale. He observed that the rainfall was erratic and that if it had fallen at the right time, crop gains would have been substantial. He also noted that lines of clouds would gather in the afternoons and drift to the east. It seemed to him, as it does to many today, that just a little disturbance of some kind would cause it to rain. Post thereupon decided to send explosives into the clouds via kites. Once properly located they would be detonated, thereby causing rain. These trials were carried out in 1911 and 1912, some of which were followed by rain; some not. Post made his experiments on the basis of observations and study; he followed definite procedures and secured reports from all of his associates. His research, however, was not continued after his death in 1914.[6]

The activities of rainmakers outside of Texas, such as Frank Melbourne in Australia, and W.B. Swisher and A. B. Montgomery of Kansas, attracted the interest of Texans. A. B.

Montgomery sold what he called the Melbourne idea to a stock company in Temple, Texas, for $50,000. He also suggested that rainmaking districts be formed in western Kansas just as irrigation districts were formed, but this idea was not accepted.[7] This eventually would be adopted for the hail suppression areas in Hale and Lamb Counties in Texas.

The period from 1915 to 1946 marked a growth in knowledge about the properties of the atmosphere, which heightened the expectations of weather modificationists and their followers. Swedish chemical-meteorologists of the 1920s developed a theory of condensation on hydroscopic nuclei and showed the importance of sea salt particles. Scientists in the 1930s in Germany and the United States measured the numbers and sizes of condensation nuclei. These breakthroughs led to experiments on the initiation of precipitation in clouds containing a mixture of liquid and ice. Quartz crystals were successfully used as the nuclei responsible for precipitation. In Germany, evidence was obtained on the growth of raindrops by the collision-coalescence process in warm clouds; and in 1932 August Veraart of the Netherlands produced rain by seeding clouds with dry ice from a small aircraft.

Eight years earlier American scientists at Harvard University had worked on the possibility of making rain by sprinkling electrically charged sand over clouds with tops of 5,000 to 10,000 feet near Aberdeen, Maryland. These efforts were successful. Partially successful experiments on the dissipation of fog were conducted at MIT in the 1930s under the direction of Henry G. Houghton. Fog was cleared by using sprays of water-absorbing solutions, particularly calcium chloride, as well as fine particles of dry hydroscopic material.[8]

World War II interrupted the work on weather modification, but the experimentation began again in 1946. The uses of dry ice and silver iodide as seeding media were tried, and General Electric field experiments in the Cirrus project from 1947 to 1953 demonstrated that clouds could be deliberately modified.

It was during this period, 1946 through 1955, that several commercial firms became operational. These firms had been encouraged by the Cirrus project and contracted with individuals and governmental units to increase or produce rain by airplanes or by ground generators. Most placed silver iodide into the clouds to start rain. It was estimated that 10 percent of the United States was covered by contracts with these firms. The area of West Texas from Lubbock to Abilene and west to Big Spring had many ground generators scattered around at various locations. Supposedly, they were turned on at the proper time and silver iodide crystals were released into the atmosphere. Nothing could be seen, and many comments were made about the black boxes. Some skeptics went so far as to believe they were empty.[9]

Drought in the early 1950s further stimulated the interest in commercial rainmaking, and it was also during this period that several governmental projects were started for the purpose of evaluating the prospects of rain augmentation. Various federal agencies and many scientists actively opposed this experimentation. The federal Weather Bureau, from the very first hint of operational rainmaking, had attempted to thwart governmental participation.[10] The bureau seemed to be saying that weather was too important to be left to amateurs, and they were certain that rainmaking was part of the magic and witchcraft of the past.

One scientist who fought for rain augmentation projects, however, was Vannevar Bush. In 1951, he observed with satisfaction, "Man has begun for the first time to affect the weather in which he lives." But by 1957, he noted carefully, "We do not know whether it will be practically feasible for man to control weather or favorably alter the climate in which he lives." David I. Blumenstock another modification observer, cautiously concluded,

Perhaps it is possible to increase the rainfall slightly through cloud seeding in certain preferred areas under certain preferred conditions. Perhaps even this is not possible. In any event, it is questionable that large-scale weather modification is possible today or will be possible at a reasonable economic price in the decades yet to come.[11]

Official skepticism was rooted in three scientific tests: the U.S. government's experiments of 1953-1954; the Arizona mountain cumulus experiments; and Project Whitetop. However, these tests were not without criticism. The people conducting these experiments were not objective, rainmakers stressed. This was borne out by statements made in the conclusions of the Whitetop Project in which scientists admitted there were inadequate rain gauges over the area.

Even with hostility having been generated from some parts of the scientific community since 1946, there have been private and commercial operations over the entire United States. These have extended from New York City to California and have included rainmaking efforts as well as snowpack escalation, fog dissipation, and hail suppression. These have varied with public interest in the subject, and the extent of various droughts. Most support has been confined to the Pacific West where utility companies have contracted for precipitation efforts for their watersheds and on the Great Plains where droughts are apt to be more severe. This is not a large business from a dollar standpoint; it is estimated to be no more than $4 million annually.[12] Results from these operations have not always been made public, but since many of the contracts have been renewed, it is possible to assume that the customers have some degree of satisfaction. The results reported by Water Resources Consultants, Inc., of Denver Colorado, and its predecessor companies would seem to illustrate this.[13]

Texans have been remarkably persistent in their quest for more water. This, of course, is due in part to the semiarid nature of much of the state. Yet not everyone has been willing to recognize this fact. Historian of the Great Plains, Walter Prescott Webb, wrote an article in the May 1957 issue of *Harper's Weekly* in which he referred to the American West as having at its heart eight states and then referring to the desert rim states, which included Texas. This created a large furor and he answered part of this in an essay "The West and the Desert " which appeared in *Montana: The Magazine of Western*

History in the winter of 1958. He asked the following questions of those who would question that the state was a desert:

1. Has your country recently been affected by drought?
2. Is there within fifty miles of your home, land too dry to be cultivated without irrigation?
3. Does the city in or near which you live have a serious water problem?
4. Is there any arable land within fifty miles of your home that could be productive if there were water for irrigation?
5. Do you watch with anxiety the clouds that seem to promise rain?
6. Is the surface water supply you have furnished by mountains that rise at least 5,000 feet?
7. Does the sound of rain on the roof affect you emotionally, make you want to go out in it as an expression of your thankfulness?
8. Does bank credit loosen up in your town after a rain?
9. Have the people in your state ever prayed for rain?
10. Have the people in your state ever raised funds for artificial rainmaking whether by explosives or chemicals?

If you answer seven of these questions in the affirmative, then you are subject to the desert influence. If you answer all of them in the negative, then the desert need be of no concern to you.[14]

During the 1954 drought, a meeting was held at Southwest Texas State College, called by Lyndon B. Johnson, in which the water problem was discussed. Webb attended this and participated in the discussions. From these and other ideas, he developed the book *More Water for Texas*. In this monograph, he felt there was no hope of transferring water to West Texas and that the people there would have to learn to get along with what they had.[15]

Such pessimism made waterless Texans turn to private concerns to augment rain. Some have been reported as successful; some have resulted in lawsuits that would indicate that someone thought they were successful; some have been continued in the effort to study the problem further. Since 1967, though, permits for weather modification have been required from the Water Resources Board in Texas.[16] Recorded permits by year are as follows:

1970-1971	9
1972	9
1973	12
1974	6
1975	5
1976	8
1977	8

Permit activity from 1970 to 1977 was limited but constant. Included in these permits were the hail suppression efforts in Hale and Lamb Counties, the operations of generators by Water Resources, Inc., for Oklahoma and Louisiana projects, and the High Plains Experiment, known as HIPLEX.

HIPLEX is a federal comprehensive weather codification research program designed "to develop a practical, scientifically sound, and socially acceptable technology for precipitation management applicable to summer convective cloud systems in the High Plains regions of the U.S." The overall goal of HIPLEX is stated as follows:

. . . to establish a verified, effective cloud seeding technology and a policy and management background for responsibly producing additional rain in the semiarid U.S. This goal includes improving the current operational cloud seeding methods, transferring the techniques and results to concerned groups, and enhancing public confidence in their use.[17]

Research in HIPLEX is being conducted at three field sites— Miles City, Montana; Goodland, Kansas; and Big Spring, Texas—which represent the northern, central, and southern High Plains. The cities were chosen in view of known variations of cloud characteristics over the extent of the High Plains. Seeking an understanding of the social, political, and agronomic differences across the High Plains and their implications for effective technology transfer was also instrumental in field sites selection.

HIPLEX was initiated in 1973 when the Office of Management and Budget (OMB) assigned to the Bureau of Reclamation the responsibility for mounting an experimental program to test scientific concepts for augmenting precipitation in the High Plains. The $1 million first appropriated for HIPLEX in fiscal year 1974 grew to about $4 million in fiscal year 1977, with each recent year's appropriation also including a congressional write-in that has increased OMB's programmed budget. About 80 percent of the fiscal year 1977 budget was for contracted research and 20 percent for in-house management and support. Universities received 29 percent of the contracted research funds, private firms were awarded 31 percent, and 20 percent went to state and federal agencies.[18]

HIPLEX includes the coordinated efforts of state agencies, local groups, and federal agencies. Field research is conducted primarily through contracts with private firms and universities, and these activities are meshed with related research sponsored by the National Science Foundation and the Departments of Commerce and Interior. To maximize water development potential, pertinent state and local organizations in the High Plains have joined with the Bureau of Reclamation in the planning, funding, and implementing of this broad research program. It is designed to accomplish the following:

1. Develop and test more productive seeding methods and evaluate results.

2. Resolve the remaining cloud dynamics and precipitation physics uncertainties on seeding effects.

3. Help prepare public weather modification backgrounds and local expertise and establish working relations among concerned nonfederal entities.

4. Assess the actual economic value of cloud seeding and the possible social and ecological impacts.

Anticipated overall costs for state cooperation and cost-sharing in HIPLEX are estimated to be about $3 million. This contribution amounts to 10 to 15 percent of the total HIPLEX research budget, since the total federal portion of the project is projected at about $20 million.[19]

HIPLEX is envisioned as a five- to seven-year program, running first at least through 1982. Earliest attention was given to the site at Miles City, Montana, where seeding was first conducted during 1976. Studies and cloud measurements are also underway at the other sites. Field facilities and research teams have been established at the three field sites, active participation and cost-sharing with the states is underway, and major equipment systems have been installed and tested. Agricultural, economic, and environmental assessment studies are also underway in all areas.

The experimental design for HIPLEX consists of two components—an atmospheric effort and an socioeconomic and environmental effort—which are divided into three overlapping phases consistent with sequential scientific efforts. In a fourth phase, the developed technology is to be transferred to applicable areas in the High Plains region. The details of this four-phase design and tentative dates associated with the overall schedule are optimistically planned to conclude in 1991.[20]

Texans and many residents of the Great Plains are closely watching the results of HIPLEX. But this is not surprising. Weather modification has been a consuming interest of many Americans, and from C. W. Post's modest kite projects to the HIPLEX experiment in Big Spring, augmented precipitation has been desired by Texans. For agricultural and industrial development, water has been a constant struggle for many Texans, a struggle that has sought out the nineteenth-century rainmaker and continues to place faith in twentieth-century modification science.

NOTES

1. Sir James George Frazer, *The Golden Bough*, abridged ed. (New York: Macmillan, 1951), pp. 72-89.

2. *Bible*, 1 Kings 18:44-45.

3. W. J. Humphreys, *Rain Making and Other Weather Vagaries* (Baltimore: Williams and Wilkins Co., 1926), pp. 3-92.

4. David M. Emmons, *Garden in the Grasslands* (Lincoln: University of Nebraska Press, 1971), pp. 128-161. See also U.S.

Table 12.1
Components of HIPLEX Rainfall Enhancement

Year	Phase	Atmospheric	Socio-Economic & Environmental
1973	*Phase 1*. Exploratory Studies	Establish, rain characteristics, cloud characteristics, seeding technologies, measurement techniques, reasonable hypotheses	Delineate, political attitudes, economic models, legal requirements, downwind impact, undesireable atmospheric impact
1974			
1975			
1977	*Phase 2*. Modification Hypotheses Formulation: Single-Cloud Rain Modification Experiment	Pre-POC: Develop, test of hypotheses, field test seeding techniques, physical statistical design	Monitor impact
1978		Sharpen hypotheses and select for experiment	Evaluate
1979		Proof of Concept Experiment: Monitor semi-isolated clouds, physical changes in clouds, precipitation, physical statistics	Evaluate

1982–1985		Evaluate continous physical statistics	
1983–1986		Conclude when design criteria are met	
	Phase 3. Hypothesis Development: Area Rain Modification Experiment	Physical Design: Develop, Launch experiments, continuous evaluation performance, Redefined initial hypothesis	Monitor Impact Evaluate Benefits & Disbenefits
1986–1991		Conclude when design criteria achieved	
	Phase 4. Transfer of Technology of High Plains States & Other Users		

Table 12.2
Fiscal Year 1977 HIPLEX Funding Breakdown by Function

Function	Percent
Field Operations	44.1
Analysis	28.7
Management, planning, design, data management	22.5
Social, legal, and environmental studies	4.7
Total	100.00

See also U.S., Department of Commerce, National Oceanic and Atmospheric Administration, *1980 Budget Request* (Washington, D.C.: 1979); and Department of Interior, Bureau of Reclamation, *1980 Budget Request* (Washington, D.C.: 1979).

Senate, Committee on Commerce, Science, and Transportation, *Weather Modification: Programs, Problems, Policy, and Potential*, 95th Congress, 2d sess., 1978, p. 28.

5. Robert G. Fleagle, ed., *Weather Modification: Science and Public Policy* (Seattle: University of Washington Press, 1969), p. 7.

6. Charles Dudley Eaves and C.A. Hutchinson, *Post City, Texas* (Austin: Texas State Historical Association, 1952), pp. 14-30.

7. Jeff Townsend, *Making Rain in America: A History*, ICASALS Publication No. 75-3 Lubbock: Texas Tech University, 1975, p. 21.

8. Fleagle, *Weather Modification*, p. 9.

9. Ibid., p. 11.

10. Donald R. Whitnah, *A History of the United States Weather Bureau* (Urbana: University of Illinois Press, 1961), p. 35.

11. National Science Foundation, *Weather Modification Report No. 40* (Washington, D.C.: National Academy of Science, 1968), p. 40.

12. U.S. House of Representatives, Committee on Science and Technology. Statement of Abram Chayes on *Review of the*

Table 12.3
Summary of HIPLEX Funds Provided by States and by the Bureau of Reclamation, Fiscal Year 1974 through 1978 (Estimated)

Fiscal Year	State			Totals	Bureau of Reclamation
	Kansas	Montana	Texas		
1974	$ 6,000	$ 0	$ 0	$ 6,000	$ 1,250,000
1975	100,000	0	25,000	125,000	1,821,000
1976	100,000	0	81,500	181,500	3,482,000
1977	100,000	25,000	65,000	190,000	4,110,000
1978	100,000	25,000	75,000	200,000	4,000,000
Total	$406,000	$ 50,000	$246,500	$702,500	$14,663,000

National Weather Modification Board, 95th Congress, 2d sess., 1978, p. 44.

13. Irving P. Krick, "Increasing Water Resources through Weather Modification," an address before the American Water Works Association, May 7, 1952, Kansas City, Missouri, pp. 4-6.

14. Walter Prescott Webb, *The West and the Desert* (Boston: Houghton Mifflin, 1959), pp. 175-193.

15. Walter Prescott Webb, *Texas Water Problems Conference* (Austin: University of Texas Press, Southwest Texas State Teacher's College, 1954), p. 10.

16. Texas Water Resources Board, *Annual Reports* (Austin, 1971-1977), Reports 175, 187, 193, 219.

17. U.S. Senate, *Programs, Problems, Policy, and Potential*, pp. 258-263.

18. Experimentation in the field has been the primary focus of HIPLEX. See Table 12.1, pp. 216-217.

19. Ibid. See Table 12.2, p. 218.

20. Ibid. See also State of Texas, Water Resources Board, *Institutional Constraints and Conjunctive Management of Water Resources in West Texas* (Austin: 1976), WRC-1. See Table 12.3, p. 219.

Bibliographical Essay

NATIVE AMERICANS AND THEIR LAND

Sovereign land use—the control of Indian reservations and Indian homelands—is the stated goal of most organized Native American groups today. The desire to do with one's own land what one wants to do without outside governmental and private interference is a crucial portion of the modern American Indian's drive for economic self-sufficiency, particularly in agriculture.

The best general legal surveys of the struggle of Native Americans to protect their land base include Felix S. Cohen, *Handbook of Federal Indian Law* (Washington, D.C.: Government Printing Office, 1942) and subsequent revision, and Monroe E. Price, *Law and the American Indian* (Indianapolis: Bobbs-Merill Company, 1973) and subsequent revision. The best general historical surveys include Wilcomb Washburn, *The Indian in America* (New York: Harper and Row, 1975); William T. Hagan, *American Indians*, rev. ed. (Chicago: University of Chicago Press, 1979); and Russel Laurence Barsh and James Youngblood Henderson, *The Road: Indian Tribes and Political Liberty* (Berkeley: University of California Press, 1980).

Recent scholarship has focused upon degrees of self-determination achieved by tribal assertiveness, court decisions, or legislative actions. Some of the best include William R. Swagerty, ed., *Indian Sovereignty* (Chicago: Newberry Library, 1979); Gilbert L. Hall, *The Federal-Indian Trust Relationship* (Washington, D.C.: Institute for the Development of Indian Law, 1979); Vine Deloria, Jr., "Self-Determination and the Concept of Sovereignty," in *Economic Development in American Indian Reservations*, ed. Roxanne Dunbar Ortiz (Albuquerque: University of New Mexico, 1979), pp. 22-28; Kirke Kickingbird et al., *Indian Sovereignty* (Washington, D.C.: Institute for the Development of Indian Law, 1977); and Michael P. Gross, "Indian Self-Determination and Tribal Sovereignty: An Analysis of Recent Federal Indian Policy," *Texas Law Review* 56 (1978):1195-1244.

Resource management with particular emphasis on agriculture and water has been the subject of several dissertations. Relevant studies include Taymon Borton, "Irrigation on the Crow Reservation: Tribal and Community Benefits of the Proposed Hardin Unit, Big Horn County, Montana," Montana State University, 1964; Victor Uchendu, "Seasonal Agricultural Labor among the Navaho Indians: A Study in Socio-Economic Transition," Northwestern University, 1966; Robert Stahl, "Farming among the Kiowa, Comanche, Kiowa-Apache and Wichita," University of Oklahoma, 1978; and James Vlasich, "Pueblo Indian Agriculture, Irrigation, and Water Rights," University of Utah, 1980.

Other useful case studies of Indian agriculture and related subjects include Paul Jones, "Reclamation and the Indian," *Utah Historical Quarterly* 27 (1959): 51-56; *Toward Economic Development for Native American Communities* (Washington, D.C: Government Printing Office, 1969); William O. Roberts, "Successful Agriculture Within the Reservation Framework," *Applied Anthropology* 2 (1943): 37-44; James Vlasich, "Transitions in Pueblo Agriculture, 1938-1948," *New Mexico Historical Review* 55 (1980): 25-46; and Thomas R. Wessel, "Agricultural on the Reservations: The Case of the Blackfeet, 1885-1935," *Journal of the West* 18 (1979):17-24.

No modern comprehensive history of American Indian agriculture exists, but three reference tools deserve note. Most useful for seeking further information are Cecil L. Harvey, *Agriculture of the American Indian: A Select Bibiliography* (Washington, D.C.: Department of Agriculture, 1979); Imre Sutton, *Indian Land Tenure: Bibliographical Essays and a Guide to the Literature* (New York: Clearwater Publishing Company, 1975); and Reginald Horsman, "Recent Trends and New Directions in Native American History," *The American West: New Perspectives, New Dimensions*, ed. Jerome O. Steffen (Norman: University of Oklahoma Press, 1979), pp. 124-151.

LAND SPECULATION

The widespread practice of the accumulation of large hunks of land for personal or corporate gain proved an attractive lure to the first Europeans in the New World and to subsequent migrations. The frontier era in particular witnessed the frenzy of speculative activity that was especially prevalent in farming and ranching areas.

The westward movement has been chronicled in any number of works, and land speculation has been prominently featured. The French and Spanish experiences are best presented in William J. Eccles, *France in America* (New York: Harper & Row, 1972) and *The Canadian Frontier, 1534-1760* (New York: Holt, Rinehart and Winston, 1969); Charles Gibson, *Spain in America* (New York: Harper and Row, 1966); Herbert E. Bolton, *The Spanish Borderlands* (New Haven: Yale University Press, 1921); and John F. Bannon, *The Spanish Borderlands Frontier, 1513-1821* (New York: Holt, Rinehart and Winston, 1971).

Frederick Jackson Turner's call to explore the various frontiers of the American experience has resulted in a myriad of syntheses. Among the best that contain significant material on land speculation include Douglas E. Leach, *The Northern Colonial Frontier, 1607-1763* (New York: Holt, Rinehart and Winston, 1966); Charles E. Clark, *The Eastern Frontier: The Settlement of Northern New England, 1610-1763* (New York: Harper & Row, 1970); Verner W. Crane, *The Southern Frontier, 1670-1732* (Durham: Duke University Press, 1928); Jack M. Sosin, *The Revolutionary Frontier, 1763-1783* (New York:

Holt, Rinehart and Winston, 1967); Thomas P. Abernathy, *Western Lands and the American Revolution* (New York: Appleton-Century, 1937) and *From Frontier to Plantation in Tennessee* (Chapel Hill: University of North Carolina Press, 1932); John D. Barnhart, *Valley of Democracy: The Frontier Versus the Plantation in the Ohio Valley, 1775-1818* (Bloomington: Indiana University Press, 1953); Frederick J. Turner, *Rise of the New West* (New York: Harper, 1906); Malcolm J. Rohrbough, *The Trans-Appalachian Frontier* (New York: Oxford University Press, 1978); John A. Caruso, *The Great Lakes Frontier* (Indianapolis: Bobbs-Merrill, 1961); Francis S. Philbrick, *The Rise of the West, 1754-1830* (New York: Harper, 1965); Robert P. Swierenga, *Pioneers and Profits: Land Speculation on the Iowa Frontier* (Ames: Iowa State University Press, 1968); Allan G. Bogue, *From Prairie to Corn Belt: Farming on the Illnois and Iowa Prairies in the Nineteenth Century* (Chicago: University of Chicago Press, 1963); Seymour V. Connor, *The Peters Colony of Texas: A History and Biographical Sketches of the Early Settlers* (Austin: University of Texas Press, 1959); Bobby D. Weaver, *Castro's Colony: Empresario Development in Texas, 1842-1865* (College Station: Texas A & M University Press, 1984); Nels Anderson, *Desert Saints: The Mormon Frontier in Utah* (Chicago: University of Chicago Press, 1942); Leonard J. Arrington, *Great Basin Kingdom: An Economic History of the Latter-Day Saints, 1830-1900* (Cambridge: Harvard University Press, 1959); Rodman Paul, *Mining Frontiers in the Far West 1848-1880* (New York: Holt, Rinehart, and Winston 1963); Robert E. Reigel, *The Story of the Western Railroad* (New York: Macmillan, 1926); Oscar O. Winther, *The Transportation Frontier: Trans-Mississippi West, 1865-1890* (New York: Holt, Rinerhart, and Winston, 1964); Fred A. Shannon, *The Farmers' Last Frontier* (New York: Farrar & Rinehart, 1945); Gene M. Gressley, *Bankers and Cattlemen* (Lincoln: University of Nebraska Press, 1966); Lewis Atherton, *The Cattle Kings* (Bloomington: Indiana University Press, 1961); W. C. Holden, *The Espuela Land and Cattle Company: A Study of a Foreign-Owned Ranch in Texas*

(Austin: University of Texas Press, 1970); Paul Sharp, *Whoop-Up Country: The Canadian-American West, 1865-1885* (Helena: Historical Society of Montana, 1965); Carl C. Rister, *No Man's Land* (Norman: University of Oklahoma Press, 1948); Gilbert C. Fite, *The Farmer's Frontier, 1865-1900* (New York: Holt, Rinehart, and Winston, 1966); Howard Lamar, *Dakota Territory, 1861-1889: A Study of Frontier Politics* (New Haven: Yale University Press, 1956) and Frederick W. Rathjen, *The Texas Panhandle Frontier* (Austin: University of Texas Press, 1973).

The best case studies highlighting recent methodological advances include those works previously cited by Swierenga and Bogue. Similarly, the best brief summations of the land speculator as an institution include Ray A. Billington, "The Origin of the Land Speculator as a Frontier Type," *Agricultural History* 19 (1945) 204-212; Allan G. and Margaret B. Bogue, "'Profits' and the Frontier Land Speculator," *Journal of Economic History* 17 (1957):1-24; and Paul W. Gates, "The Role of the Land Speculator in Western Development," *Pennsylvania Magazine of History and Biography* 66 (1942): 314-333.

LAND POLICY AND ENTREPRENEURSHIP

Federal land policy was predicated upon the encouragement of economic development. Such development was supposed to give the greatest good to the most people. This goal was not always realized, but policy was designed with it in mind.

The history of federal land policy has resulted in a number of overview works. The best include Vernon Carstensen, ed., *The Public Land: Studies in the History of the Public Domain* (Madison: University of Wisconsin Press, 1963); Paul W. Gates, *History of Public Land Law Development* (Washington, D.C.: Government Printing Office, 1968); Benjamin Hibbard, *A History of Public Land Policies* (New York: MacMillian, 1924); Malcolm J. Rohrbough, *The Land Office Business: The Settlement and Administration of American Public Lands, 1789-1837* (New York: Oxford University Press, 1968); and

Roy M. Robbins, *Our Landed Heritage: The Public Domain, 1770-1936* (Princeton, N.J.: Princeton University Press, 1942).

Specific case studies have also been generated. Noteworthy are Paul W. Gates, *Fifty Million Acres: Conflict over Kansas Land Policy, 1854-1890* (Ithaca, N.Y.: Cornell University Press, 1954); Richard E. Greenleaf, "Land and Water in Mexico and New Mexico, 1700-1821," *New Mexico Historical Review* 47 (1982): 85-112; and Thomas Le Duc, "The Disposal of the Public Domain on the Trans-Mississippi Plains," *Agricultural History* 24 (1950):199-204.

The use of land policy by individuals and groups for private gain has led to the rise of entire frontier industries. On mining, see Rodman Paul, *Mining Frontiers in the Far West, 1848-1880* (New York: Holt, Rinehart, and Winston, 1963) and Lewis Atherton, "The Mining Promoter in the Trans-Mississippi West," *Western Historical Quarterly* 1 (1970): 35-50. On cattle and ranching, see Gene M. Gressley, *Bankers and Cattlemen* (Lincoln: University of Nebraska Press, 1966) and David H. Murrah, *C.C. Slaughter: Rancher, Banker, Baptist* (Austin: University of Texas Press, 1981). On sheep, see Charles W. Towne and Edward N. Wentworth, *Shepherd's Empire* (Norman: University of Oklahoma Press, 1945) and Alexander C. McGregor, *Counting Sheep: From Open Range to Agribusiness on the Columbia Plateau* (Seattle: University of Washington Press, 1982). On farming, see Theodore Saloutos, "The New Deal and Farm Policy in the Great Plains," *Agricultural History* 42 (1969): 345-355; John T. Schlebecker, *Whereby We Thrive: A History of American Farming, 1607-1972* (Ames: Iowa State University Press, (1975); and Carl C. Rister, *Land Hunger: David L. Payne and the Oklahoma Boomers* (Norman: University of Oklahoma Press, 1942).

ENVIRONMENT AND LAND MANAGEMENT

The impact of humans on the land and the subsequent environmental alterations have been the subject of recent concern and inquiry. Modern scholars must begin with the works of James C. Malin, and in particular, *The Community and the*

Grassland of North America: Prolegomena to Its History (Lawrence: by author, 1947) and *Winter Wheat in the Golden Belt of Kansas: A Study in the Adaption to a Subhumid Geographical Environment* (Lawrence: by author, 1944). Other works of significance on the American relationship to land and environment include Samuel P. Hays, *Conservation and the Gospel of Efficiency: The Progressive Conservation Movement, 1890-1920* (Cambridge: Harvard University Press, 1959); Roderick Nash, *Wilderness and the American Mind*; rev. ed. (New Haven: Yale University Press, 1973); and Gene Marine, *America the Raped: The Engineering Mentality and the Devastation of a Continent* (New York: Simon and Schuster, 1969).

Recent case studies of import include Richard White, *Land Use, Environment, and Social Change: The Shaping of Island County, Washington* (Seattle: University of Washington Press, 1980); Calvin Martin, *Keepers of the Game: Indian-Animal Relationships and the Fur Trade* (Berkeley: University of California Press, 1978); and Donald Worster, *Dust Bowl: The Southern Plains in the 1930s* (New York: Oxford University Press, 1979).

For studies on water and the environment, the best include Norris Hundley, Jr., *Water and the West: The Colorado River Compact and the Politics of Water in the American West* (Berkeley: University of California Press, 1975); Donald E. Green, *Land of the Underground Rain: Irrigation on the Texas High Plains* (Austin: University of Texas Press, 1973); and Clark C. Spence, "A Brief History of Pluviculture," *Pacific Northwest Quarterly* 52 (1961): 129-138.

Index

Landrum, F.O., 140
"Lapse-lease practice," 91
Law of Consecration and Steward-
ship, 159
Lawrence, William (Representative),
48
Legislation, U.S.: conservation, 170–
71, 174, 182 n.40; land, 113–24,
131, 133–34, 187–203; (see also
Texas land law); Indian rights, 7, 9,
13–19, 20–21, 39–40, 43, 47–53.
See also Indian Peace Commission
"Legislative ouster," as congressional
tactic, 192–94, 202
"Legislative rider," as congressional
tactic, 202
Lenroot bill, 19
Leonard, Samuel, 69
Lincoln, Abraham (President), 39, 43
Livingston, Robert, 61
Livingston, Robert, Jr., 60, 63–64
Llano Cattle Company. See Curry-
comb Ranch
Llano Estacado. See High Plains of
Texas
Llano Livestock Company, 92
Loftin, Oliver, 86
Lone Star Real Estate and Coloniza-
tion Company, 86
Lone Wolf v. Hitchcock, 52–53
Lucero, José Juan, 7
Luhan, Antonio, 16
Lynn, George Washington, 84
Lynn County, Texas: census of 1880,
87, 96n.23; establishment of, 84–
85; land speculators, 85–87; and
ranching economy, 85–94; and
settlers, 90–93

McCord, James, 88
McDonnill, A.C. and Margaret, 87
McKellar, Kenneth M. (Representa-
tive), 195–99
Madero, Francisco, 101–2
Manor lords of colonial New York:
families of colonial New York, 60–
64, 72; as political bloc, 59–61, 64,
68, 72, 74; on taxation, 71–72
Manors of colonial New York, 60–61

Manti National Forest, 171
Marshall, John (Chief Justice), 41–42
Maynard, Horace (Representative),
48
Melbourne, Frank, 108–9
"Melbourne idea," 209
Mexican Constitution of 1917, 105–7
Mexican Revolution of 1910, and
effects on Warren ranching, 101–7
Middlesex County, New Jersey, 62,
65, 69
Military District of New Mexico, 26,
32
Military land warrants, 133, 135
Miller, Ebenezer, 70
Miller, George P. (Representative),
190
Mix, Charles E., 29
Mohair: overseas competition, 148–
50; popularity of, 144; production
of, 139, 141–42, 147–49
The Monkey Wrench Gang (Abbey),
174
Montana: The Magazine of Western
History, 211–12
Montgomery, A.B., 108–9
More Water for Texas (Webb), 212
Mormon Church: and communalism,
159–60, 163–67, 174; and United
States conservation policy, 170–71,
182n.40
Mormon Cutoff, 168
Mormon doctrine: continuing revela-
tion, 164; cultural origins of, 159;
stewardship and communalism,
159, 164, 166–67, 173–74, 178n.22,
182n.40
Mormon settlers: Americanization of,
167, 172–74; and regulation of nat-
ural resources, 164–66, 168
Morrill Land Grant College Act, 133
Morris, Lewis, 61, 64, 77n.8
Morris, Lewis, Sr., 62–63
Morris, Robert H., 62–63
Morrisana Manor, 61, 64
Mucho, Ganado, 32

National Forest Reserve System. See
Forest reserves, U.S.

About the Contributors

DONALD ABBE, research associate, History of Engineering Program, Texas Tech University, has written "Borger: First Oil Boom Town in the Panhandle," in *Panhandle Petroleum*, ed. Bobby D. Weaver (Canyon, Tex.: Panhandle-Plains Historical Society, 1982), pp. 55-70; and "Spanish Anti-Anglo-American Defensive Policy of the Northern Frontier of New Spain from 1763 to 1829," *Studies in History*, I (1976): 29-41. He is currently compiling an architectural and historical survey of the Texas Panhandle and South Plains.

PAUL H. CARLSON, professor of history and chairman of the Department of History, Texas Lutheran College, has written *Texas Woolly-backs* (College Station: Texas A & M University Press, 1982) and "Shepherds and Cowboys: A Comparison of Life Styles in West Texas," *West Texas Historical Association Yearbook* 58 (1982): 19-38.

DAN L. FLORES, associate professor of history, Texas Tech University, is the editor of *Jefferson and Southwestern Exploration: The Freeman-Custis Accounts of the Red River Expedition of 1806* (Norman: University of Oklahoma Press, 1983) and "The Red River Branch of the Alabama-Coushetts Indians: An Ethnohistory," *Journal of Southern Studies* 15 (Spring 1977): 55-72. He is currently completing a manuscript entitled "Islands in the Desert: An Environmental History of the Rocky Mountain West."

DELMAR HAYTER is a Ph.D. candidate in history at Texas Tech University. He wrote a master's thesis entitled "South Plains Agriculture: 1880-1950" (Texas Tech University, 1981) and is currently researching his dissertation, "The Pecos River," and investigating the history of cotton harvesting equipment development and early twentieth-century dairying in West Texas.

DAVID LANEHART, formerly a teacher of social studies for the Abernathy (Texas) Public Schools and currently a law student at St. Mary's University, wrote a master's thesis entitled "The Navajos and the Peace Commission of 1867" (Texas Tech University, 1981). He is presently researching the history of irrigation in the Southwest.

DAVID J. MURRAH, director of the Southwest Collection, adjunct professor of museum science and associate professor of history, Texas Tech University, is the author of *C. C. Slaughter: Rancher, Banker, Baptist* (Austin: University of Texas Press, 1981) and *The Pitchfork Land and Cattle Company: The First Century* (Pitchfork Land and Cattle Company, 1983). He is presently investigating the history of agriculture in Lubbock County, 1945-1980.

RITA NAPIER, associate professor of history, University of Kansas, is the author of *Squatter City: The Construction of a New Community in the American West*, under publication consideration, and served as historical consultant for the book and film, both entitled "Neshnabeck: The People," a history of the Kansas Potawatomi. She is currently writing a text on the Plains Indians with Peter Iverson and John R. Wunder for the University of Oklahoma Press.

BENJAMIN H. NEWCOMB, associate professor of history, Texas Tech University, is the author of *Franklin and Galloway: A Political Partnership* (New Haven: Yale University Press, 1972) and is currently preparing a manuscript entitled, "Political Partisanship in the Middle American Colonies, 1730-1776."

WILLARD H. ROLLINGS is a Newberry Library postgraduate Fellow. He is the associate editor of *HOPI: Contemporary Challenges* (forthcoming) and is currently preparing his manuscript "Hegemony in the Middle Mississippi Basin: An Ethnohistorical Study of the Osage from Earliest Times to 1840" for publication.

STEPHEN P. SAYLES, assistant professor of history, University of LaVerne, California, is the author of *Clair Engle: The Forging of a Public Servant, A Study of Sacramento Valley Politics, 1933-1944* (Chico, Calif.: Association for Northern California Records and Research, 1976). He is currently studying the career of early California editor, politician, and reclamationist Will Semple Green.

HOMER E. SOCOLOFSKY, professor of history, Kansas State University, is the author of *Arthur Capper: Publisher, Politician, and Philanthropist* (Lawrence: Regents Press of Kansas, 1962) and *Landlord William Scully* (Lawrence: Regents Press of Kansas, 1979).

JOHN R. WUNDER, professor, and head of the Department of History, Clemson University, is the author of *Inferior Courts, Superior Justice: A History of Justices of the Peace on the Northwest Frontier, 1853-1889* (Westport, Conn.: Greenwood Press, 1979) and "The Chinese and the Courts in the Pacific Northwest: Justice Denied?" *Pacific Historical Review* 52 (May 1983): 191-211. He is currently researching the history of the abolition of Indian treaties by the United States and law and the Chinese on the trans-Mississippi West frontier.

Recent Titles in
Contributions in Economics and Economic History
Series Editor: Robert Sobel

The European Community and Latin America: A Case Study in Global Role Expansion
A. Glenn Mower, Jr.

Economics and Policymaking: The Tragic Illusion
Eugene J. Meehan

A Portrait Cast in Steel: Buckeye International and Columbus, Ohio, 1881–1980
Mansel G. Blackford

The Strategic Petroleum Reserve: Planning, Implementation, and Analysis
David Leo Weimer

United States Oil Policy and Diplomacy: A Twentieth-Century Overview
Edward W. Chester

The Emergence of Giant Enterprise, 1860–1914: American Commercial Enterprise and Extractive Industries
David O. Whitten

The Marshall Plan Revisited: The European Recovery Program in Economic Perspective
Imanuel Wexler

The Rise and Decline of the American Cut Nail Industry: A Study of the Interrelationships of Technology, Business Organization, and Management Techniques
Amos J. Loveday, Jr.

The Dynamics of Development and Development Administration
Kempe Ronald Hope

Moving and Shaking American Medicine: The Structure of a Socioeconomic Transformation
Betty Leyerle

The Age of Giant Corporations: A Microeconomic History of American Business, 1914–1984; A Second Edition
Robert Sobel

The Anti-Monopoly Persuasion: Popular Resistance to the Rise of Big Business in the Midwest
Steven L. Piott